"The life and times of award-winning journalist and producer Pat Mitchell is an inspiration for all who wish to see positive change in the world. . . . Pat is a tour de force whose continued advocacy for access and equal opportunities for women is to be applauded."

—Deborah Calmeyer, founder and CEO of Roar Africa

"Dangerous women are the antidote to dangerous times. Thank you, Pat Mitchell, for your courageous work and enduring leadership—you inspire us all to put aside our fears so we can do the work needed to fix our broken world."

—Jessica Zitter, MD, author of *Extreme Measures*

BECOMING A DANGEROUS WOMAN

BECOMING A DANGEROUS WOMAN

Embracing Risk to Change the World

PAT MITCHELL

SEAL PRESS
New York

Seal Press
Hachette Book Group
1290 Avenue of the Americas, New York, NY 10104
www.sealpress.com
@sealpress

Printed in the United States of America

First Edition: October 2019

Published by Seal Press, an imprint of Perseus Books, LLC, a subsidiary of Hachette Book Group, Inc. The Seal Press name and logo is a trademark of the Hachette Book Group.

The Hachette Speakers Bureau provides a wide range of authors for speaking events. To find out more, go to www.hachettespeakersbureau.com or call (866) 376-6591.

The publisher is not responsible for websites (or their content) that are not owned by the publisher.

Print book interior design by Jeff Williams.

Library of Congress Cataloging-in-Publication Data

Names: Mitchell, Pat, 1943– author.
Title: Becoming a dangerous woman: embracing risk to change the world / Pat Mitchell.
Description: First edition. | New York: Seal Press, 2019.
Identifiers: LCCN 2019011265 (print) | LCCN 2019981408 (ebook) | ISBN 9781580059299 (hardcover) | ISBN 9781580059312 (ebook)
Subjects: LCSH: Mitchell, Pat, 1943– | Women television journalists—United States—Biography. | Television journalists—United States—Biography. | Television producers and directors—United States—Biography. | Women chief executive officers—United States—Biography. | Mass media and women—United States.
Classification: LCC PN4874.M545 A3 2019 (print) | LCC PN4874.M545 (ebook) | DDC 384.55092 [B]—dc23
LC record available at https://lccn.loc.gov/2019011265
LC ebook record available at https://lccn.loc.gov/2019981408

ISBNs: 978-1-58005-929-9 (hardcover), 978-1-58005-931-2 (ebook)

LSC-C

10 9 8 7 6 5 4 3 2 1

To all the dangerous women—and the men who stand with us—who have inspired me to share my stories, and whose work compels me to embrace the risks necessary to make the world a safer, more equitable place for all women and girls

To our children and grandchildren—for whose futures I have become a dangerous woman

Contents

Preface

The Most Dangerous Woman in the Room

Instructions for living a life:
Pay attention.
Be astonished.
Tell about it.

—MARY OLIVER FROM A STITCHED NOTE "SOMETIMES"

"YES, I'LL BE there."

Eve Ensler was calling with an invitation to what she described as "the meeting of movements," planned for the first week of January 2017. In the wake of a polarizing presidential election in the United States, Eve had decided it was time for activists to come together to shape strategies that could unify and leverage the collective power of a wide range of social-justice organizations.

"Who else is coming?" I asked.

"I'm not releasing the invitation list," Eve replied, "but you'll want to be in the room."

Indeed, I did want to be in that room, knowing from past experiences that any meeting or event that Eve organized would be meaningful. So I showed up, as the invitation indicated, at a nondescript building in Stone Ridge, New York, and surrendered my cell phone to the smiling young volunteers at the front door.

"Best to have all communication devices outside the room," was the explanation, which of course heightened my anticipation about what would transpire within the room.

I entered a large room and saw Eve standing at the front, with folding chairs in a circle. Mingling about the room were some familiar faces: the meeting's other conveners, Kimberlé Crenshaw of the African American Policy Forum; Naomi Klein, award-winning author and activist; independent media entrepreneur and journalist Laura Flanders; and Jane Fonda, actor and activist.

We were asked to find our seats, and Eve began.

"We are living in dangerous times," was her opening line, "and such times call for new levels of activism from all the communities represented in this circle. Let's begin by identifying who's in the room."

One by one, the introductions began: "I'm one of the founders of the Women's March." "I'm the executive director of 350.org." "I run Project South." With each introduction, the level of leadership and activists' credentials became more impressive, and for me, more intimidating.

I could feel my anxiety building. How was I going to identify myself? I had no title and was no longer running an organization, having left my last CEO position at the Paley Center for Media the previous spring. I could say that I was the CEO of Pat Mitchell Media, with its grand total of two employees (including myself). But that felt wholly inadequate to explain why I belonged in that room.

I mentally rehearsed some other options. I could say I was a lifetime advocate for women—true enough, if a little vague. I could list some of my previous titles—but why make a point of being the *former* anything? I was struggling to come up with how to identify myself in the present, an identity that would hopefully give some indication of why Eve had included me in this circle of activists and leaders.

Finally, it was my turn. Before I knew it, I heard myself saying, "I'm Pat Mitchell. And I'm a dangerous woman."

I'm not sure exactly what prompted this personal declaration of dangerousness, but I could tell from the looks of surprise that I needed to add a bit more context.

"At this time in my life, about to turn seventy-five," I continued, "I have nothing left to prove, less to lose, and I'm ready to take more risks and to be less politic and polite. As Eve said, these are dangerous times, and dangerous times call for dangerous women."

That got a big, sisterly "YES!" from Eve and others in the circle, including Jane Fonda, who was sitting across from me and stood up, declaring, "Well, I'm older than my friend Pat, so that makes me even more dangerous."

Laughter erupted, of course, and I could sense that others were contemplating exactly what becoming more dangerous to meet the challenges of dangerous times would mean for each of us and for the work we had convened to consider.

Certainly, Jane Fonda's life of activism is a textbook case for being bold and brave. During our many years of friendship, I've witnessed her willingness to take risks for a good cause, to speak out and show up, even when it meant personal peril or sacrifice. At eighty-one, she is still on the front lines, campaigning for domestic and restaurant workers' rights, standing with the American Indian communities protesting natural-resource exploitation at Standing Rock, and busier as an actor than ever. In her book, *Prime Time*, Jane advanced the idea that older women have the potential to become the most powerful population on the planet. She's a great example of how we embrace that potential at every age.

My personal potential for becoming more dangerous is perhaps most directly linked to my friendship with Eve Ensler.

From our first conversation in war-torn Sarajevo in 1998, I have been deeply inspired by her courage and her commitment to doing whatever is necessary to end violence against women everywhere. Taking risks comes easier to Eve than to many: writing and performing *The Vagina Monologues,* making it the centerpiece of a global movement, V-Day, to end gender-based violence is a transformative approach to activism that I feel privileged to have experienced. Yes, I was an activist and women's advocate before I met Eve, but through my relationship with her and as a board member of the V-Day movement, I've met activists facing dangers every day to create change in some of the most difficult places on earth to be a woman.

But until that day, I had not felt dangerous myself.

DECLARING MYSELF A *dangerous woman* still feels a bit, well, *dangerous,* and I readily admit to some second thoughts about declaring it even more widely and boldly as the title of this book. But every day since that convening, I'm discovering more about what being dangerous means in my life and why I believe that it's time for us—women and the men who stand with us—at whatever age or place in life's journey, to embrace risks and engage with renewed passion and collective purpose in the truly dangerous work of making the world a safer place for women and girls.

I have had to face my own questions and those of others about the definition of *dangerous* in this work. For me, it doesn't mean being feared but being more fearless; it does mean speaking the truth when silence is safer; showing up for one another even within the patriarchal construct that encourages us to compete and compare; and it does mean speaking out about the politics and policies that divide us and diminish our individual and collective power. It also means optimizing that power to be effective in allying with those who don't have access to opportunity, influence, or privilege. It also means, for me, sharing our stories as women have done for generations to survive, thrive, and move forward.

That's why I'm sharing my journey from small-town South Georgia girl with big dreams but little means to realize them—no money, no connections, no power or sphere of influence—to media executive with influence, to where I am today, more prepared to leverage my privilege, platforms, and connections; to optimize every opportunity to elevate other women and their stories; and to support their struggles and celebrate their accomplishments.

MY STORY BEGAN in an unlikely place, on my grandparents' small cotton farm with no electricity or indoor toilets. But what I had in those early years was a grandmother who could wring a chicken's neck with one arm and churn butter or pump water with the other, while telling me fanciful stories of places she had never seen—stories that ignited an intense curiosity that is at the heart of everything I have done in my life and work.

By taking some early risks and leaps of faith in myself, I escaped the limitations of resources and pushed past barriers, sometimes helping to dismantle them, while often coping with the challenges of being the first or only woman. Very early on, I learned the value of nurturing connections, of building and sustaining a support network of women friends and colleagues, and of being an advocate for other women in every room and for every opportunity. Now I'm ready to join a global community of women and girls stepping into our power, redefining it by how we use it and share it. It's time—prime time—for the good we can do by becoming more dangerous together.

After all, when we're watching *The Handmaid's Tale* on television as the last abortion clinic is removed in the state of Louisiana; and when reproductive rights and access to health care are under threat in many places, including my home state of

Georgia, which passed legislation in 2019 that will make it one of the most restrictive places in the United States to end an unwanted or unhealthy pregnancy; when extraordinary numbers of refugees are roaming the world without a safe place to call home; when political extremism, racism, and sexism are on the rise in all corners of the world; and when protections for our mother earth are being dismantled by climate-deniers, we need bold responses and brave women willing to speak up, to show up, and to embrace our collective power.

I am encouraged, even in this time of fears about the future, by the many women and girls embracing bigger risks to confront a growing number of global challenges. I'm privileged to know many as friends, and as I set about to share my journey to becoming more dangerous, I asked some of them about their journeys, and have included their responses in the book.

To the many more women warriors on the front lines of change, innovating, defending, protecting, and problem solving, you, too, strengthen my belief that when we come together as a global women's community, extend our admiration for each other, sustain our advocacy for each other; when we march together, protest, and rise together; when we dance, sing, laugh, and take risks together, we can and do move forward toward a more equal and just world.

This is a future we have the power, the responsibility, and the opportunity to create, and if it means becoming more dangerous to do so—and I believe that it does—my purpose in sharing my stories is to inspire you to become more dangerous, too.

Chapter 1

Falling Forward

"WAIT!!"

But it was too late. The New York City cabbie peeled off in the driving rainstorm, taking with him the purse I'd left on the seat. The purse with all my identification, maxed-out credit cards, and the cash I'd only just borrowed to pay my rent.

The signs were clear: time to give up, pack up, and head back to Georgia.

My big break had finally come—I'd been assigned a story for *LOOK* magazine on Chinatown's hidden gang wars—but I'd just found out it wasn't going to be published because the magazine was bankrupt. And so was I. The dream of a big-city journalism career that inspired me to jump at the opportunity to leave my secure job as a college teacher and move to New York City was fading fast.

I was twenty-seven years old, a single mother with a five-year-old son, and no prospects for a new job. Well, except one. I had a tentative connection to television through a political reporter from WNBC-TV named Gabe Pressman. Gabe is the one who had delivered the news to me that *LOOK* was going out of business.

"Magazines are dying," he'd observed on the early morning call to tell me I was unemployed. "Maybe you ought to try television. We need writers, and I hear the station is looking for women, too."

Within days after the farewell Bloody Marys were passed around at *LOOK*'s offices and television crews had come to cover the closing party—for me, more like a wake—Gabe came through for me, setting up a meeting with WNBC's news director.

"Any television experience?" the news director asked without smiling. I'd been sitting outside his office all day, and out of pity or his promise to Gabe, he finally motioned me in.

"No, but I know how to tell a story," I said, hastily handing him a photocopy of the Chinatown story.

He glanced at the provocative title, read a few paragraphs, and asked, "Can you do this story for television?"

"YES" was my answer, although I had no idea what that meant.

I was back in Chinatown the next day, with a full television news crew who had to show me how to hold the microphone when doing an interview, how to do a *stand-up* on camera, even how to pretend to be listening during the *cutaways*, another new term I filed away for future use, as I was hopeful I would be doing this again.

The story got almost three minutes, an eternity in television news, and I was hooked! Immediate gratification. No waiting for publishing dates. The story was seen by a much larger number of people than would have read it in a magazine, and I had produced and reported it for NBC News—with a lot of help, of course. My total time on camera was less than thirty seconds, but former colleagues at *LOOK* called to congratulate me on landing a new job—and career—so quickly.

I waited for the next assignment.

What I got instead was this advice from the news director: 1) become a blonde, 2) lose some weight, and 3) find a small town somewhere and learn the business. "You don't start in New York," I was told with a distinct note of finality.

So I made the rounds to every TV station that took my call or request for an interview.

"Already got a brunette; would you become a blonde?"

"Just not ethnic enough . . . we need *twofers* . . . woman *and* minority."

"You're too young to be credible."

"Too old" (at twenty-seven!). "Too inexperienced." "Too educated"—painful to hear as I was still paying off my student loans for my graduate degrees.

It was three months after my TV debut, after a long string of "not quite right" rejections and waitressing for cash, that I was watching the red taillights of that NYC taxi flicker in the downpour as it disappeared down the street with my rent money in the back seat.

Dejected and drenched and fighting tears, I told my five-year-old son, Mark, "Time to pack up and head back to Georgia." Then the phone rang.

"Hello, this is Rabbi Goldberg. I got in the taxi after you, and I have your bag. Your number was inside. Would you like me to return it now?"

Within a half hour, there he stood, handing over my small, black bag with the borrowed money and with it, the chance to keep moving forward—at least for another month. When I tried to explain how meaningful his act of kindness was, he took my hands and said, "Well, Patricia, at some point in everyone's life, they need a rabbi, and tonight, you got yours."

I got something else that night, too. I had experienced the singular goodness of another human being whose gift of showing up at my door, giving me back my bag, and restoring hope and possibilities inspired me to make a silent promise to be someone else's rabbi, mentor, sponsor, and advocate.

Each time I have had that opportunity in the many decades since that stormy, life-defining encounter, I remember my promise and think of Rabbi Goldberg with deep gratitude.

IT'S BECOME ALMOST a cliché that life journeys begin with grandmother stories, and as I referenced in the preface, so does mine. My mother and I spent my earliest years about eighty miles west of Savannah, Georgia, with my grandparents on that small farm without electricity or indoor plumbing. My father was overseas in the army during World War II.

I have warm and wonderful memories of those first three years with a doting grandfather who would feed me homemade biscuits and sing me back to sleep and a grandmother whose long, raven-black hair I loved to brush as she told me stories next to the pot-bellied stove that provided heat in the kitchen, where we spent most of our time. She had only finished sixth grade and had never lived anywhere but small tenant farms, but her stories seemed to come from deep in her memory and contained special meanings for me. One story stands out in my memory, a story that I later found exists in many forms in many cultures.

Her version went something like this:

Once upon a time, there was a little girl who was always running and falling. She would run in the fields through the cotton and tobacco, falling among the rows. But one day, the running girl found herself outside the fields: no cotton or tobacco, only high mountains.

A beautiful horse galloped by with a friendly boy on his back, a boy with a feather in his hair. He offered her a ride.

They rode and rode through green fields and flowers and women sitting in circles around small fires.

When they came to the end of their journey, the boy turned to her.

"I will grant you one wish," the boy said. "What will it be?"

The running girl said, "I want to be able to run far and wide and never fall."

"That wish," the young brave said, "I cannot give you, because there will be times when falling is your only way forward. You must run on rough ground, through barriers sometimes, and you will take wrong turns and become lost, and you will fall. You must fall. And from time to time, you will.

It's in the falls that you will learn to breathe, to recover, to get up, and to continue moving forward.

No matter how often I stumbled or fell, which was often, as I seemed always to be in a hurry as a child, and even now, I would hear Grandmother comforting me with that familiar line adapted from the story: "Falling on your face is at least a forward movement." I never thought of slowing down or stopping—that was never her advice. She just gave me unconditional love through the falls and the failures—something it would take me nearly a half century to find again.

My grandmother had to hide her American Indian heritage—which her papers, discovered when she passed, indicated was Creek-Cherokee. There was little information about her family, but it's likely that her mother, like many other Creek and Cherokee women in the Southeast who were landowners in those matrilineal cultures, had married a white farmer to avoid extradition by the US government's 1838 Supreme Court decision—a decision that forced relocation of the American Indian communities in the South to newly formed reservations in the West. Because so many died on what was truly a death march, history refers to this movement as the Trail of Tears.

I knew none of this until my grandmother's death, and however distant this connection to her heritage, the discovery of my grandmother's background led to a personal interest in the history of the American Indian nations, an interest that would play a big role later during my years of working with Ted Turner and Robert Redford. I also believe that my grandmother's legacy of storytelling as well as her personal strength and resilience gave me an early portrait of what a woman could do and be, even with very limited resources. Imagine how pleased I was to discover that my grandmother's native language, which I never heard her speak, has no gender pronouns, no *hes* or *shes* to distinguish what is male or female.

One day, a tall, dark-haired *he* appeared in the yard, a stranger dressed in a green army uniform. My grandmother hugged him, clearly overjoyed. Granddaddy said, "Patsy, honey, this is your father! Go welcome him home!"

My father approached and tried to hug me, but I turned away, and even today, I can remember feeling sad while everyone else, especially my mother, seemed so happy about this stranger's presence. Each time he would reach for me and say, "Come, hug Daddy," I would run to the more familiar arms of my grandfather or grandmother.

It was not an easy homecoming. A few days later, in spite of my tears and begging to stay, we left the farm in his borrowed '45 Ford and headed for Fort Stewart outside of Savannah, Georgia, where this man who said he was my father would continue his military service.

FOR THE NEXT several years, we moved to a succession of army bases, averaging one or more moves a year. Mother soon tired of the moving, but I thrived on being the new girl at school and in the neighborhood, making new friends fast because no sooner were they made than we would move again. Finally, Mother convinced my father to leave active military service, and they decided to settle in Swainsboro, Georgia, a small town just thirty miles from my grandparents' farm.

Swainsboro (population then and now around five thousand) was once called "The Crossroads of the South" because the north-south and east-west national highways actually crossed there. When Interstate 15 was built to connect Atlanta and Savannah, bypassing Swainsboro altogether, there were even fewer reasons to visit a town that had once been named Paris. The Swains family, who had a lot of influence in the town's early days, had thought that Paris sounded "too foreign" and changed the name. What didn't change for me from the beginning was the feeling that I didn't belong there.

Except once a year, when the excitement of the annual Pine Tree Festival parade suspended my complaints about small-town boredom. I would arrive early for the best spot along the parade route, and as the high-school band approached, trying to play in tune and march in step, and accomplishing neither, my heart raced, anticipating the colorful floats to follow. I fell in love with parades and their disruption of routine, their movement forward—although in the case of this parade, the forward movement was transiting the ten blocks from the county courthouse to the city limits sign. From that first parade encounter, I had a strong urge to be *in* parades, not just standing on the sidelines, watching them—and life—pass by. I couldn't have articulated why at that age, but I must have realized that being an observer, even to something as transitory as a parade, just wasn't enough. Not for me. Then or now.

To get into the Pine Tree Festival parade, I entered the beauty pageant for Pine Tree Festival queen as soon as I was old enough—fifteen—and I won! I was delighted at the time, but looking back, winning a beauty pageant at such a young age wasn't such a good move. It seemed to set me apart from the other girls my age, and I spent a lot of the rest of my high-school years battling the beauty-queen stereotype and all that it meant in the South of the fifties, where being pretty was valued much more than being smart.

I felt pretty in the royal-blue, off-the-shoulder, full-skirted evening gown based on a photo of a former Miss America's gown that my mother had stayed up night after night sewing for me to wear on the big day of my ride in the parade as Miss Pine Tree Festival. The skirt was so large that it took five heavily starched crinolines (please google *crinolines* if born after 1960) to hold it up in a huge circle.

Suddenly, the tractor driving the float jerked to a stop, and the abrupt jolt threw me off my pine-box throne. I fell forward on my face, my royal-blue evening gown skirt falling forward too, like a deflated balloon.

Laughter floated up from the crowd in the streets, and I was mortified. The first face I saw when once again upright was, of course, my grandmother, who was visiting for the big day. At the end of the parade, as she helped me dismount from my throne, she whispered, "Well, honey, at least falling on your face is a forward movement."

I wanted to laugh, or at least smile conspiratorially, but I was too sad. The magic of the day had faded, and the Pine Tree Festival queen's parade ride felt shorter that day, and the town felt smaller, a phenomenon that I've observed other times when the reality didn't quite live up to the expectations.

I WAS DETERMINED to get past the expectations of what was possible for a young girl who was told she was pretty enough to get by without money or connections—past the emotional scars of a mother who displayed my pageant trophies as if they could have been hers. And they could have been, had she not abandoned her own dreams to marry my father. While I struggled with the tension between what I valued in myself and what my mother wanted me to become, I lived in fear of my father, whose silent anger hung like a heavy cloud over our house. My brother, who was born when I was seven, was too young to be my confidant, and his relationship with our parents always seemed easier than mine.

School was always my happy place. I loved learning and my report card reflected my determination to be as close to number one in every subject as I could. Straight As meant I might qualify for a college scholarship, and I intended to go to college, even though my parents had not gone beyond high school and only three in their large farm families had gone to college.

I had big plans but no idea how I was going to implement them . . . until Miss Shirley Roundtree swept into my eighth-grade English class at Swainsboro High School wearing a full-skirted dress that swayed as rhythmically as Loretta Young's did during her dramatic descent down the staircase every Sunday night on *The Loretta Young Show.* Miss Roundtree was beautiful by anybody's standard, with shining dark hair that was perfectly coiffed, bright red lipstick that I soon learned was her signature, and gorgeously coordinated outfits.

Beyond Miss Roundtree's stylishness, however, I loved the way she commanded respect, clearly the boss from the moment she set foot in the classroom. I didn't just want to look like her; I wanted to *be* her.

I didn't have any other role models, so I pursued Miss Roundtree after class, day after day, with endless questions: "How can I get into college? What do I need to do to make that possible? Can you help me get a scholarship?"

"If you could do anything you wanted, what career would you choose?" she asked one day, realizing that I was not going to stop asking her questions.

"I want to be an actress—like Vivien Leigh!" I said, thanks to annual showings of *Gone with the Wind* at the one movie theatre in town.

"Okay," she responded. "Let's start a theatre company at school." She cast me in every play she directed and produced—usually as the lead. We didn't do the usual high-school dramas; Miss Roundtree believed in challenging us and the audiences. I won best actress in the state, playing an unmarried mother in a rarely performed theatre piece by poet Carl Sandburg.

Then, in my junior year, my attention suddenly turned to politics. I was inspired by a story during the Saturday newsreels about Margaret Chase Smith, the first woman ever to serve in both the House and Senate as well as the first female candidate nominated for president from a major party. I didn't know that she was a Republican, and in fact, I had never met a Republican since everyone I knew was a Democrat in those days, including my parents and grandparents; Southern Democrats then were closer in ideology to the Tea Party now. I only knew that I was ready to put acting aside and focus on my new dream—becoming a senator.

My interest in politics was ridiculed by everyone—except Miss Roundtree, who encouraged me and even started a debate team at school. We thrived, winning debate competitions around the state. This training turned out to be the best preparation for the teaching jobs to come. I also had begun to give youth sermons at the Baptist church where we went twice every Sunday, Wednesday night for prayer meetings, and every other Saturday for "hate Catholics" sessions—Bible studies intended to convince us only Baptists would get to heaven. I enjoyed giving sermons and was told that I was a natural at the pulpit, and at one of the yearly tent revivals, I even promised to dedicate my life to full-time Christian service. But since everything I was beginning to enjoy doing, such as dating and dancing, was a sin according to the Baptist view of the Bible, I began to have doubts.

Clearly, I wasn't all that sure exactly what I wanted to do or be—shifting from big-screen star to Baptist missionary in one year—but one thing I was absolutely clear about was that I wanted to move forward from where I was and what was expected that I could become.

"I THINK YOU should apply for a drama scholarship to the University of Georgia," Miss Roundtree—now Mrs. Reid—suggested as she had noted my flair for the dramatic, my love of public speaking, and my ease with an audience, probably all good qualifiers for a stage career.

She wrote a recommendation and I got the notice to come to UGA and audition.

"Absolutely not!" my father said, denying my request to go to the audition. When he'd retired from the military and gone to work for an appliance store that sold televisions, he had refused to get one for our family, explaining that he worried about the influence of TV on my life. (Little did he know!) Just the mention of an audition for a life in the theatre was out of the question for him.

"Don't you worry," Mrs. Reid told me conspiratorially when I ran to her with the bad news. "We'll figure out a way." Then she drove me to Athens herself, and sat in the back during my audition.

A couple of agonizing months later, the thick envelope arrived: I'd been accepted with a fully paid scholarship to study drama at UGA.

Still, my father was adamant. "You can go use that money to go to the state teachers' college down the road, like my sister," the only person in his family to go to college. Once again, Mrs. Reid interceded, assuring my parents I'd be safe in Athens, Georgia.

"I promise I'll visit often to make sure she's doing okay," she assuaged. "It's a great opportunity for Patsy," as I was called then—and in spite of efforts to get people to call me "Patricia," no one did, then or now! At last, Mrs. Reid prevailed, and off I went to UGA.

My father came to see me at university only once, unexpectedly, just in time to see my performance in the role of a prostitute dying of syphilis in *Hello from Bertha*, a one-act play by Tennessee Williams. He watched in horror as, clad in a revealing black slip, I cursed and threw gin bottles onstage.

"That's it," he told me afterward. "You're coming home with me."

"I'm not," I told him levelly. I loved my life at the university, and I had started my journey away from a home where I didn't feel safe, understood, or loved, and beyond the small-town limitations. I would do what I had to do to stay, so I threatened him with words I had never spoken before. "And if you try to make me leave school," I told him, "I'll tell Mother about what you did to me."

He froze. He knew what I meant. He had threatened me into keeping "our secret"; now I was threatening him with revealing it.

My voice was calm, but inside I was shaking. Still, I spoke my truth, even for a fleeting moment, and the abject fear in his eyes told me that I had gone far enough. As he turned to leave, I knew I was staying—and to keep moving forward, I buried our secret for the next twenty-eight years.

DANGEROUS TIMES CALL FOR DANGEROUS WOMEN

In Conversation with Stacey Abrams

Stacey Abrams has made history more than once in her life. She is the first African American woman to become the Democratic nominee for governor in any state—and she almost became the governor of my home state, Georgia. Amid allegations of voter suppression through political maneuvering by her opponent, who was Georgia's secretary of state at the time, Abrams demanded that every vote be recounted in the days after the election. Ten days later, she announced the end of her gubernatorial campaign. There's no question for those of us who witnessed both her effectiveness as the Democratic leader in a conservative, Republican-dominated state assembly and the way that her campaign ignited support and interest across the United States and around the world that she will continue to move forward as a leader.

Stacey's life story is one defying expectations and limitations at every step in her journey from rural Mississippi. A daughter of Methodist ministers who taught her the values of giving as well as leading, she inspires all those who hear her and meet her with how smart and strategic she is, how committed and courageous, and yes, dangerous, too. She's clearly not afraid to take risks, to put herself on the line, to disrupt, and to be as daring as she needs to be to make the changes she sees as possible.

Stacey had only had a few days to rest and reflect on her historic campaign when I sat down with her and asked her what it means to her to be a dangerous woman.

What resonates for you in the statement that "dangerous times call for dangerous women"?

Stacey: Central constructs motivate people to action—the core notion of autonomy, the resilience of democracy, the opportunity for success—yet recent years have eroded our confidence in their truth. We wake, we work, we dream, believing that our efforts will bring them to fruition. In these times, when our basic beliefs are at stake, we must have women who are willing to defy convention, to take calculated risks, and to build infrastructure that will serve a broader community and withstand assaults on our freedoms.

Do you think of yourself as a dangerous woman and, if so, how has this been manifested in your life and work?

Stacey: A dangerous woman is one who understands the traditions and conventions, may even operate within them, but she is also willing to defy them when necessary. I ran for governor as the first black woman to receive the nomination from a major party, and after questionable actions that eroded access to the ballot for thousands, I refused to offer a concession speech, instead challenging the structure of our elections. More importantly, I launched an organization to pursue legal reforms to our electoral process, even though the results would not change the outcome of my election. This moment is an example of how I have consistently tried to confront challenges: identify the problem, understand why it's a problem, and then work to solve it. I would say there are few things as dangerous as a woman with a plan and the perseverance to execute.

Is there an age component to feeling dangerous? Was there a particular incident or moment or time in your life when becoming dangerous felt essential, and why?

Stacey: I do not believe age is a necessary factor. As we can see from the young women at the heart of Black Lives Matter or the Parkland survivors, to the tenacity of an Edith Windsor or Maxine Waters or Mazie Hirono, the issue is not age; the question is the necessity of the moment. At the age of twelve, I was selected for a prestigious honor that included a trip to Arizona from my hometown in Mississippi—and I was the only African American selected from my state. Unfortunately, when my parents brought me to the airport to travel with the other participants, we discovered they'd intentionally given us the wrong information and left without me. My parents tried to take me home, but they'd raised me to not allow others to dictate my future. So I convinced them to let me go alone, on my very first flight, to the event. I was nervous, terrified of flying, and not exactly certain of my reception when I arrived, but I did it anyway. Being dangerous is an act of imagination—deciding your goals and pushing through pain and angst.

Who are the women in your life who inspire you to be more dangerous?

Stacey: My mother, my three sisters, Johnnetta Cole [the first female president of Spelman College], Lauren Groh-Wargo [Stacey's campaign manager and the CEO of Fair Fight Action], and those countless women who stepped up to help me pursue my bid for governor.

What are the biggest remaining danger zones for women worldwide?

Stacey: Poverty, reproductive health care access, academic education, property ownership, and access to technology.

Chapter 2

Starting Over

"I'LL BE *DAMNED* if my own daughter is going to sit in classes with one of *them*," my father roared.

When news broke that the University of Georgia was about to admit its first black students, my father tried everything short of imprisoning me to keep me from accepting my scholarship to study there.

When UGA made its historic decision a few weeks before I started my first semester, I thought it was the best news I'd heard. The civil-rights movement had already won some other victories, most significantly the battle to integrate the schools of neighboring Alabama. On June 11, 1963, Governor George Wallace—who had declared "segregation now, segregation tomorrow, segregation forever" in his inaugural address—had famously stood on the steps of the University of Alabama campus to try to stop black students Vivian Malone and James Hood from coming through those doors until the federal authorities, the Alabama National Guard, stepped in.

The governor of Georgia, Ernest Vandiver Jr., decided to try to keep his state, the home of Dr. Martin Luther King Jr., from becoming a battleground, and integrating the University of

Georgia was one big step forward. Three days after Charlayne Hunter (later Hunter-Gault) and Hamilton Holmes arrived, an angry mob hurled bottles and bricks at Charlayne's dorm—the very one I was assigned to.

As Charlayne would later write in the *New Yorker*, "The town police threw around tear gas, ostensibly to disperse an already-thinning crowd. By the time the state troopers arrived, the protesters were long gone. The university suspended me, they said, for my own safety." That's right—Charlayne and Hamilton got suspended, not their racist hecklers! A quick protest from hundreds of teachers and students restored them to campus.

I met Charlayne Hunter my first week on campus, and while understandably cautious, she seemed to appreciate somewhat my overly effusive welcome and offer to walk with her to class from Myers Hall.

I knew what she had already been through—more than eighteen months in court simply to attend UGA, which she chose for its strong journalism program, for which she was highly qualified. From day one on campus, she endured racial slurs, her car tires were slashed, and even some professors refused to address her in class. In all the clear demonstrations of racism, I never saw her express anger or fear, even though she told me later that she felt both often. Outwardly, she always appeared composed, prepared, and purposeful toward those who opposed her presence as well as to those who welcomed it.

I easily remember the fear I felt but never saw in her face during the times I and other supportive students walked with her through the rock-throwing, angry groups of students. She never lost her composure or deviated from her purpose. In a moment that must have felt somewhat redemptive, she returned in 1988 as UGA's commencement speaker—the first person of color to give the speech in the university's 185-year history—and in her stirring words, she told a new generation of students that "I stand before you now . . . because we have had our justice after all."

Forty or more years after we marched together in Georgia, Charlayne and I reconnected on one of my first trips to Africa. She had married a South African and was NPR's African bureau chief—just another plaudit in a career that has included positions at the *New Yorker* and the *New York Times* (where she got them to stop using the word *negro* to refer to African Americans), national correspondent and anchor positions at PBS's *The MacNeil/Lehrer NewsHour*, and CNN. She's also written several highly acclaimed books—and even started a South African wine company!

When we met for coffee in Johannesburg, Charlayne wore a traditional African caftan, her hair now a beautiful Afro, and looked every bit the warrior woman she had been at nineteen. At seventy-six, she's as dangerous as ever; just check out her Twitter feed!

MORE THAN ONCE, marching for African American civil rights in the South in the 1960s, I would hear a shout from fellow white southerners on the sidelines: "If they don't rape you, we're going to kill you."

It was an ugly, scary time, and it was hard to find equilibrium between all the diverse parts of my college life, which was, not unexpectedly, crammed with activities. I joined a sorority to help me navigate social life in a big university where I knew so few people. Through Phi Mu, I made lifelong friends, especially my roommate at the sorority house, Glenda Grimsley. She has been my best friend from college until now. Like Glenda, I was also active in campus politics and activities, running, unsuccessfully, for class president my sophomore year. "Pick Patsy" was my campaign slogan, with posters that featured my face inside a daisy. I didn't get picked.

I worked part-time at a dress shop, and I joined the civil-rights protests whenever possible. I lost my balance between what really mattered and what was popular more than once while trying to find where I felt I belonged and where I felt a sense of real purpose.

I wanted to focus on something more than getting through college as fast as possible to avoid more of the accumulating student loans that were necessary to augment the scholarship.

Fortunately, I had a new mentor, a new rabbi, in the form of my college advisor, who helped keep me focused during tumultuous and transformative times for this small-town girl.

"Education is your ticket to being in all the parades that matter," Dr. Boyd McWhorter reminded me. "Focus on that first—learn, *then* do. If you try to do everything, be everything, right now, you could lose yourself."

It was good advice—but I didn't fully adopt it. There were too many exciting opportunities everywhere around me, so I did it all. Or tried.

I was being pushed and pulled between a strong urge to be an activist, wanting to be on the front lines to right the many wrongs I witnessed close-up during those years in the South, and a desire to be popular and accepted within the dominant culture, which, to say the least, was not an activist or feminist one in the sixties at UGA.

That tension between wanting to fit in and fighting for change that began in college has continued, as I have often straddled (and sometimes bridged) different worlds and perspectives: I've juggled being an activist and a journalist, and not always successfully, especially since I often worked with people whose views on race, gender, and politics were opposite to mine. Sustaining relationships with family and friends across political differences, geographic divides, and life experiences was always challenging.

ONE SUSTAINING UGA relationship is with Tom Johnson, who became Lyndon B. Johnson's press secretary, publisher of the *LA Times*, and later president of CNN where we reconnected. Tom was an early role model, friend, and advocate—putting me forward more than once for the right career opportunities. He's a world class connector, but his first connection—introducing me to a man I would marry—wasn't as successful as some that followed.

It was one of those hot, sticky, early fall nights that people who grew up "below the gnat line" in Georgia know well. (The *gnat line* refers to the part of Georgia where those irritating little creatures live all year long because it never gets cold enough in the winter for them to hibernate or die.)

My college boyfriend and I were on Tybee Island, off the coast of Savannah, for a friend's wedding, where I was one of the bridesmaids. We'd been dating for two years—"pinned"—which was considered the step before engagement.

On the long drive down from Athens to Tybee that day, he talked about getting married, while I silently contemplated how to break the news that I planned to end the relationship. He was the perfect college boyfriend, fun-loving and a great dancer, but I wasn't thinking about marriage. I was far too curious about the world, too serious about my growing activism, and already committed to graduate school with plans to go for a PhD. I wanted to write and travel the world, not follow the BS with MRS or MOM, which was the expected path for Southern good girls. I was definitely a good girl, committed to being a virgin when I did get married.

That night on Tybee Beach, after too much champagne, I allowed him to pull off my bridesmaid's dress, which stuck to my body in the midnight heat. The kissing and fondling that always ended didn't stop. I remember the pain of entry and an immediate feeling of fear that was almost paralyzing as I was sure, that instant, that I was going to get pregnant. After all, I had just sinned, according to the Baptist preachers I heard every Sunday in Swainsboro.

I'm being irrational, I told myself as I rather frantically tried to get back into my sticky dress. No one gets pregnant the first time they have sex! The fear was palpable; the reality of what had happened, nauseating. The next day, visiting my parents in Swainsboro, I could barely look at my father; the shame and fear that I often felt in his presence were more intense than ever.

I was certain that something had happened on the beach that would change my life forever.

I WAS RIGHT. I was pregnant.

In my final quarter of living in the Phi Mu house, my body already felt like it no longer belonged only to me, and my mind raced with ways to fix this situation, trying to remember all the remedies I'd heard supposedly bad girls used when they got pregnant. It was the dark ages for women in terms of reproductive rights—no birth control pills, no legal abortions. Being pregnant *out of wedlock*—another quaint phrase—meant that marriage and babies were a lock, to be sure. A lock on all my dreams.

Castor oil. I'd heard taking a large dose of the popular laxative would work. It didn't, but it surely made me sicker. After another month of almost constant sickness, I finally drove myself to Atlanta and saw a gynecologist. "Mrs. Greenfield," he said, with a tone that indicated he knew I was using a fake name, "congratulations, you're going to have a baby."

Bursting into hysterical tears, I called Glenda, my best friend and roommate, who quickly went into battle-plan mode. "You've got to tell your parents . . . and him," she said. "And arrange a quick wedding. I'll help put it together. No one has to know."

"There has to be another solution," I protested and heard myself say the words, "I'll get an abortion." Just the word conjured up images of dark alleys with dimly lit rooms where so-called physicians helped girls in trouble for a few thousand dollars. I'd seen those films, usually ending with the girl bleeding to death.

But I'd also heard of the girls who had survived them and went on with their original life plans; maybe that could happen for me too. Glenda wasn't supportive of this option but offered to help. We asked around discreetly "for a friend" and got a name and number. One week later, I was driving to the appointment, having borrowed the cash from an unsuspecting and generous sorority sister, but Glenda had decided that she couldn't let me go through with it.

"I told him," she explained. "He's on his way to Atlanta to ask you to marry him." I'm not sure I would have gone through with the plan even if she hadn't intervened, but suddenly I felt completely out of control of my life.

"YOU'LL LOSE YOUR graduate fellowship if you get married," the dean of graduate school told me when I said I was getting married. Male students didn't lose their fellowships if they got married, but females did. At home, my announcement created a scene. My father remained stoic and silent while my mother focused on what people would say. We decided on a story for the public, that we had had a secret marriage in the summer.

Sometime in the fall of that year—how telling that I can never recall the date—we got married in a small chapel in Athens. I can't remember anything about the day except that I cried throughout the ceremony. How sad for the man who loved me and never wavered in his commitment to "do the right thing."

On June 5, 1965, our son, Mark, was born in Piedmont Hospital, now called Piedmont Atlanta Hospital. As was the custom then, I was knocked out with drugs and have no memory whatsoever of his birth. I woke up to find a big, round baby sucking on my breast, something else no one prepared me for. In fact, I was so unprepared for childbirth that I actually went into the hospital with my hair styled in a beehive, with dozens of hairpins that had to be extracted, one by one, when I went into labor. *Plink. Plink.* After eleven hours of labor, I looked like Phyllis Diller.

Mark was perfect. Motherly love took over, pushing away the anger and disappointment of missing my graduation ceremony, which was that same day. I'd so wanted the chance to march across that stage and be handed the evidence that I had, indeed, graduated with honors. But I also loved my son, fully and deeply, and gave myself over to that feeling.

Still, I was nowhere near where I had imagined myself to be at twenty-two. I had made a mistake, and I had to make the most of the unexpected fall on the journey and keep moving forward.

Within two short years, I knew that the marriage wasn't going to work. I was juggling teaching sixth grade in a challenging middle school on Atlanta's south side, finishing graduate work at Georgia State University, and also caring for a baby. My husband was looking for a good job and trying to transition from being considered the most likely to succeed, according to all our college friends, to the financial challenges of supporting a family without having completed a degree. We were both unhappy, and I didn't see this changing even if we kept trying.

My mother advised me to accept my fate and stay put. "You made your bed; now you have to lie in it."

My friends worried for me, and what would come of my life if I left. "What will you do as a single mom?" "Who will pay your bills?" I was already paying the bills.

This was my "problem that has no name," as Betty Friedan had called it in her book *The Feminine Mystique,* where she'd written, "I had a hunger that food cannot fill." I had read her book and was captivated by the news about women's marches for equality going on in New York and Washington, and I was experiencing a profound AHA moment about inequality as well.

With Mark nearly three, I went for the divorce—mutual agreement, split of the assets (which was zero), taking half the bills (which were big!).

AFTER THE DIVORCE, I signed up, along with Glenda, to take a group of students to Europe on one of those "if it's Tuesday, it must be Belgium" tours. It was my first trip outside the United States, and I discovered a passion for travel that has only increased every year since. As a divorced working mom, I also discovered that much of what I wanted to do would often conflict with my new responsibilities. I had custody of Mark and was receiving the state minimum for child support ($350 a month at the time), which didn't even cover the babysitters necessary for me to both teach and finish my coursework for my PhD. I was hired as an instructor at UGA to teach two courses while finishing my thesis and had to delay my doctorate plans as my student loans had run out.

I discovered that I loved teaching; my theatre training paid off big time as I kept my students' attention with dramatic readings of contemporary poetry or Herman Melville's *Moby-Dick*, the subject of my master's thesis. "You're one of the most popular instructors," my graduate advisor told me at my first semester's review. "Students are competing for your classes!"

When one of my colleagues shared with me that he'd gotten a raise for his second year, I asked for one, too. We had the same credentials and experience. The head of the English department smiled serenely at my request even as he denied it: "John's a married man with a family to support." No matter that I had a child to support as well. It was my first direct experience of equal work for unequal pay, and it further radicalized my fermenting feminism.

I poured myself into the social-justice protests of the day and was soon arrested for participating in a civil-rights march. Along with several of my freshmen students, I was herded into a holding pen at the Clarke County Jail. When the police discovered my faculty card, I was released without charges after a lecture from the sheriff about how we "liberals" needed to just move north and stop corrupting the young people we were supposed to be teaching.

THE CLARKE COUNTY sheriff's moral compass was despicable, but his sense of direction was keen; it was indeed time to move a bit farther north.

Virginia Commonwealth University had once been dubbed the "hippie's college," and joining the faculty there the following year was, for me, another big step away from what civil-rights activist Virginia Durr dubbed the "magic circle" of Southern womanhood: playacting the well-brought-up, conformist Southern belle; going crazy (if she had any spark of creativity whatsoever); or becoming the rebel and cutting ties with all expectations and "privilege."

Mark and I lived in a big house in the Fan district, Richmond's "Greenwich Village," with Dr. Casey Hughes, another divorcée and friend from UGA, and her two children. We quickly became the center of a growing student revolution happening on many college campuses where students, passions fueled by other social-justice movements of the time for black Americans and for women, began to make demands to have a louder voice, more freedoms.

Our house was like an ongoing consciousness-raising session with groups of students, other faculty, and regular out-of-town visitors crashing on various sofas and extra beds. There was rarely a night when there wasn't a group meeting or civil-rights or student-rights demonstration or an antiwar rally, and sometimes all of them rolled into one continuous house party.

Casey and I also ran the community women's consciousness-raising sessions, while holding down jobs that paid us less than our male colleagues and fending off the sexual overtures of so-called liberals who took up the label only when it became associated with sexual freedom. It was the time of communes, communal sex and drugs, love and peace, but for me, it was a year of financial challenges, anemic paychecks, and a son who needed more attention than he was getting.

I enjoyed teaching but the salary was not really enough to cover my bills and pay back student loans. I also longed to have time to write or go back to graduate school for my doctorate. And while I was as engaged as I could be in many activist activities, being in Virginia still felt like being in the backwater of a rising tide elsewhere. So when a college friend who had gone to work for the popular weekly *LOOK* offered to introduce me to the editor to pitch a story about the student uprisings that were big news at the time, I leapt at the opportunity to share my experiences as one of the faculty sympathizers. I drove to New York for the interview, and although the story idea was turned down, I got an offer for a job as a researcher with a salary that was more than I made as an assistant professor.

Even more important to me at the time was what I perceived to be a chance to start over in the city of my childhood dreams. I had been there once before, a brief visit as part of my studies as a drama major at UGA, and I had felt immediately at home, in sync with the city's rhythms that matched my own so much better than those of a college campus. I said good-bye to Casey and our communal home, and Mark and I headed for New York.

DAVE MAXEY, *LOOK*'S managing editor, gave it to me straight.

"Listen, Pat, I'd love to guarantee that this is going to work out for you, but you'll have to turn in some stories that you pursue on your own, and if I like them, I'll publish them. Meanwhile, your job will be to do research for the other writers and occasionally, maybe I can get you an assignment with one of our photographers. You can learn a lot by watching them cover a story."

It didn't take but two of the martini lunches typical of the day to discover why everyone slumped over their typewriters between 3 and 5 p.m.—yes, typewriters, with actual desk phones and desks and offices, think *Mad Men* with our own "Jon Hamms" and romantic intrigues and pretty out-front competitiveness. In this totally foreign world of New York journalism, where most of the women went to Smith or Barnard and carried a certainty about them that I clearly lacked, I was anything but confident. I was scared that any minute I would be found out to be a small-town girl whose only experience at this point had been teaching freshman English.

I had to fake confidence and channel Mrs. Reid's words ("speak up because no one else is going to do that for you") more than once when challenged to step back or step aside. I channeled Grandmother, too, and just kept moving forward, as fast as my too-high heels would carry me. (Later, a fellow writer, Pat Carbine, said without looking up, "New York streets are better navigated in more sensible shoes. And they're less noisy, too.")

Navigating motherhood in NYC was another challenge entirely. The cheap loft I sublet over a Chinese restaurant in lower Chinatown—on the Bowery, actually—wasn't a great place for Mark, who was four years old and eager to explore. After the first weeks, my mother suggested he live with her and my father until I got settled. Mark liked that plan, given that the grandparents spoiled him, and they would laugh and smile when he was around, rare events during my own childhood. He could also visit more easily with his dad, who was still living in Georgia. So I agreed, and Mark went to Swainsboro for the summer.

Alone now in the big city, I began to see a big story developing in my neighborhood in Chinatown. Gangs were being formed among different groups of new immigrants, and fights began to break out over who controlled a block or got to sit on a certain stoop outside a particular restaurant.

"It's getting violent there," I explained to the skeptical-looking editor when I pitched the story, "but I've been volunteering at one of the community centers for new residents, and I think I can get the kids to talk to me about what's going on."

I did manage to get two key gang leaders to talk to me, and after a few conversations that revealed the story of two rival gangs and their families, my editor encouraged me to keep listening and writing. Maxey also realized the story was gaining in importance as the violence in Chinatown was making headlines in the *New York Post* and *Daily News.*

By mid-September, my story had been approved; the storyboards were put up for the editorial staff, a practice in those days for magazines. I can still visualize the photographs and headline: "Chinatown: A Family Divided." My first story with a byline was scheduled for the October issue, and I was moving forward faster than I had imagined toward being a bona fide writer in the city of my dreams.

I had moved uptown, too, out of the Chinatown sublease to a ground-floor apartment in a townhouse on the Upper West Side, at that time the less expensive side of Central Park, and Mark had returned from Swainsboro. I had a downtown artist boyfriend, an uptown apartment, a son in a public school that I could walk him to every morning, and a job I loved. Success!

Until one morning, only a month or so later, when the news came over the loudspeakers at Cowles Communications, the company that owned *LOOK*, that the magazine would not be publishing another edition; the business was bankrupt. Tubs full of ice and Bloody Marys were offered to the stunned staff, and realizing that I was now unemployed and with no idea what was next, I passed on the drinks and started making calls. In the chaos of the next few days, as the television cameras showed up to cover the dismantling of the offices, I was asked by a television reporter about what I would do next. Noting that she was employed and I wasn't, I looked straight into her camera and said, "I think I'll try television!"

I DID TRY—AUDITION after audition followed my onetime, brief television report on the Chinatown story—but Christmas came and went and there were no offers. I was broke and still unemployed.

But before giving up entirely, I made one more call—to David Garth, the political media guru I had met while reporting a story on the US Conference of Mayors for *LOOK*. Garth was going to run the media for former New York mayor John V. Lindsay's newly announced campaign for the presidency.

"Want to help me elect a president?" David asked when I explained my plight.

A job! "Yes, when do I start?"

David Garth already had a reputation as a great propagandist, and I'd join his media team alongside a young Yale graduate named Jeff Greenfield, who had already worked for Robert Kennedy as a speechwriter. Our assignment was to conceive, write, and produce political ads that would secure wins for Lindsay in the Wisconsin and South Carolina primaries.

Jeff and I produced more than thirty campaign commercials for Lindsay, and I learned fast how to conceive, write, and edit political television commercials that at that time were starting to transform all political campaigns. It was a high-stakes, high-pressure environment and a learning opportunity that would serve me well post campaign, even though I wasn't sure how at the time.

Even then, Garth Associates had better equipment and more advanced technology than the networks I'd been auditioning for. We had a state-of-the-art Avid editing system inside a mobile truck, and we wrote, edited, and got thirty-second commercials on the air within hours, not days. I learned more during three months on the road with Jeff and more from David Garth about how to tell a story than I would have learned in months, maybe years, at a television station.

I loved it, too, but I didn't like being away from Mark as much as I was. Fortunately, Mrs. Weiner, the kindly babysitter who lived upstairs in our brownstone, had moved into our small apartment to care for Mark while I was on the road five days a week—until, that is, this new career also came to an abrupt end.

Lindsay lost the primary elections, and he called it quits. Garth had other campaigns and I could have continued to work on his team, but my dream was still to get a job in television and hopefully one that would allow me to be a more present parent. When I told Jeff Greenfield, my Garth colleague who had become a close friend, that I was leaving to pursue a job in television, he predicted, "Television will ruin your life!" Ironic words from a man who later became a network television star political correspondent and analyst.

Mayor Lindsay's quixotic campaign became memorialized the next year on the big screen in one of my favorite Robert

Redford films, *The Candidate*, inspired by David Garth's dictum that "any campaign can be won with the right media campaign." Redford's character in the movie had that right media campaign and won his election. At the end of the movie, the winning candidate looks up after his victory speech and asks, "Now what?"

I had the same question! I was at yet another crossroads and ready to once again risk starting over.

DANGEROUS TIMES CALL FOR DANGEROUS WOMEN

In Conversation with Ai-jen Poo

When Ai-jen found herself volunteering at a domestic violence shelter for immigrant women, she was struck by how difficult it was for the women—all of whom were working full-time—to make ends meet. Many of the women worked in low-wage service occupations, caring for the families of others, yet were finding it impossible to care for their own families. Later on, when Ai-jen's family was no longer able to care for her grandfather, they were forced to place him in a nursing home, and it was at the nursing home that Ai-jen observed close-up the challenges for caregivers, 90 percent of whom are women and disproportionately women of color, and the impact on people in need of care, like her grandfather. It's been her life's mission to fight for the rights of caregivers—nannies, housekeepers, home health aides, and all the others who, while caring for our most vulnerable, are themselves undervalued, underpaid, and subjected to discrimination and harassment. In 2010, she helped get the first Domestic Workers Bill of Rights passed, which has brought protections to more than 200,000 domestic workers in New York.

Many caregivers, of course, are undocumented immigrants, and Ai-jen has pushed tirelessly to create a path to citizenship for them. She speaks for the caring economy; she represents the people who care for the rest of us and to win them legal rights recognizing and protecting their dignity and humanity.

A recipient of a MacArthur "Genius" Award, Ai-jen is the director of the National Domestic Workers Alliance, codirector of Caring Across Generations, and author of The Age of Dignity: Preparing for the Elder Boom in a Changing America. *I talked with Ai-jen about her journey to becoming a dangerous woman, determined to change the world for caregivers.*

What does becoming more dangerous mean to you and your work?

Ai-jen: While I'm not sure others see us this way (yet), the domestic workers movement is dangerous. Fighting to recognize the value of the care economy is dangerous. Building power of poor women of color is dangerous. It disrupts conventional wisdom about what we value and who has power, which gets to some pretty fundamental questions about society and how we've organized it. Much of our world has been designed by and for rich and powerful white men. The idea that we should not only empathize with but see domestic workers as powerful is a dangerous idea.

I've personally felt the most dangerous when working collectively with other women in a way that challenges or threatens the existing logic or consensus that keeps power in the hands of those who already have it—it can be through pushing new ideas, new ways of doing things or being, and certainly when demanding new configurations of power.

Has age been a factor for you in this journey to embracing risk and speaking up for others, many of whom don't have a public voice?

Ai-jen: Because I'm a "younger" woman—well, that's all relative—and a woman of color, an Asian woman in particular, and because of the way Asian women are racialized, I don't think most people think of me as dangerous. At least, not initially. Maybe disruptive, more like an annoyance than actually dangerous. I associate danger with risk, fear, and threat. I don't think I inspired those emotions in people until I was older and much more established. People always underestimate women, especially women of color.

What are the biggest remaining challenges to your creating the changes you set out to do?

Ai-jen: I've certainly had challenges in my work, but I think of it like this: most change that's worth fighting for, that's truly meaningful in people's lives, requires some disruption and will instigate some level of backlash. Some people will not be happy, and they may even attack you, try to undermine you. Every action causes a reaction. It just means you have to stay really grounded in your sense of purpose, anticipate and prepare for the reactions, and have practices that keep you focused on purpose. I also prioritize keeping people around me who I trust to keep me on purpose. The beautiful thing about danger and risk is that you never have to do anything alone.

Do you agree with the idea that we are living in dangerous times and dangerous times call for dangerous women?

Ai-jen: I think we're living in dangerous times. I often compare it to a sun storm, a weather pattern that's common to parts of the Midwest and the Southeast. It's when it's pouring down rain and the sun is still shining brightly through. We are living in a political sun storm, and women are the sun—we keep showing up to march, to call Congress, to support survivors, to run for office, and to vote. We are holding the democracy up and together. And yet the forces pouring down rain are powerful. More than a challenge, women—all of us—are in the fight of our lives for the soul of the country. And it's dangerous.

Chapter 3

Saying Yes

"PAT, BECOME A blonde. It'll help get you a job in front of the cameras."

So said Raysa Bonow, a sturdily built woman with red hair pulled back into a tight bun—not exactly a fashion ideal herself—but I knew enough to listen to her, the executive producer at WBZ-TV in Boston. If I wanted to be hired for an on-air position, I needed to do something about my hair. It seemed to come up in every conversation with a television executive.

I had joined the station as an associate producer of a weekly show about local politics, not the job of my dreams, but at least a step inside the door of a television station—and in this case, the most popular station in Boston.

As it turned out, being a woman or a minority was an asset when it came to getting hired to work in television in the late sixties and early seventies. The Equal Employment Opportunity Commission (EEOC), established in the wake of the civil-rights and women's movements, required companies to document nondiscriminatory hiring practices. These were not quotas, exactly, but the impact of the FCC on one side, requiring regular review and renewals of broadcast licenses, and the EEOC as a new monitor of hiring practices, led to new opportunities for women and minorities in television and radio—opportunities that might not have come so quickly without these incentives and accountability.

WBZ actually had two women on the air, one anchoring a noon news program and one hosting a morning talk show. And of course, Raysa Bonow was the Mother Superior to us all. A veteran of consciousness-raising groups, in 1970, Raysa had helped launch *For Women Today* (later redubbed *The Sonya Hamlin Show*). Forget advice on getting out tough stains or landing that man, Raysa and the show's host, Sonya Hamlin, made sure the show tackled balancing career and motherhood, fighting for equal pay, a week-long exploration on gay and straight sexuality, and even a live self-examination to alert women to the dangers of breast cancer. It's almost impossible to convey how revolutionary this was in the early 1970s.

RAYSA QUICKLY BECAME a mentor, one who knew how to get what she wanted from the men with decision-making power. I took her advice, streaked my hair blonde, and sure enough, a few months later, was asked to audition for a job as theatre and movie critic on the 11 p.m. news and got it. I knew a little bit about theatre, given my earlier focus in college, but not a clue about how to review film. But I was now a blonde and had the ability to talk live on television without nerves—an ability I attribute to keeping eighteen-year-olds interested in eighteenth-century poetry. Of course, I continued my producing position, too. After all, the news director explained, I was lucky to have both jobs, and I didn't disagree, even though I was paid for only one.

My day started early with meetings for the weekly show, essentially producing minidocumentaries on political campaigns and candidates. I'd finish those assignments, rush home for a quick dinner with Mark, change my clothes, and zip off to opening night at the theatre or a film premiere, after which I'd taxi back to the station (I didn't own a car for the first two years) to write up a review with seconds to spare before I slid into place next to the big, handsome, popular anchorman Tom Ellis, who always welcomed me on the set with a wink and boomed in his Texas drawl, "Well, here's Pat back from another glamorous opening."

Not exactly *glamorous*, but it didn't take me long to realize that my ninety-second critiques were sometimes deciding the fate of theatre productions trying out in Boston before heading to Broadway or determining whether movies would deliver the much needed opening-weekend box-office punch. The power of the medium would dawn slowly and dramatically over my first year of mistakes, mishaps, and misgivings.

Within the first month on the 11 p.m. news, I was called in to a meeting with the news director.

"You're using too many big words, Pat," he told me. "You have to learn to write in simple sentences—and sound less Southern. Also, wear brighter colors and lower necklines, so you look like you just came from the theatre." He looked pointedly at my outfit. "And for god's sake, ditch the ugly scarves."

Raysa worked on my vocabulary so I'd sound less professorial and tried to smooth my Southern accent by having me repeat over and over Yiddish words that began with *s-c-h—schlep, schlemiel.* Unfortunately, she didn't instruct me about what those words meant. One night I was reviewing the latest Woody Allen film: "Woody Allen plays his usual schmuck," I told our viewers, and right away, the switchboard lit up with outraged Jewish viewers who knew exactly what schmuck meant.

"You just called Woody Allen a penis!'" one viewer thundered over the phone. I apologized on the news the next night, and after consultations with leaders from the Jewish community, I agreed to get instruction from a local rabbi who became another mentor of sorts. He gave me an impressive, acceptable Yiddish vocabulary that has served me well from time to time, and with his support, I got past my first televised blooper. Imagine the longer-term damage of this cultural appropriation and misuse of Yiddish on television in the Twitter/meme world!

That wouldn't be my last misstep. No one could have prepared me for the fame that comes with being on television. Boston was as passionate and as personal about their television reporters and news anchors as they were about their hockey and basketball players. I could feel eyes on me when I ate at restaurants; sometimes my name filtered into the gossip pages, with speculation about whom I might be dating.

No doubt about it . . . I was experiencing a meteoric rise. Within two years, I was reporting, anchoring an afternoon news program, and reviewing film and theatre on the 11 p.m. news—but I was still being paid as if I were the political producer for one weekly show.

Raysa prepped me for asking the boss for a raise.

"Ask to double your salary," she insisted, "because you are more than doubling the work you were hired to do."

That seemed pretty gutsy to me. Sure, this man had hired me to do both roles—but not before telling me that, at age twenty-nine, I was too old for television. And being a single mother was strike two. Still, I was feeling confident about my popularity and value to the station. So the next day I walked into his office, my spine straight.

"I'm doing more than twice as much as you hired me to do. I love it, I don't want to give it up, but I'm working from 6 a.m. to 11 p.m. I feel like it's time to talk about what I'm worth to the station."

Deadly silence. Then, the man who had hired me in spite of his misgivings about my age and motherhood, who had advocated for me when new opportunities arose, walked over and sat in the chair beside me, frowned reflectively, and said, "You know, I was walking through the grocery store last week and noticed that hamburger is now $1.39 a pound. Just a couple weeks ago, it was $1.98. The value of that hamburger meat varies a lot. Talent in television is like hamburger meat. You never know when people are going to lose their appetite for hamburgers and look for something new."

Everything I'd prepared flew out of my head in an instant. Why were we talking about hamburger meat? I envisioned myself inside that Styrofoam plastic-wrapped package with the sell-by date and price stamped on it.

"Many young women"—emphasis on the *young*—"would kill to have any of your jobs," he said, standing up to indicate the meeting was over.

But he had one final item on his agenda.

"How about dinner between the early and late news?" he asked. "I'm free tonight and maybe we can discuss the raise a bit more over a glass of wine?"

Sadly, I wasn't surprised by the overture. Nearly every interview during my months of unemployment in New York had ended with similar invitations. In those days, we seldom, if ever, shared our fears or our truths, and in our silence, out of fear of reprisal or loss of job or promotion, we were complicit in the abuse of power that was widespread—then and now.

I knew what was at risk in declining the invitation to dinner, and I wasn't wrong. After all, I was now working without a contract, and the prior discussions about getting my own talk show stopped cold. I worried that the slightest misstep, the smallest error, would seal my sell-by date. And of course, I didn't say a word about the negotiation that became an inappropriate invitation, nor did I tell anyone about the remarks about my breasts or legs or probing questions about my personal life or the "breast touches" when mics were adjusted. I'd bet the raise I didn't get that the other women at the station were getting the same sexual innuendoes and personal invitations and intimidating power plays.

Imagine how many future #MeToo stories we might have prevented had we shared our experiences and taken collective actions to expose the abusers. Silence and fear kept us in self-protective silos. Today, as more and more women have gone public and some high-profile perpetrators have faced the consequences, we have an opportunity and a responsibility, in my opinion, to end our silences, to talk about what happened and continues to happen, and to work collectively to end the power dynamic that was used then and now to dominate, diminish, and create environments where women were and are unsafe and exploited.

In those earlier, silent times, I dropped my push for a raise and continued to do four jobs and get paid for two—a familiar story for women in nearly every sector of business, even today. While I believe that being the one who volunteers to step up for a new responsibility is important, there's a line between being eager and being exploited, and it wasn't always clear then, but I'm clear about it now. Wanting to advance, being eager to learn, and proving that we could handle the responsibilities was part of being among the first in any profession. And while it's still true that there is an expectation that we have to continue to work twice as hard for half the money, it's critical to support all efforts for equal pay for equal work so that can become a reality for all women.

Reality shifted for me when the competing station offered me a job. "Have your agent call me," was the message that changed the personal power dynamic in my life.

I didn't have an agent, so I decided to call the only agent I knew personally—Bob Woolf, a prominent sports agent whom I had met through mutual friends and who had kindly hosted me at Bruins and Celtics games. Even though he only represented athletes at this time (later, he would represent Larry King and a lot of other big names in television), he agreed to take me on. Without even talking to me about salary and going on the scale of sports salaries he had negotiated for his star players, he asked for three times what I was making. The general manager at the competing ABC station agreed without much discussion, and Bob Woolf then took that offer back to my boss, who matched the salary on the spot, with no mention of the price of hamburger meat that week.

I learned from that first real negotiation that it was better for me to have someone else make the salary ask for me. Like others, particularly in my generation, I was less likely to put as high a value on my work as others did, and having agents negotiate salaries over the years was a better option for me. But when I did have to negotiate for myself, I became much braver about asking for fair value.

Later in my career as an executive, I observed that men, in general, ask for more money than women applying for the same positions, and that men definitely ask for raises more often.

I believe this lag in our personal-value proposition has a lot to do with the *imposter syndrome*—the internal doubt about our own success or accomplishments that makes us wary of asking for more, sure that we're not as good as others believe we are. And the reluctance to push for a promotion or a raise is also the hangover of exhausting, energy-sapping turf battles that make us, as women, reluctant to make waves or to support each other, having been assured that the spaces for women are more limited and our sell-by dates can be moved forward if we appear too ambitious or aggressive. And of course, many of us still wage the secret battle internally to navigate the sexual power plays that often occur during negotiations about our value.

For millions of our sisters working in jobs that don't begin to pay what their labor is worth, working twice as hard for half the pay or less, there are other barriers to fair and equal earnings. They don't enjoy the freedoms or opportunities to negotiate for raises or to stand up to the power plays or sexual threats that also threaten necessary livelihoods. We have a responsibility to speak up for them. To raise our voices, to use our collective power and experience in negotiating to obtain better guarantees and protections for all working women.

In my working life, I've been fortunate (or shortsighted, according to my accountant) to sometimes put other considerations ahead of money—doing what I love, learning something new, having new adventures, and creating something of value.

As a result, I don't have a huge retirement fund or even the luxury to cease work for pay altogether, but in my new "less to prove or lose" place in life's journey, I'm making work choices the same way I'm making life choices: based more on time spent than money made. And I discovered, late in my working life, that knowing my worth and asking for it didn't narrow the options; it increased them. Believing that was a big step that felt risky for a long time, but it's a risk I wish I had taken earlier on my journey to becoming more valued in the marketplace, and importantly, on my journey to believing in my own value.

"DO *NOT* VOLUNTEER to cover women's stories of any kind. And for goodness' sake, don't call yourself a feminist!"

That was the advice from everyone at WBZ, but it was the seventies and the women's movement was front and center. It was a time when the problems with no names got names and coalitions were forming across sectors of work and life, and I wanted to play a part. As a news reporter, I couldn't become the story by joining the marches, but I wanted to make the story better known and understood. My female colleagues and I wanted to get *more* stories about women on the air, and in 1974, the women of WBZ achieved something that the *New York Times* called "history making for women."

Yes, We Can was the bold name we gave to our idea of a marathon day of programming for women, produced and directed and hosted by women. Raysa headed up the production team, which by now included a woman or two behind the cameras and on the technical crews and more in front of the cameras too. WBZ's male management turned over the station and twenty-four hours of valuable broadcast time to a bold and audacious idea that we could get an audience for a full day and night of programming focused on women's issues and that women and men would show up in person at the venue for live panels, demonstrations, presentations, and a *happening* that we really didn't even know how to describe.

I tried to describe it to Gloria Steinem, whom I invited to cohost the event. I'd met her at one of the early women's movement marches in New York through her friend and my colleague at *LOOK*, Pat Carbine. Gloria agreed to come but was skeptical that such an event would really have any impact. She did offer to invite other activists and friends, and I promised that we would make this a meaningful step forward for women—at least in Boston and, we believed, throughout television—if we were successful.

As the host of the black-tie gala that launched our twenty-four-hour television marathon, *Yes, We Can,* I looked out of sync in my sparkling pink pantsuit (that Raysa had insisted I wear) while introducing such feminist icons as Gloria, African American activist Florynce Kennedy, Betty Friedan, and other women leaders who were more appropriately attired for the seriousness of this groundbreaking event. We wanted to use television's power, at least for twenty-four hours, for women—for our stories, our challenges, our accomplishments. Singer/songwriter Helen Reddy performed "I Am Woman," which had become something of an anthem at that time, and as we all sang with her, "I am woman, hear me roar!" we felt the power of sisterhood that had brought us to that moment.

Of course, the women's movement isn't one voice, one song, or even one agenda, and there were differences of opinion about what it meant to be a feminist, even then (and of course, now). Reflecting on what happened the next day, we should have been more alert to the differences in opinion and the need to be more inclusive.

We had taken over the Hynes Auditorium in downtown Boston for a full day of workshops, panels, a job fair, and relevant information shared live on television on everything from women's health to work-life balance to job training. More than 25,000 women (some reports said 75,000) showed up on what turned out to be the coldest day of the year, creating a traffic jam in downtown Boston and a crisis in the overcrowded on-site daycare we had announced we were generously providing.

Women ran everything: the cameras, the lighting, the sound, directing, producing. At one end on a large stage, we held interviews and conversations that were being broadcast live. Each of the on-air personalities took turns on stage, moderating the panels. I had the noon panel with the fabulous Flo Kennedy. Wearing her signature black cowboy hat and boots, Flo sat down next to me on the stage.

I was thrilled to be interviewing her; Flo had busted through so many barriers. She'd graduated from Columbia Law School in the early fifties and become an activist for feminist and civil-rights causes, eventually touring the country with Gloria Steinem. Now Flo gave me a skeptical if not downright disapproving look, running her eyes over yet another girly pink pantsuit (at least it wasn't the sparkling one) and my perfectly coiffed hair, and said, "Honey, am I supposed to look at you or the cameras during this interview?"

I knew she was making a point that had nothing to do with camera angles, but she quickly laughed that huge, cackling laugh of hers, slapped my upper leg, and said, "It's okay, honey. I can see beyond your color." Flo would use her quick wit and humor to defuse many tense situations during those days of marches and protests, and on this day of groundbreaking television, too.

Our interview was just starting when a loud commotion in the auditorium clearly signaled a problem. Looking past the stage lights, I saw a large crowd moving quickly toward the stage, carrying huge white signs reading "Liberation, Not Tokenism" and "Abortion on Demand." As they moved closer, I could read four-letter words on some of the other signs and hear curses being shouted. A similar torrent of four-letter words was streaming in my ear through the communications device connecting me to the control room at the station. Pandemonium broke out in the auditorium as nonprotesters and protesters shouted at each other, and there was a panic back at the station, since all of this was being broadcast live!

"Go to commercial!" I kept shouting over my headset, which gave me time to assess the situation. The biggest group of marchers, dressed in jeans and combat boots, were protesting the lack of lesbians on the program and the fact that gay rights weren't being represented anywhere in the materials being distributed. They were right, of course. We had made a significant blunder and were as guilty of not being inclusive as we were accusing television, in general, of being.

Now we had a big challenge. How to keep this day for which we'd worked so hard from falling apart? We knew that *the optics,* as they'd come to be known, would be the women protesters shouting four-letter words at other women; women against women.

We agreed that the protesters should be heard and Sonya Hamlin, my experienced WBZ colleague, Flo, and I made another seat on the panel for one of the parade leaders, who also gave my pink suit a once-over, rolling her eyes as she sat down next to me. I took on the challenge to try to keep one group of unhappy women, regrettably excluded and rightfully upset about it, from dominating the rest of the day and distracting everyone from the positive interchanges we were witnessing all over the room. Flo was masterful in negotiating past the anger to a place where the panel ended with hugs and high fives.

When the event was behind us, over late-night drinks and laughter, we organizers talked over the stories we were sure we'd see in the press the next day. Would it be all the job opportunities? The health-care options? The interviews with feminism's leading lights? Instead, sure enough, the protesters grabbed the headlines, and the photograph of me in my pink suit facing off with the parade leaders was front-page in some places.

Yes, We Can proved that a group of women could put together a full day and evening of informative, relevant programming and that women would show up and tune in. But it had also reinforced the disempowering narrative that women don't agree among themselves about important issues and that we don't support each other's efforts. It's certainly true that women as a global community are not monolithic in values, opinions, or shared goals and aspirations. But I believed, even then in 1974, that we have more in common than the political, religious, and cultural differences that sometimes divide us, and tapping into that resource—the power of collective action—sustains my commitment to optimize every opportunity to tell a different story about women and what we want, need, and can give to each other.

REGRETTABLY, THE STORY of our differences continues to push through the most positive stories of the accomplishments of collective actions toward common goals over the years since *Yes, We Can.* The response to the call for women to march in 2017, following the election of Donald Trump, created a collective action that moved millions of women all over the world into the streets in unified protest.

The convergence delivered a powerful message. But after time, as too often happens, discord arose among some of the organizers, and differences of opinion divided communities. Leading up to the Women's March in 2019, stories in the press focused on the disunity, but still women showed up all over the world to march again, together. Women intent upon change are not always of one mind on any single issue, and while I admit to feeling deep sadness when the differences distract us—and the media—from the purpose of the work or action, I prefer to focus on what is accomplished, and above all, to stay connected even when our ties are tested.

According to sociologist Jo Reger, who studies social movements, "sometimes the ways we begin to change these things is when we begin to talk about them, and to examine the world around us to see: What have I been allowing? What have I not noticed? What have I been accepting? What has my privilege blinded me to? And how can I begin to address it?"

I emerged from the *Yes, We Can* experience committed to asking those questions about how we, privileged women inside media, were going to use media's power to bridge differences and convene difficult conversations.

"HOUSEWIVES AREN'T INTERESTED in hearing other women's stories or learning about issues or watching other women on television," was the response I got from the head of programming when I proposed a new daily talk show that would continue in the spirit of *Yes, We Can*, an effort he had dismissed already as proof of the theory that women won't show up for each other.

"Women love their daytime dramas," he continued, pointing out that the so-called popular soap operas, like *Guiding Light* and *General Hospital*, "are giving women what they want." Yes, that was the prevailing theory of programming in the seventies, but as I tried to point out to the closed-minded male executive, women watching television in the daytime had few if any viewing options. I went on to suggest that this was a narrow and possibly outdated view of the women in the audience and why not try an optional format—one that offered women content with more relevance to their lives?

I also pointed out to the skeptical executive that I had tested high on the audience likability scores—yes, there were and are such measurements of television personalities—so if I hosted such a show, I could possibly bring in more women viewers. I wasn't asking for more money, after all, just more television time and an opportunity to devote more of it to substantive programming for women.

After a few more meetings, I got permission to pull together a team and launch *Woman 74*—an hour live every day featuring interviews and conversations with women about women. With a small but evolving sisterhood at the station, we moved into new, and as it turned out, risky territory.

On a show about aging, a well-known pediatrician and family therapist named Dr. Eleanor Hamilton was asked about the biggest challenge for older women and calmly replied, "They think they can't fuck after sixty." Pandemonium broke out in the studio with the director shouting, "Go to commercial!" We did, but it was too late. The four-letter word, forbidden in the tightly regulated and pre-cable world of the seventies, had gone out to the large regional New England audience. The phones started ringing as Dr. Hamilton, wearing her signature wire-rimmed specs and looking like the grandmother she was, wondered, Why the fuss?

The FCC and FBI arrived to investigate and explained that we had violated an interstate-commerce law that regulated the transport of content, including language. The station was fined and the show was put on a hiatus for a few weeks. Because of this incident and others, stations and networks instituted a seven-second delay on all live broadcasts—time enough for a television director to delete a word or a comment before it was transmitted.

We also took on the issue of abortion, knowing that this subject always means controversy, given the great divide of opinions. I had decided to interview Dr. Kenneth Edelin, a doctor who had performed a late-term legal abortion, as well as the woman who elected to have the abortion. The state of Massachusetts had brought manslaughter charges against Dr. Edelin, ultimately convicting him even though he'd performed the procedure shortly after *Roe v. Wade* legalized it. The fact that Dr. Edelin was black and the jury was all white certainly made race a factor in the trial and debate that followed. The conviction was eventually overturned on appeal, but the program created more trouble than even we anticipated.

The next morning, protesters surrounded WBZ, calling for the show to be canceled. Negotiations with them didn't go well. The station offered them time on the show, but unlike the lesbian leaders who rightfully protested their omission from programming at *Yes, We Can*, this group wasn't convinced to trade television time for appeasement. So WBZ suspended live broadcasts for another few weeks, and I got a lot of press, some praising my courage, others condemning the use of public airwaves for advocating my clearly liberal and feminist point of view.

Both opinions had validity, but so did the newsworthiness of the subject and the importance of an open conversation about what was at stake, not just in the case of one doctor who told the *New York Times* in 1975, "Nobody likes to do abortions, but the least we can do is make it safe and humane," but what's at stake again right now. More than forty years later, in the United States, we are witnessing state legislators, governors, and Congress pass laws and enact policies that are diminishing (many with the goal of ultimately eliminating) a woman's right to choose when or if to have children and what is the best health outcome for herself and her family.

Reproductive justice and a woman's right to control her own body are still a battleground, one that feels far too familiar to those of us who came of reproductive age when there was no legal access to a safe and humane abortion in cases of unwanted pregnancies, incest, rape, or threats to a mother's health. The generations since *Roe v. Wade* who also have access to many forms of safe contraception have perhaps taken the freedom to control what happens to their bodies for granted. I hope they won't be silent about the real consequences of losing reproductive rights because it feels like we are closer to that reality than I could have imagined we would ever be again.

MY REALITY AT this time in my life, approaching thirty, was a far cry from the fears I had felt in coping with an unplanned pregnancy, getting through an early divorce without support from friends or family, and putting together a life as a single mother. I had landed in a career that satisfied my drive to learn—nothing better for an innately curious person than journalism, which presents each new assignment as a learning opportunity. I was making more money than I ever imagined and doing work that I felt was important. I was discovering a natural inclination to lead and a love of working with women.

I was proving more fearless than I would ever have predicted in taking on challenges and controversy in my work, but still not fearless enough to expose the unwanted sexual advances that continued for me and most assuredly for others. I regret that I didn't use my personal power resulting from my position and popularity to speak out, to go public and name names, to take the risk of not being believed, and to losing hard-fought gains with a distracting controversy and confrontation. Today, witnessing the brave women who come forward, risking so much—and still not always being believed (and often losing more than their perpetrators)—I feel shame for my silence then and anger that this dangerous power dynamic still exists.

Looking back, I had enough personal power to take that chance. I had made myself almost indispensable with my highly visible positions on early-morning drive-time radio, on a daily talk show, as an anchor of a daily news program, and as the high-profile entertainment reporter on the 11 p.m. news. Little wonder I tested high on audience surveys. I was on television a lot.

And I was not home enough. I remember sitting in 6 p.m. staff meetings, feeling guilty that I was missing early dinner with Mark—again—and at the same time, feeling guilty that I wasn't giving the meeting my full attention either. This was a dilemma that I didn't dare discuss then with my male colleagues or with most of the women I knew who were either single or without children. I didn't know anyone who had a nanny either, but I had hired a graduate student to live with us and be with Mark when I wasn't—which was too much of the time. She was a kind and loving companion for many years, but she wasn't his mother.

He needed more from me, and I needed more help balancing the opportunities at work and my responsibilities as a parent—a balance that is still, for so many working parents, a question with no simple answer. It is the one question that I never feel I answer well when asked, as I often am, how I navigated my career while being a single parent. "Not well enough" is the most honest answer.

Like other women, I looked everywhere for role models on how to balance the work-life challenge better, so I was listening closely when Katherine "Kay" Fanning, the first woman to become editor of a national newspaper, the *Christian Science Monitor*, was asked whether women could have it all—a successful career and a satisfying personal life. She replied, "Yes, we can have it all—just not all at one time."

An important insight, but I didn't stop trying to have it all and at once, at least not during this time of professional and personal growth, challenges, and opportunities. I embraced each one and became more and more committed to the idea that I could make a difference through media's power—and this became the touchstone for all my subsequent choices as a journalist, independent producer, talk-show host, and ultimately, as a media executive.

SOME THIRTY YEARS after *Yes, We Can*, I was invited to a meeting one rainy Sunday afternoon in Gloria Steinem's apartment with several other veterans of media and various social-justice movements. The subject was media and what we could do about the consolidation of its power among fewer and fewer owners as well as the lack of regulation in a game-changing technological revolution that was transforming the media landscape and all our lives, even then, in 2005, with consequences that we couldn't anticipate. As the CEO of PBS at the time, I was experiencing these challenges up close and was ready to support any efforts to address the negative impact of media's underrepresentation and misrepresentation of women.

We agreed that it was time to do something; after all, women were the most important consumers of all media, including the new technologies, and were, in fact, shaping the power of social media as its earliest adopters. Our attributes as communicators and storytellers aligned well with the social-media tools. Facebook, Twitter, Instagram, and LinkedIn kept us connected with family, friends, and colleagues, and women became, quickly, the most highly valued consumers of the new digital-media platforms. But women weren't leading or owning any of the new media companies, and the number of women in *clout positions*—those with decision-making power—in any media or technology company was still appallingly low.

After an afternoon of complaining and pointing out the problems, an action plan was presented by three women who already had lifetimes of frontline leadership in movements for change: Robin Morgan, Gloria Steinem, and Jane Fonda. They proposed a new advocacy organization to act as a monitor of the media, documenting the need for changes, and to be an advocate for increasing the numbers of women on-screen and behind the scenes. The group, which included committed feminists with media experience and resources to support a new nonprofit—Loreen Arbus, Carol Jenkins, Helen Zia, Regina Scully, and others—stepped up and with Robin, Gloria, and Jane as founders, launched the Women's Media Center (WMC).

I signed on for the board, too. I then became chair, and now I'm cochair with Maya Harris. Since 2005, WMC has effectively used interconnected strategies of research: issuing comprehensive annual reports on the status of women in all media and technology as well as evidence of the need for greater diversity and higher numbers; promoting more women's voices and opinions through the SheSource database; training progressive women to be media ready; and recognizing and celebrating the women in media who are leading change and having positive impact.

Every year, at the WMC awards, I get to present the Pat Mitchell Lifetime Achievement Award to a woman whose media work reflects a commitment to improving the status of women in media. It's deeply meaningful to me to publicly recognize and honor another woman and her work, and so far the award has been given to Christiane Amanpour, Katie Couric, Judy Woodruff, the late Gwen Ifill, Regina Scully, and Abigail Disney—women using media's power to further empower other women—a commitment shared and strengthened by this acknowledgment. What a privilege for me!

As chair of the board of the Sundance Institute, I have witnessed the progress in bringing more women storytellers into our lab programs and exhibiting their work at the Sundance Film Festival. What began over a breakfast and conversation hosted by Sundance board member Jacki Zehner is now a fully deployed strategy, shaped and led by the exceptionally effective CEO of the Sundance Institute, Keri Putnam. This strategy has helped to open up opportunities for women writers, directors, and producers, and to advance greater access to financial resources and distribution options. This has had an impact not only on Sundance Institute and the Sundance Film Festival in terms of representation in all our programs, but also on the media landscape at large.

The numbers of women-led projects and films directed by people of color selected for the Sundance Institute labs as well as the Sundance Film Festival over the several years of this initiative are proof that a strategy with accountable outcomes, powered by a team committed to be more inclusive, works. At the 2019 Sundance Film Festival in Park City, the numbers of women directors and producers almost reached parity—a new and important benchmark in progress toward equalizing opportunities for women in front of and behind the cameras—and the numbers of films directed by people of color also increased significantly. The more inclusive lineup led to some of the most positive reviews for the films and the festival experience.

When my twenty-one-year-old granddaughter, Laura Elizabeth, a film student at UCLA, arrived for the final weekend at the 2019 festival, she asked about the positive comments she was hearing about this year's lineup of films. I pointed to the increase in women and people of color who were storytellers, noting that different storytellers tell different kinds of stories. The value of diversity in this case was further supported by the fact that some of the women-led projects broke records for distribution deals.

The numbers overall, however, documented in research conducted by Sundance and USC's Dr. Stacey Smith of Annenberg Inclusion Initiative, indicate we still have a long way to go to level the playing field, especially at the intersections of money and market. We have definitely made progress, but the numbers fall off dramatically when it comes to the measurement of who gets financing to make their films and which films reach the largest audiences and bring in the biggest box-office revenues.

In 2017, director Patty Jenkins broke through one significant barrier to women's progress in movies: *Wonder Woman* surpassed $800 million at the box office, proving that a woman can direct a blockbuster. In 2018, Ava DuVernay became the first woman of color to direct a $100 million movie, *A Wrinkle in Time*, for Disney, and later that same year, she signed a multimillion-dollar production deal with Warner Bros.

These two success stories won't lower all the barriers or end all the stereotypes that continue to block women as directors or as engineers or as CEOs. As media makers and as media consumers, we all have a role to play in changing this picture, in creating new narratives and stories, in advocating for more women's voices, ideas, opinions, stories, and importantly, women's leadership where decisions are made. The power of media is in our hands, now more than ever, and women, as one of the most influential users of social media, can use it to support women's stories, women-led projects and initiatives, and each other. As one of the most important media-consumer groups, we can make sure our decisions about what we watch, listen to, tweet, Instagram, blog, connect, celebrate, or condemn in media reflects our values, individually and as a global community. Media matters and *Yes, We Can* make it better.

DANGEROUS TIMES CALL FOR DANGEROUS WOMEN

In Conversation with Ava DuVernay

Ava DuVernay, as a director, producer, screenwriter, and leader, has been making the media landscape better for women her entire career, which is on a fast track to unprecedented success. From pro-

moting and celebrating women's stories, especially women of color, to the creative choices she makes as a director and producer, to the leadership she puts into action through her nonprofit, ARRAY, Ava is one of the most courageous and committed women I have the privilege to know and celebrate.

Her accomplishments are many; most notably, in 2012, she became the first black woman to win the Sundance Film Festival prize for directing Middle of Nowhere. *She's also the first black woman director to have a film nominated for best picture—*Selma, *which chronicles how the 1965 marches in Alabama led by Martin Luther King Jr. catalyzed the passage of the Voting Rights Act. Ava received another Academy Award nomination for best documentary for* 13th, *a devastating film that painstakingly exposes how our prison system disproportionately targets and punishes African Americans. Ava returned to the subject of injustices in the legal system with the recent Netflix documentary series* When They See Us.

Through ARRAY, her distribution collective dedicated to films by people of color and women, she is committed to centering independent voices from the margins of the mainstream. I was eager to hear what she would say about the notion that danger is necessary for progress.

Do you agree with the statement that dangerous times call for dangerous women?

Ava: For women, the times are always dangerous. Always have been. Cultural, sexual, social, emotional, historical, political, and physical violence has permeated the lives of women for as long as the history books can chronicle the state of our world. Few countries or cultures or communities have been immune. The situations have been even more threatening to women of color, divorced from proximity to patriarchy and power. And so dangerous times have necessitated the innovation, ingenuity, inspiration, and imagination of women at all turns. To defend ourselves. To protect ourselves. To help ourselves. To heal ourselves—and each other.

How does being a dangerous woman play out in your work and life?

Ava: I consider myself a dangerous woman. If you are working outside of the dominant culture, there is no easy place for you. There is no safe space for you. Your voice and vision and presence are always at risk. So just the literal act of asserting your voice and vision and presence is dangerous. And brave. And necessary if you can muster it. I don't think the bravery that we are speaking of is related to age. It's all an evolution. And everyone is different.

Who were your dangerous role models or inspirations?

Ava: My mother and grandmother and Aunt Denise are my role models of defying expectations and living dangerously and as truthfully as they could. I'm lucky to have been raised in a family dominated by women. Women who stood up for themselves and loved and helped each other and taught me and my sisters to do the same.

From your perspective, where are the danger zones for women now?

Ava: Sadly, the range of remaining danger zones for women is wide and deep. From domestic and sexual violence to unjust laws and policing, from harmful workplaces to environmental injustice in our communities that affects families and well-being. The rate of death of black mothers in childbirth being more than double that of our white counterparts . . . in the United States . . . in 2019! Like I said, the range is wide and deep. And so the solutions and resistance must be the same.

Chapter 4

Playing the Power Game

"I'M TAKING THE job," I told my agent, who had just negotiated a new five-year contract for me to stay at WBZ-TV.

"What?" Bob Woolf practically yelled into the phone. "You're doing *what*? I've just negotiated more money for you than you thought you'd ever see in your life! You're one of the most popular television personalities in Boston, and you're going to Washington, DC, a much smaller market, for less money? This is not smart, and if you take this offer, I can't represent you."

My own agent fired me!

The next day, I notified the general manager at WBZ-TV that I was taking a job in Washington, DC, hosting *Panorama*, a live, ninety-minute, midday talk program, and anchoring the noon news. The GM was as incredulous as my agent had been.

"It's all downhill for you," he predicted. "You're going backward from the great opportunities I've given you."

Given me? I'd earned every penny. Why was I leaving? I responded to my unhappily surprised boss, "I just have a feeling that this is too good an opportunity to pass up." That was my unsatisfying answer. I wasn't dissatisfied or unhappy in Boston, but I was feeling a bit too comfortable, perhaps. I needed a new challenge and was, admittedly, curious about the world of politics and power. I had a lot to learn about both.

IN TWO SHORT weeks, Mark and I were in Washington, looking for a middle school and an apartment, and attending some of the inaugural activities for the country's thirty-ninth president, Jimmy Carter. A reporter noted that two Georgians began new jobs in the nation's capital on the same day, January 20, 1977, albeit with very different spheres of influence and responsibilities. Being in Washington and observing President Carter's leadership was a model of how to use power from an "outsider" perspective. This created challenges for him in working with Congress, but in many ways also led to some of the most notable accomplishments of his presidency. He has become the most admired former president for his peace-building work through the Carter Center in Atlanta, where I continue to observe his values-based leadership.

I replaced a very popular host at *Panorama*, Maury Povich. The person who made this risky hire of putting a woman in the host chair was Phyllis McGrady, barely thirty, who was already getting quite the reputation for being a risk-taking, talented producer.

Phyllis and I knew every decision we would make about *Panorama* would be judged through the lens of "what are those women doing?" We were making some changes, for sure—booking more women writers, activists, and leaders, and putting women forward on our small producing team for open positions and promotions. Having more women on-screen and on the production teams was starting to shift the focus, the stories, and the issues. *Panorama*'s audience wasn't predominantly women, however, as my talk programs had been in Boston, making many of our decisions to focus on women risky in terms of ratings and reputation. It's hard to envision just how much influence and impact *Panorama* had in those pre-CNN and no internet days.

Before 24/7 cable-news channels, our ninety-minute live TV program was the closest to current news in DC at the time. Political power players, White House aides, Cabinet secretaries, and congressional leaders all showed up when invited, and the program was viewed daily in the White House press room, congressional offices, and in the places where televisions now are most likely tuned to CNN or Fox.

HOSTING *PANORAMA* WAS like getting a PhD in political theory as well as marketing. Some days, I didn't feel nearly informed enough to be cross-examining the Speaker of the House about proposed legislation or a senior White House official about the president's prescient call for environmental regulations, but by this time in my life, after the challenges and successes of Boston and New York, I had experienced the reality that *being ready* could mean being ready to learn quickly while doing. I had also discovered that with each job, there were elements of the work I'd done before that I could incorporate or draw from. So while I had never hosted a live, two-hour program with guests who ranged from members of Congress to movie stars, often on the same program, I'd road-tested the interviewing and researching skills I'd need to do a credible job. And if the research hadn't been deep enough, I'd rely on my own curiosity. *Panorama* confirmed for me that the best interviewers are the best listeners and the most curious, and to this day, that's the advice I give anyone for how to get the best results from an interview: listen well and questions will naturally follow from a curious mind.

In addition to the politicians and actors, lots of book authors coveted a seat on *Panorama*'s sofa because in those days, when people bought books exclusively from bookstores, it was widely believed that landing a *Panorama* interview sold more books than any of the network TV talk shows. And unlike many in those heady days of publishing, I actually *read* the books before interviewing the authors! The stack by my bed reached from the floor to well over my nightstand. I always asked the authors before the show where in the book tour they were. If they were at the beginning, they'd be fresh-faced and brilliant; by the end, they were all pale zombies, repeating the stock answers they had said too many times to count on too many local TV and radio programs. The challenge was to ask something they hadn't been asked before, and I had to read the books to do that!

I took my job so seriously that Clare Boothe Luce, playwright, politician, and powerhouse, told me, "You are the perfect dinner guest at a Washington dinner party; you can talk about almost anything for fifteen minutes, and that's all the knowledge you need."

She was my Virgil to the dynamics of the Washington elite, inviting me to the exclusive Jockey Club, the place where *the* powerful had their assigned power tables for lunches. Ms. Luce (and yes, I called her that as she was already in her seventies and far too intimidating to be "Clare") had once been the managing editor of *Vanity Fair* and gained fame as a playwright for *The Women*, which was largely derided as antiwomen, and I avoided the subject altogether at our first lunches so I wouldn't be asked my opinion.

She had also been the first female ambassador and was famously witty—"no good deed goes unpunished" was a favorite line. She treated being a social hostess as the power position it was, and at our every encounter, she emphasized the importance of doing your homework—whether for a dinner party, meeting, or interview. We couldn't just *google them* then, but the investment in preprep could have life-changing consequences and, if nothing else, would make for a more engaged conversation.

Staying away from religion, politics, and sex in mixed company, as my first mentor, Mrs. Reid, once counseled me, was quickly dismissed by Ms. Luce, who advised, "Just stake out your position and defend it." My debate training came in handy at these dinners; at that time, you could have informed debates and civil differences of opinion. Clare Boothe Luce and I were worlds apart in our political leanings; although as a journalist I couldn't take a partisan position publicly, I was already out of the closet as a feminist and a Democrat. What I observed in these early encounters in one of DC's social power circles at that time was a truly dangerous, courageous woman who was prepared to use her power and influence—and being in her circle certainly widened mine and added to my growing list of dangerous women role models.

Thanks to my high-profile position, I was invited to a *lot* of dinner parties and pitched a lot of ideas for interviews. In Washington, the celebrities were people in political power; journalists came next in the power parade, especially if you had ninety minutes of free air time to offer them to promote, advocate, debate . . . or as happened once, make demands while holding AK-47s pointed at the heads of hostages.

I was barely two months into my job when, on March 9, 1977, seven men from a former Nation of Islam rival group called the Hanafi movement took hostages at B'nai B'rith, the Islamic Center of Washington, and the District Building. Hanafi's leader was a man named Hamaas Khaalis. Five years earlier, five of his children had been murdered and he held the Nation of Islam responsible. Now he was demanding that the men convicted of the murders be turned over to his group. He wanted *Panorama* to be the messenger.

We were the only live program in those pre-CNN days. The captors knew that and put in a call to us. I was interviewing someone when my station manager passed me a note: "There's been a takeover at B'nai B'rith. They're demanding to be heard on the air. We have to acknowledge that this is going on; they're threatening to kill the hostages." With no other instructions, I stopped the interview and turned to the camera to explain to our viewers what was happening as calmly as I could and with as little information as I had. Going to commercial to regroup, Phyllis and I assessed our options as more calls came from the gunmen. "Tell her we have our guns trained on fifteen people," the voice on the phone said over our audio system, demanding that his message be broadcast. What if we said one thing that they misinterpreted and someone died?

"The FBI wants you to take the call and try to keep them on the line." The message was delivered to me, now alone on the sofa, guests having been dismissed. With absolutely no training or further instructions, I was on the air, taking a call from a man holding hostages a few blocks away. I just started asking questions—like the reporter I was—about who the group was, their purpose, trying to keep him talking, which he did, explaining their cause and his intention to kill the people he was holding if his demands weren't met. After what seemed like an eternity, the call was disconnected. The FBI had the number and information they needed.

The ordeal lasted through the next day as three Muslim ambassadors pleaded successfully with the hostage takers to spare their victims. Tragically, a reporter for WHUR FM radio, Maurice Williams, had already been fatally shot; a security guard later died in the hospital. Marion Barry, then a councilman and later mayor of Washington, DC, was injured when a bullet ricocheted. The captors eventually released their hostages. Khaalis died in prison in 2003.

Since that first event, there have been many instances of live takeovers of media in attempts to get publicity or issue threats. Thirty years after my first encounter with the outsized power of the media to make news as well as cover it, we're facing a different kind of power play. With news organizations sometimes being barred from the Trump White House, the president referring to the press as "the enemy of the people," and with media becoming more partisan, the very existence of independent media as a source of facts is threatened, as is the democracy that depends on its independence.

THE FIRST TIME I stepped into the White House press room, a much saner place then than it is today, it felt to me like a sacred place. I was in awe and more than a bit intimidated by the network news anchors and White House reporters I had watched and admired for years. For the first two press briefings, I sat there in silence—surprising for someone who'd already been on television for nine years.

Then NBC's Tom Brokaw introduced himself, leaning in to advise, "It's important to ask questions in this room or no one's going to take you seriously."

I went home and read every shred of anything I could find to prepare myself for the next day's briefing. When Press Secretary Jody Powell opened the floor for questions, my hand shot up, forgetting that Helen Thomas, as the senior reporter in the room, traditionally got the first one. A glare from her, a frown from others, and my raised hand was ignored by Powell. Toward the end, I tried again and got the nod to ask a question, which I did in a voice that didn't sound like mine. But I had broken my silence and conquered that fear.

From that day forward, I've encouraged women to be prepared for all opportunities to ask an early question. If you wait, either your question gets asked by someone else or you start obsessing—which means you stop listening—or you just get more and more intimidated and lose your turn. Speaking early also helps calm the nerves so that once you hear your voice in the room, you can be more focused on the active listening that is as critical as the speaking.

I HAD MY share of encounters with famous people during my tenure at *Panorama*. One day a pale blue envelope arrived with "Elizabeth Taylor" emblazoned on the letter inside. In beautiful handwriting was written, "I'm a fan of your show. I'm a Washington housewife now, sitting at home, watching television. *Panorama* is keeping my mind from going totally to waste."

Elizabeth was married to Senator John Warner of Virginia, and the gossip was that she wasn't exactly having the best time of her life in her new role. A few weeks later, I was invited to a soiree at the home of Ambassador Ardeshir Zahedi, Iran's prerevolutionary, peripatetic host whose parties at the embassy were legendary, and found myself sitting next to Mrs. John Warner. Even this world-famous movie star was experiencing the power dynamic of Washington that made her senator husband a more desirable dinner companion for many, but not for me.

We talked all evening about everything from the women we admired and to the politicians we didn't. She was funny and even profane, and I almost forgot that I was having a conversation with one of the most famous people on the planet—certainly among the most beautiful, too.

Mrs. Warner—Elizabeth—and I were now both on the same dinner party list and as she sometimes requested to sit next to me, my Washington celeb status was on the upswing on the social circuit. I was told by one hostess in the know, "Elizabeth knows you don't need anything from her and won't expect anything from her or her husband, and that's rare in this town."

But what did people want and expect from *me*? What was the motivation for an invite to dinner or an embassy or even the White House? Seldom did or *does* anything happen in our nation's capital without a motive. What, for example, was I to think about the huge tins of Iranian caviar from Ambassador Zahedi that began arriving at my apartment? I had to request that the deliveries cease, reminding Zahedi's staff that it's not appropriate for journalists to receive gifts from people whose lives and work could be newsworthy.

The very next year, 1979, Ambassador Zahedi's life became newsworthy for sure. A revolution began in Iran, overthrowing the shah and sending the ambassador into exile—a revolution that transformed that country from top to bottom and contributed in no small way to the end of Carter's presidency.

CAVIAR DELIVERED TO my apartment! State dinners! Celebrity interviews and dinner partners! I should have been feeling a little of the power drug by now, but it all felt very fragile. I was observing power up close and personal in the bubble that's our nation's capital, then and now. The power paradigm in the late seventies felt audacious and feels even more so today as "government of the people, by the people, for the people"—the purpose of our representative democracy—seems to be less representative of the people it governs.

The way power is used in Washington is one of the most significant reasons why women in particular distance themselves from the association with power or with being seen as powerful. There have always been women with power in DC, but power is still largely defined as white and male, reflecting George Orwell's comment: "No one ever seizes power with the intention of relinquishing it."

After the 2018 midterm elections in the United States, we have more women leaders in Congress than ever in our history, including more women of color and more women from different generations, ranging from the youngest-serving member to the oldest ever elected—and seventy-eight-year-old Nancy Pelosi was reelected to be the Speaker of the House, the third most powerful position in the US government, after the president and vice president. These new women in Washington have an opportunity to redefine what power looks like and acts like.

Will they work together across political and ideological lines to shape important policies that will serve all women? We can expect that some will approach their responsibilities with a gender lens and some will not, but I am counting on this largest coalition ever of women to dismantle the divisiveness, shape new legislation, and perhaps even finally secure equal-rights protections under the US Constitution by passing an Equal Rights Amendment. Already, by their presence, Congress is a lot closer to looking like the American population, and for the world, they offer a new and potentially transformative paradigm of power.

I didn't feel powerful during my early years in the power game of Washington, but I surely learned a lot about how it can distort and distract. I did feel watched and judged, and I was always aware that my value in a room, at a dinner, at a press conference, and even on television was dependent, at least in part, on what I did or what I could do for someone else or how close I was to someone with real power. That part about living in DC didn't change when I returned twenty years later to lead PBS—but more on that story later.

My status as a single woman started to feel more and more like a liability, too. On my own, I was more tempted by the whirlwind of activity, often choosing to go out rather than have a quiet dinner at home. Meanwhile, I was worried about Mark; he'd recently become a sullen, seemingly miserable twelve-year-old. He wasn't doing well, socially or academically, in Washington; in his school, sixth graders were already smoking dope at recess, and his environment was taking a toll. It should have been clearer to me earlier that Mark needed more than he was getting in terms of direction and attention.

One New Year's Eve in Washington, I decided to stay home with him. I had considered going out on the town, but without a steady companion, I could either go out on a casual date that could turn out sour or so-so, or go to a party where I wanted to hide at the dreaded celebration moment of kissing—or having no one to kiss—as the clock struck midnight. Forget it! I chose to forgo the invitations and planned an evening with my son.

I had thought a fun New Year's Eve would be going to a concert and the fireworks on the Washington Mall, but he wasn't interested. Since I was unable to engage, let alone excite him, with the idea, we ended up at home with one of my special frozen-food meals. Mark's cat, a female feline he named Frank, stalked up and down the back of the sofa, shredding it with her claws as we sat in silence, with me occasionally reverting to my interviewer role and asking questions he didn't want to answer. Suddenly I was overwhelmed by an incredible sense of sadness and failure, feeling emotionally separated from my only child.

I felt as if I'd failed as a mother and decided then and there to find a man who might like to join our lives—a companion for myself and a fatherly influence for Mark.

The very next month at another Washington dinner party, I was introduced to Adam, a charming, smart, stable lawyer with four seemingly well-adjusted children. We moved quickly into a committed relationship, though my time with Adam felt more like a solution than a romance. Still, within six months, we moved in together.

My fantasies of our becoming one big happy family evaporated pretty fast. Instead of flourishing with a male role model at home, Mark was becoming more and more miserable and showing it. Finally, his school psychologist suggested a boarding school might be the best solution to get him back on track academically and socially. Mark liked the idea, and we chose Cardigan Mountain in New Hampshire, near the slopes where he had learned to ski during his much happier days in Boston.

"It's the right decision," I told Adam, joyfully. "Mark will love it there. And the timing is great because I've been asked to audition for a pilot for CBS that's being shot in Los Angeles, so Mark will have the stability of boarding school and not having to move schools again."

"You're going to *what*?" Adam's face darkened. "You're considering moving to Los Angeles? And this is how you tell me?"

He was furious—and with good cause. He felt blindsided, and I understood his frustration. But I'd been offered a chance to cohost a new primetime TV show based on the wildly popular *People* magazine for CBS. It would be my first spot on network TV. Since I knew that Adam had a temper, one that seemed to be growing, I didn't want to provoke him when I hadn't even been offered the job.

"It's unlikely I'll be chosen," I reassured Adam, but inside I felt much more optimistic that I would. "And if I am, I'll commute back and forth." This sent Adam into a rage. I had good reason to question whether I could marry a man who didn't understand or support my need to pursue a career opportunity; he had good reason to question whether or not he—and his children—would ever be a priority for me. This was not the first and would not be the last time that I pursued a job at the expense of a relationship.

I GOT THE job. I'd be hosting along with Phyllis George, a former Miss America, and Alan Hamel, known primarily at that time as Suzanne Somers's husband. Even better, CBS had hired my old friend Raysa Bonow, my producer from Boston, to do the show.

At our first production meeting in New York, I felt like a beginner again. I had to learn a lot, fast, about being in the big time with the big boys and girls, proving myself again, competing again. Raysa took me aside for a talk.

"Pat, I know I told you this before in Boston, but here, at the network level, it's even more important to think about your hair and your clothes. When there is a brunette and a blonde on the screen at the same time, the blondes get more attention, and since Phyllis is a brunette and your hair is sort of in between, I think you should become a blonde or maybe a redhead." During the pilot production, I changed hair color on a weekly basis, seeking that blonde-but-not-too-blonde or red-but-not-quite-red color that would compete but not be too distracting.

This started a pattern that I am sad to observe characterizes my entire television career—changing hair color and styles to suit some producer, to respond to some viewer's criticism, or to respond to my own growing sense of insecurity about how I looked on television. Eventually, this preoccupation with looks rather than substance initiated my move away from being on television to becoming a producer and eventually an executive.

Many of the activities surrounding the production of television programs have very little to do with going for mindshare or meaningful content, and everything to do with marketing and publicity. Perhaps you've heard of the *upfronts*—the show-your-hand moment where the network executives present the next season's shows to advertisers and the media? Lining up alphabetically with all of the network's stars, I found myself going on-stage next to Mary Tyler Moore. Thunderous applause erupted as MTM, one of television's most beloved stars, walked with power-filled strides across the stage. My heart filled with dread as I heard my name called, followed by what felt like a funereal silence and a few people loudly whispering, "Who's that?"

The next day, David Susskind, the executive producer, called me to come see him. I was sure I was going to be fired.

"So I've got good news and bad news," he told me. "Phyllis is going to be called the host. You and Alan are going to be cohosts. The good news is that you get to travel around the country reporting the interesting stories and she'll be stuck in the studio. Okay?"

It was a strictly rhetorical question.

WE PRODUCED AND broadcast four episodes of the *People* show. Alan and I traveled coast to coast for stories that I don't remember now—and that says everything you need to know about why the show didn't make it beyond the first four. "Thank you very much, but we won't be renewing the show" was the not-at-all-unexpected news from CBS.

Meanwhile, a big-time ICM agent reached out to say he wanted to represent me after the *People* gig. "Can you move to LA?" he asked. "There are so many opportunities out here for you. NBC is looking for a cohost or correspondent for a new daytime talk program, and you'd be perfect for it."

I hired him, officially broke up with Adam, and officially resigned from *Panorama.* I felt badly about leaving the show, but it turned out to be a good choice; a year later, *Panorama* was replaced by reruns of *Alice* and a syndicated home shopping show. As TV critic Tom Shales wrote in the *Washington Post,* "Canceling *Panorama* was a supposedly sound business decision that also happens to be morally indefensible." He placed the blame at the feet of the FCC, which had abolished public-service requirements for stations four years earlier.

"Stations now have no official mandate to air regular, locally responsive, public-affairs programs," Shales wrote. "They are free instead to turn that pesky old public-service time into moneymaking time—say, with tired off-network reruns or home shopping sprees." That was the beginning of a power shift inside media companies who no longer had to be responsive to community needs but could focus on the ever-increasing profits to shareholders . . . until the power shifted again through technology's transformation of the media landscape.

IN MY NEXT move, to Southern California, I was experiencing a new landscape and, in many ways, a new life of freedom. Mark was settled into his boarding school and thriving. I was feeling good about having made the move because I felt it was right for me, even though there had been pressure from Adam to give us another shot. I was living alone for the first time, now that Mark was away at school, and for the first time, I wasn't feeling guilty. I was feeling independent.

With my new cohosting spot on *America Alive!*, I was at last on *national* TV, and my mother and father could finally see what I did for a living! I invited my mother into the NBC studios for a mother-daughter program in New York (her first plane ride) and sent my parents on their first cruise and an anniversary weekend at the Plaza Hotel. I was finally a success that they could somewhat understand.

My father, visiting a television studio for the first time, observing me in the spotlight, noted afterward, "Looks like an easy job to me. You're just reading." After nearly twelve years of working hard not to be dismissed or denigrated, his comment almost unleashed the rage I had never allowed to surface. But I ignored the pain and pushed down the memories, again.

My job was best described as the *active cohost*, since I was live every day doing something exciting—or at least I had to make it appear to be so. From driving a race car at the Indy 500 to walking with flamingos at Disneyland to sailing with Walter Cronkite—and yes, that was exciting—I was contributing my time and talents to a television show the *New York Times* described as "comfortable placebo entertainment for those who like to turn their sets on in broad daylight." Far from satisfying after the heady and more substantive fare of *Panorama.*

I wasn't connecting to the work I was doing, and I wasn't feeling all that comfortable in LA, even though the power dynamics were similar to those in DC. Both are one-industry towns, and your power is pretty much determined by your latest appointment or election in DC or your latest movie or TV series in LA. In DC, I'd been in the power circle because of my job and what it meant in that ecosystem of politics and policy. In LA, I orbited in and out of the power circle, not because of my job or its importance but because my agent, who was also my live-in partner, was powerful. And I was losing a lot of myself in that relationship.

We weren't married, but this relationship was the first full capture of my heart and mind in the nearly twenty-five years since my divorce. We lived among the elite in Montecito, commuted to Los Angeles and New York for work, wrote a film script that was optioned by Columbia Studios (never produced), wrote a Broadway-bound musical (never performed), and traveled by train through the newly liberated Eastern Europe interviewing writers, artists, filmmakers, and world leaders for a project never completed. When we finally separated, after several attempts, it took me some time to recover my balance. I had lost some emotional independence, but I had gained a better understanding of what I wanted from a life partner. So had he, apparently, as he was married within a year.

Old friends commented on how much less confident and less free I seemed as a person, devoting so much of my time and energy to his happiness and not my own. After too long a time, I confronted the reality within myself and with him and ended what had been more than a decade-long commitment.

I was also asking a lot of questions about my career choices. I had stayed with television because I believed in the potential to make a positive difference, but nothing I was doing now felt that it made any difference to anyone, least of all, me. I wasn't unhappy when the show got canceled. I needed to stop and reassess my next choice.

I didn't. I got a job offer from the new cable network, went right into cohosting *Daytime* (which later became *Lifetime*), and then the nationally syndicated daily talk show, *Hour Magazine*, another program intended for women hosted by a man. The title card blared "*Hour Magazine* with your host, Gary Collins" in *huge* type followed by, in tiny little print, "with Pat Mitchell."

I didn't know whether to laugh or cry, seeing my name in those tiny letters, when in fact I did more than half the show. Once again, I was in a supporting role—the attractive, articulate, vivacious personality who was good at bringing out the best in people I interviewed and being able to wing it live when things went wrong, which they did all the time—all to make someone else look better and not, in any discernable way, to make the world better. Time to move on again in my pursuit of media that mattered.

I needed to get back to my original commitment to telling the stories of women, to providing a media platform for substantive conversations and for raising awareness of the many challenges I knew were a part of the lives of the women we were supposedly programming for. I believed there could be a new kind of daytime television program to connect women to women. With my producer from *Hour Magazine*, Mary Muldoon, we began to shape a new format and a different option to soaps, game shows, male hosts, and giddy studio audiences: to produce instead a real conversation with real women.

My agent and all the men I worked with said, "You'll never sell it."

They were wrong.

DANGEROUS TIMES CALL FOR DANGEROUS WOMEN

In Conversation with Mary Robinson

Mary Robinson was advised by many that a woman would never be elected president of Ireland, but she proved them wrong. I met her during her first campaign for the presidency and went with her door to door as she told voters what she intended to do as their leader. And after she was elected, she delivered on her campaign promise to transform the presidency to make it more relevant at the local, national, and international levels.

Following Mary's term, she was appointed a UN high commissioner for human rights, then founded Realizing Rights: The Ethical Globalization Initiative, whose objectives included strengthening women's leadership and encouraging corporate social responsibility. She's now chair of The Elders, an independent group of global leaders convened by Nelson Mandela and others to fight for peace and human rights. In 2010, she started the Mary Robinson Foundation—Climate Justice to fight for the often-overlooked victims of climate change. She also has served as a UN envoy for climate change.

Mary is one of the most effective leaders I have ever observed, and when I asked her whether she thought of herself as dangerous, she answered in her usual forthright style.

Do you think of yourself as dangerous?

Mary: I haven't always described myself as dangerous; I always thought it better not to be too explicit about what I wanted to achieve at various stages of my life! But when I served as president of Ireland, I operated on the principle of "seeking forgiveness, not permission"!

I did like the description of me in my absence by Laurence Tubiana at a women's leadership conference on gender and climate change in Ottawa last May. There was a discussion about bad girls, and Laurence referred to me as a "sophisticated bad girl"!

Did becoming more dangerous have anything to do with age for you?

Mary: As I get older, I find it easier to feel dangerous. The breakthrough moment for me was when I introduced a bill to legalize family planning in Ireland in 1971 and suffered a huge backlash of public criticism and denunciation by bishops. I wobbled a bit at first, but then realized it was important to be prepared to pay the price of being unpopular. When you fight for what you believe in, you may risk being unpopular, but in the end I think you gain people's trust.

Who or what has inspired you to become more dangerous?

Mary: I am very inspired by women who live in difficult circumstances and fight for the rights of their community. I met many when I served as UN high commissioner for human rights. It is no accident that nine of the eleven stories in my book, *Climate Justice: Hope, Resilience, and the Fight for a Sustainable Future,* are about women.

If you agree that these are dangerous times, how do you see the role of women in such times?

Mary: These are dangerous times, and they require passion and courage from everyone. We also need to find smart ways to communicate our messages—hence my recent podcast series, *Mothers of Invention*, with its tagline: "Climate change is a man-made problem—with a feminist solution!" Women need to take seriously the existential threat of climate change. The recent Intergovernmental Panel on Climate Change report makes it clear that limiting global warming to no more than 1.5°C above preindustrial levels is the only really safe level for the future, so this needs to become a priority of the women's movement worldwide. We need to change people's behavior and begin to live sustainably with Mother Earth—and who changes behavior in the family and community? Women!

In September 2014 I took part in the big climate change march in New York as an elder, alongside fellow elder Gro Brundtland. I spotted another banner too far away that I would like to have marched behind: "Angry Grannies!" We need angry grannies, mothers, daughters, aunts, nieces to rise up and fight for a safe world for our children and grandchildren. They need us to take action during the window of time we have, which will be gone if we don't use it.

Chapter 5

Connecting Woman to Woman

"YOU'RE NOT SERIOUS about this idea? Women sitting on a couch *talking* to each other?"

At this point in our pitch, the Chicago media executive wasn't buying the concept or the program. "Who do you think is going to watch this show?"

"Your wife," I answered. "And all her friends."

Still not convinced. "Why not famous women? And what's your role?"

"I'm going to be sitting in the circle with them, and we'll have famous women if the subject calls for it. But it's not *The Phil Donahue Show.* It's not interviews. *Woman to Woman* will be a conversation like women have with their friends all the time."

"You've got to get a better name. No woman will watch a show called *Woman to Woman,*" and with that, he stood up to end the meeting.

I held out a copy of the pilot show on videotape. "Take the show home to your wife, and if she says she'll watch it, will you consider taking the series for Chicago?"

He took the tape and agreed to show it to his wife. She loved it. We'd made one sale.

I'D FIRST MET Mary Muldoon, who became my producing partner for *Woman to Woman*, when we both worked for *Hour Magazine*. We had an idea that women watching daytime television wanted a show that talked *with* them, rather than *about* them. We wanted to produce something entirely different from anything else on TV at that time, from the way it looked to the subjects and guests.

For the pilot, I sat on a nubbly, beige-colored semicircular couch in a set of arched windows that looked somewhat like someone's living room. A dozen other women sat beside me or on adjoining peach and mauve (very eighties) couches and easy chairs. Grammy-winning duo Burt Bacharach and Hal David wrote our theme song, and Dionne Warwick recorded it and every day that distinctive voice opened the program with these lyrics:

"Woman to woman / face to face / coming together / from many places / asking the questions one at a time / bonding at the answers that were there all the time."

The subject for the first show was a careful choice: "The Myth of the Happy Housewife." I asked my guests, all of whom had been selected carefully for their opinions and personal stories, "What makes you happy?" to get the conversation going.

"A drink with my girlfriends," one offered and the conversation was in motion. "Being a housewife is just a role I play." "No one can do this alone." Everybody was talking . . . just like women do with girlfriends. They were really listening to each other, too, and seemed to forget the cameras discreetly recording a real conversation. Given the bad name so-called reality television has given to anything real (consider *The Real Housewives*), I hesitate to use that description, but in the early eighties, *real* was a good thing.

From the very first taping, Mary and I knew we had something special—and revolutionary. Armed with a week of shows, we started the selling process, going literally station to station, meeting the same skepticism about the appeal of the title and format. But every single time a male executive showed the programs to his wife, the station bought the show.

OUR FIRST SHOW aired on September 14, 1983. The *New York Times*'s television critic wrote that the show was "being handled with intelligence. And it beats a steady diet of game shows," which was a bit damning with faint praise. But the reviewer, a man, got the central point: "All of the women appear to be genuinely interested in one another. . . . One clue to this harmony and sympathy is that control of the program is just about completely in the hands of women."

Yes, that was the point of the program and even the way we put it together, creating the first independent and only all-women production company, a decision we had to defend from time to time. The press seemed obsessed with the fact that we were an all-women production team, and there were tiresome questions about the differences in an all-female workplace. "We put on lipstick less often," was one practiced answer, and on a more serious note, we would point out, we had no titles, no egos—just an all-women team getting a show on the air every day that would have meaning for the women watching and be a positive experience for the women participating. Not only did we want to prove that an all-women production team could be successful, but we believed it was the best model, editorially and culturally, for our show.

Mary and I had titles as co–executive producers, required for the business we incorporated for financial management, but otherwise no one had titles because we wanted to break down the usual hierarchy and invite everyone to the table equally. We remembered what it was like to have our ideas denigrated or for someone else to take credit for them because we were only assistants or associate producers, and we didn't want anyone else dismissed or their abilities judged or limited by a title. Everyone was welcome to put forward ideas at our daily staff meetings.

We paid our staff top salaries and lobbied hard to get on-site daycare; I didn't want other mothers to feel the stress or the guilt of choosing between being with their children or at work. If they wanted to have their young children with them in the office, we wanted to make that possible—and it kept us real about the challenges of balancing motherhood and work. We had a common area with changing tables and cribs and hired a professional to help out. We started out with three under the age of two and by the end of the first production cycle, there were four more between the age of six months and crawlers. Was there something in the water?

I was quite literally changing somebody's baby on my desk while a male reporter asked me some question about ratings—which in large part determined whether a show or series continued production.

"Well, changing a baby's dirty diaper certainly keeps your numbers from last week in perspective," I told him.

If someone needed to work from home because their child was sick, that was fine. All those young mothers were bringing great ideas to the table, and we were rewarded with high staff loyalty; not a single employee left our eighty-person staff while we were producing the show, unusual in Hollywood. Women were watching, too, and after the first rating numbers came in, more stations signed on to broadcast the series.

I signed off at the end of every program, "Woman to woman, that's how we learn, that's how we change, that's how we support each other."

OUR TOPICS REALLY pushed boundaries for the day: Teen suicide. Sexually abusive soccer coaches. Ageism. Sterilization as birth control. Missing children. Life after menopause. Why pornography is so damaging for women. Surviving the death of a child. Compulsive eating. Teenage runaways. Surrogate mothers. The right to die. Wives and mistresses talking (that was a fun one!). The first national TV interview with a transsexual couple.

With such subjects being discussed not by experts but by real women sharing their own stories, it was important to have women production crews for the tapings, and we did.

Not surprisingly, the topics we took on were too controversial for some stations. Some canceled the program, but we didn't change direction because the women we were programming for let us know that our shows inspired them, encouraged them to get support, helped them recognize they weren't alone, and sometimes compelled them to take action.

Running a business—managing a team, meeting payroll, paying insurance and lawyers, and negotiating contracts with every single station—was new to me. Happily, Mary *loved* doing budgets and meeting payroll! (Always find someone who shares your values but complements your skills.) She was single, came from a big Irish family but never had children of her own, and chain-smoked like a chimney. In the good cop/bad cop scenario of most working partnerships, Mary was willing to be the "bad cop," and she was a great partner.

After 180 original hours of conversations with "real women" about their lives, ideas, challenges, and accomplishments, *Woman to Woman* was nominated for an Emmy for best daytime talk series.

Mary and I went to the ceremony, which is decidedly less glamorous than the nighttime Emmys. We were just going to have a good time. After all, Phil Donahue had won almost every single year he'd been on the air, so we prepared our "it's an honor just to be nominated" posture.

Phil and his wife, Marlo Thomas, someone I knew and admired a great deal, were seated at the table next to us. Mary and I had maybe one or two more glasses of wine than we should have because we were so sure Phil would win, and when they called out our names, we sat in stunned silence for a minute before leaping to the stage with no idea of an acceptance speech. I decided to use my daily closing line from the show, to which Mary added a quick quip, "She's the one who talks. I'm the one who makes sure the shows get on the air." Well, not *exactly*, we both did that. But it was a great partnership and the Emmy was a big accomplishment!

The only person who was more surprised than we were was Phil, but he graciously congratulated us and even posed for a photo.

NEGOTIATING DEALS FOR our second year was going to be a lot easier after the Emmy win, and while I was in Boston just a few weeks later to discuss the next year's licensing contract, the general manager suggested a celebratory lunch.

"There's a call for you, Ms. Mitchell," the hostess at the Ritz-Carlton hotel said quietly. I excused myself to take the call.

It was the head of our syndication partners. "I have some bad news," he said. "We just got the call that Golden West Television [our syndication partners] has been sold, to a private equity firm called KKR—Kohlberg, Kravis and Roberts."

"What does that mean?" I asked.

"Not sure, but there's been a lot of talk about private-equity guys buying up media companies and leveraging their assets to buy bigger companies. We're small potatoes, but that might be the plan."

And so it was, a plan that began in the eighties to transform the media landscape. Our little production company, part of a small Hollywood syndication company that was started by the cowboy star, Gene Autry, by the way, was the first time a private-equity firm had bought a small media company for the sole purpose of strip-mining it to buy a larger media company. The outcome of these leveraged buyouts was that over the next thirty years, newspapers, radio, and television stations, as well as production companies and studios, were all vulnerable to being bought at a low valuation, followed by dramatic cutting of expenses and bulking up of assets to improve market valuations.

Of course, I didn't know KKR's plans at that point, but I knew that they were in the profit-making and not program-making business.

We immediately launched a big advocacy program with the new owners, showing them ratings, ad revenues, reader responses, station buy-ins. All in vain. "Close down production as fast as you can," we were told, "and because we're nice guys, you can have the rights back to the show. And if you produce it somewhere else, we'll take a cut to pay down the investment."

Woman to Woman was a balance sheet loss to KKR, but it was so much more than just another show to us—not just because Mary and I owned the title or because it had won an Emmy—but because our lives had been changed and we had changed the lives of other women. We had made a difference. The show was, for all of us who worked on the team and all the women who shared their stories with us, a powerful validation of what women could create with each other and for each other. I wasn't going to give it up.

IT WAS A mad scramble to find someone else to finance the production. The stations in our syndicated network had to know within a couple of weeks whether we would be producing more shows for them to broadcast.

My agent started making phone calls, as did I. WABC in New York said, "Come and produce the show here; you're number one in New York and we love the show and don't want to lose it on our lineup." That would have meant moving to New York, hiring new staff, and turning ownership over to ABC. We said no. I flew to Chicago to try my luck there, but another story was developing there that became the biggest media story of all time. More on that later.

Then a producer at *The Today Show*, Jacoba Atlas (called Coby by everyone), called. "We'd like you to bring the concept to us and produce it in segments." We could keep our independent production company with editorial control over the segments we produced. But there was no money to keep the team that was producing five hour-long shows a week. No option allowed the great team of women we'd hired to stay together. It was not the best choice, but for me and Mary, it was our only choice for continuing the concept for greatest reach and impact. We decided to take the NBC offer and keep the concept alive on the most popular morning show at the time.

I can still remember the profound sadness I felt the day I gathered everyone at *Woman to Woman* to announce our decision. We provided the most generous severance payments we could squeeze from the new owners. I don't think I have ever felt such a loss as the day I cleaned out my office at Golden West Broadcasting studios and drove off the lot for the last time. I knew that whatever came next, it would never equal the experience of owning my own company, creating something that mattered to me and so many others, and shaping new ways of women working together as well.

Looking back, I believe my biggest mistake here was doubting myself and our ability to put together enough financing to keep the show in production. Had I been the risk-taker I am today, I would have borrowed the money from a bank for a year's worth of shows, betting on our hitting the breakeven by end of year two. But, instead, I took the less risky course of returning to the network, giving them the financial responsibility (and any profits)—and Mary and I were right back in an old power paradigm.

Ultimately, I learned some big lessons about power. Mary and I might have felt powerful as hosts and producers, but the real power was a bunch of guys in suits who didn't really care about our mission or our production team or even the audience we had built over one year. We learned a hard lesson about control and how you get it and keep it. Every part of a team has to be aligned and committed. In our case, our partners who paid the bills weren't buying a mission; they were building an asset. We had broken new ground for women on television, but we hadn't held *our* ground.

WOMAN TO WOMAN isn't a story of failure, however. We'd taken a creative and financial risk and won an Emmy and gained a loyal following; we'd created a supportive working environment for other women and even reduced stress levels for some working mothers. We also made a deal with Lifetime cable network to rerun the first season's shows, ensuring that the programs would continue to air . . . and in fact, they were seen by millions for two more years. *The Today Show* broadcast *Woman to Woman* segments for the next four years. Today, two decades after the last segment aired on *The Today Show* and many decades since Lifetime ran the shows, someone will recognize me as the host of *Woman to Woman,* a show that hasn't been on television in any format since 1989.

What I'm especially proud of is that a selection of the original shows became the first television series ever collected by the Schlesinger Library on the History of Women at Radcliffe College, and I'm grateful every day that there are copies for students and researchers to view as windows into the lives of real women in the mid-eighties. The original master tapes were lost in a fire, but everything about this experience had lit a fire within me—to take more risks, to trust my own instincts and experience, to fight for what I believe is important.

But I did have a real sinking spell after I gave up on my dream for *Woman to Woman,* a period of depression and anxiety, feeling that I was going backward for the first time in my professional life even though I was now a regular on NBC's *The Today Show.* I had broken new ground for myself and, I believed, for other women, and it was tough to hold on to my grandmother's adage that this fall had been a forward movement.

I would later understand that letting go of my dream for what this program could be also played a role in helping another woman to move forward. Oprah Winfrey, whom I had met and admired, was hosting her local Chicago show and was the lead-in program to the nationally syndicated *Woman to Woman.* She and her producer saw an opportunity when we had to pull out of syndication, to take Oprah's local talk show into national syndication. They were able to move right into many of the time slots on stations around the country that our show had held.

What happened next is television history: Oprah quite literally transformed the media landscape, proving beyond anyone's doubt that women want to see other powerful and inspiring women on television. By the sheer force of her presence, who she is, on-screen and off—a woman who speaks her truth, who opens her heart to hear others' truths, and who communicates compassion and power—Oprah elevated a daily talk show into something no one else had ever achieved, and became media's most powerful and most well-compensated personality. Oprah—through her programming, her philanthropy, her ownership—fully captures the power of fame, fortune, and media to be a positive transformative force. During the early years, when we saw each other at industry gatherings or women's forums, Oprah would acknowledge the connection: "Pat paved the way with *Woman to Woman*, opening the door for what followed for me." That's, at least, partly true. But the bigger truth is that Oprah's story is a testimonial to the power of one individual to change the world, and she is arguably among the world's most dangerous women.

DANGEROUS TIMES CALL FOR DANGEROUS WOMEN

In Conversation with Abigail Disney

Abigail Disney (yes, of that *Disney family) inspires me, too. She grew up with fame and fortune and chose to take a different path with her life and her work. She is a lifelong activist and an award-winning documentary filmmaker who produced the Oscar-nominated* Pray the Devil Back to Hell, *about Liberian peace activist Leymah Gbowee and all the women who fought to bring peace to their country, which was divided and stricken by war. Abby made her directorial debut with the Emmy-nominated* The Armor of Light, *which spotlighted controversial pro-life evangelical minister Rev. Rob Schenck and the gunning down of an unarmed*

African American teenager in an effort to explore the question of how people might be both pro-life and pro-gun.

Having dedicated most of her career to telling important stories through her films and her foundation, and supporting other work, Abby has now set her sights on a game-changing goal: a start-up called Level Forward that aims to back projects solely driven by women and persons of color. Named for the goal of a level playing field for women and others who have been traditionally disadvantaged in Hollywood, the venture is, as Abby says, "committed to the vision of unlocking and amplifying storytelling from all corners and perspectives, to claiming the power of ownership."

In a wide-ranging conversation with my longtime friend and a woman I admire for her work and her outspokenness, Abby shared insights about her journey to becoming more dangerous.

Do you think of yourself as a dangerous woman, and if so, why?

Abby: I'm very proud to think of myself as a dangerous woman. Danger sounds like a terrible thing until you realize it's just where you belong. I wasn't brought up to be dangerous or even to speak my mind. But I felt danger all around me in the family. Now I have a postcard that says, "The older I get, the more everyone can kiss my ass." That's where I am right now. I don't care what anybody thinks of me anymore. That's an important part of being dangerous.

What have you learned about being dangerous from the films you've made?

Abby: Pray the Devil Back to Hell about the peace movement in Liberia taught me a lot about fear. Going to Liberia in my forties, not knowing what I would find or how I would tell the story, I had a lot of fear. And I learned that peace-building is the truly dangerous profession. Women peace builders in particular are dangerous and effective. When a woman says, "Stop killing my children," it is quite difficult for everybody at the peace talks to say, "No, I'd really like to continue killing your children." Women peace builders are fearless and feared. Leymah Gbowee, the Nobel Peace laureate whose story I told, knows real capital *D* danger, and is really good at anger as part of building peace. She channels it into a sort of righteousness that is really hard to deny. Anger is important for dangerous women.

How is becoming more dangerous playing out in your life now?

Abby: Recently this cabdriver just got right in my face and started screaming at me. I was watching him yell at me and I realized that he knew I was just as strong as he was; he had already shoved me. And he wasn't hitting me, so that meant he wasn't going to hit me and I thought, "Oh my god, that's all you have? That's it?" And I started to laugh. I gave a yelling man so much power for so many years, and all of a sudden it was just unmasked for me. And no man will ever yell at me again because I just saw it for everything that it is—a desperate measure, you know? I mean, years of being yelled at by my father just fell away, honestly. I spent all that money on therapy and all I had to do, all this time, was just get in a fight with a cabdriver. I tell women all the time, especially young ones, fear is your enemy; you cannot let it stop you from doing things. You're gonna feel it no matter what, but think big. Don't waste your time in half measures. Adrienne Becker, my partner, and I started Level Forward to give women-led projects a bigger voice. I could really, really fail spectacularly with it and I'm excited by that. After I mouthed off at Sundance about our plans, someone said, "Nobody will ever loan these women a hundred million dollars." And Adrienne cut it out of the newspaper and put it on our desk and said, "A year from now we want to have a hundred million dollars."

Chapter 6

Surviving the Shadows

"HE SEDUCED ME into the basement, in the dark, while the rest of the family was outside having a picnic," the young woman with the feathered haircut and large glasses told the circle of women who were assembled in a living room–like setting at *Woman to Woman.* "And I remember saying, 'That hurts me,' and he said, 'That's okay, it'll only hurt for a little while.'"

The camera moved gently from her and pulled in for a close-up on me.

"Incest is the most secret of crimes, and in many ways, it is the most tragic," I told the audience. "It betrays the innocent love of a child and it destroys all trust in a family, and it's happening much more frequently than we ever knew. I'm Pat Mitchell, and today on *Woman to Woman,* we'll talk to incest survivors and to mothers who knew too late what was happening to their daughters."

The camera returned to the group, and the next woman spoke.

"My father forced me to have sex with him from the time I was five to fifteen," she said, her eyes tearing. The faces of the other incest survivors clearly showed that this was a familiar story and a shared pain.

Another said, "My grandfather was my hero, so I did what he asked, even though I hated it. I never told anyone. I didn't feel I had a choice."

Another confessed her father's violations. "Here I'm thirty-eight, and I held it in for such a long time. Now I can talk about it and it's like giving other people permission to talk about it too."

As the stories continued, one by one, around the circle of women on set, I noticed how unusually quiet the studio was, almost church-like.

I tried not to probe beyond the details already freely shared but asked questions that might help our audience comprehend how such abuse could go on, often for years, in seemingly respectable homes, amid seemingly perfect families, in small and large cities, among the well-to-do and the poor.

There were no easy answers. One guest suggested that incest was often intergenerational—a father is abused, so he abuses. Others attributed their abuse to other causes, from male power paradigms to mental illness.

Suddenly, a wave of nausea passed over me, and I had to steady myself for a minute before moving the conversation away from the horror stories of the abuse to the inspiring stories of survival. I focused on the accomplishments of the women in this circle—physicians, lawyers, teachers, therapists, mothers, and grandmothers—who had all overcome their childhood trauma and gone on to become successful and seemingly well-adjusted adults.

In preparing for this program I'd been surprised to discover that surviving incest is uncannily aligned with becoming an overachiever. These women spoke of having to prove they were *good girls* deserving of respect and unconditional love, rather than *bad girls* hiding shame on top of shame. Incest, several of my guests reported, had driven them to spend the rest of their lives struggling to earn love since they had never received it as children themselves, as the natural entitlement expected and needed from a parent.

Suddenly, another wave of nausea enveloped me, and I felt as if I was going to faint or throw up. A quick thank-you to the guests and I ran to my dressing room, quickly closed the door, and fell to my knees, sobbing, out of control.

"Pat? Can Deanna come in and refresh your makeup?" Mary Muldoon shouted from the other side of the dressing room door. I couldn't answer. "Pat, are you okay?" More knocking, and both Deanna and Mary entered to find me in a fetal position, unable to move or talk, sobbing as if I'd never cried before.

I couldn't tell them what was wrong because I had no idea. All I knew is that I wanted to disappear or die, a frightening darkness welling up and taking over my mind and body.

MARY CANCELED THE next two shows, sending the guests home with a promise to reschedule, and called one of my close friends in Santa Barbara to confide my symptoms and seek advice.

Sylvia suggested Dr. Lambert, a highly respected psychiatrist, and the next morning I was sitting in his office when a tall, slim, tanned man with a white beard entered, incongruously holding a surfboard. "I'm so sorry for being late," he told me, taking his place in a chair very close to mine. "Surfing's my morning routine." The sight of an elder statesman psychiatrist in his late seventies wielding a surfboard was a sign that I was going on a journey with a very experienced and very fit guide.

We began to talk. At first, I relied heavily on my well-practiced skills of conversation, trying to appear as normal and likeable as if I were interviewing for a job. I recited my accomplishments to assure Dr. Lambert that I wasn't some out-of-control woman having a nervous breakdown. I wanted him to know that I was a successful woman who had no reason to be crying and canceling programs and sitting in this office.

Dr. Lambert listened with a patient smile, one that was knowing, but not condescending. Finally he leaned forward and asked very gently, “Are you ready to stop the very impressive forward movement in your life long enough to *feel* where you have been and where you are?”

That hit my panic button and I had to resist an urge to bolt. “I can’t stop! If I stopped, I’d end up back in Swainsboro, Georgia. If I stopped, everyone would lose interest in me and I would be broke and alone. If I stopped, what would keep me interesting to myself and other people? If I stopped, I’d have to think and . . . ” I paused, realizing that my voice was rising, as was my blood pressure.

Dr. Lambert leaned in closer. “If you stopped, you might remember why you’re running.”

Just like that, in our first five minutes together, this kind, compassionate, patient, and remarkably intuitive being opened the door to long-hidden memories.

DRIVING HOME, I struggled with the choice: continue with this new therapist on a journey of discovery and, hopefully, recovery from the pain I was now carrying in my head and heart, or cancel the next appointment and return to a life so jam-packed morning, noon, and night with activities and people and responsibilities that I wouldn’t have time to really think about this incident again. That seemed like a reasonable decision, I thought. I would feel better by Monday, I told myself, and we would resume taping, and everything would be as before.

But before the weekend was over, I knew what I needed to do. I couldn’t pretend my father’s abuse had never happened, or that my breakdown at work was something I could dismiss. I’d been stopped in a way I could not ignore. Dr. Lambert started me on a journey toward remembering what had happened, and until I faced that, it would be impossible to move forward.

The five-year-old girl inside me had to tell her story. Over the next six months, my memories slowly were recovered.

A memory. We are living in a small duplex in our new hometown. Mother is pregnant and sick a lot. My father is working in an appliance store and never smiles. He misses the military. My bedroom is across the hall from theirs, and I'm awake, frightened by what I am sure is a ghost at the foot of my bed. I've just turned six. My father comes into my room, slips into my bed, and pulls me close to him, whispering for me to be quiet so as not to wake Mother. Then he moves his hands all over my body, whispering that he's showing me how much he loves me. I hate the feeling of his tough hands touching me. I want to scream or run away, but what would I say? Who would believe me?

Sometimes I pretended to be asleep; sometimes I tried to believe it was a dream and not really happening. It didn't happen every night but often enough to be a nightly fear of the door opening, my father's rough hands turning my small body toward him, the forced touching. "I love you," he'd whisper each time, telling me how special I was to him. "This has to be our secret," he'd remind me each time, "because others wouldn't understand." As I grew older and he knew the day was coming when I would resist, push back, or refuse to go along, he'd repeat his dire warning: "If you ever tell anyone, terrible things will happen to our family." I'd believed him and kept the secret.

It all happened in the dark. In the light of day, no touching, no fatherly hugs, no clues that he had pressed his body against mine, almost whimpering and childlike in his own child's bed.

It went on until I became a teenager and put a lock on my bedroom door.

Keeping that dark secret led to a kind of compartmentalizing of my life, as I filed the horrible memories into a "don't think about" file, which I kept shut tight. After that one time I'd threatened to reveal the secret when my father tried to make me leave college, I suppressed the memory any time it pushed forward to a conscious level. I also did what many other incest survivors, like the ones I'd interviewed, did: filled life with nonstop activities, leaving little time for true reflection, always moving forward to leave the past behind.

But I couldn't outrun the shame. "Shame is the lie someone told you about yourself," Anaïs Nin once said. According to Beverly Engel, author of *The Compassion Chronicles,* about healing the shame of childhood abuse, "The chances are high that you blame yourself in some way for being submissive, for not telling someone, for having the abuse continue, for 'enticing' the abuser with your behavior or dress, or because you felt some physical pleasure."

All this leads to what she calls Perfectionist Syndrome, whose symptoms include "fear of being caught in a mistake, believing you don't really deserve good things—commonly known as the Imposter Syndrome"—and the one that hit hardest for me, "people pleasing." Survivors often feel "defective, worthless, bad, unlovable," Dr. Engel wrote. "Abuse victims often cope with these false yet powerful beliefs by trying to ignore them or convince themselves otherwise by overachieving or becoming perfectionistic."

Be the best. Prove yourself. Keep moving, moving, moving.

In addition to helping me understand the roots of my endless drive, Dr. Lambert helped me slowly recover more specifics of my lost memories. It was painful, and many times, I almost ended the therapy.

"Why do I need to revisit this all the time?" I asked him. "Maybe it's not going to make anything better by trying to remember now that I'm doing so well."

"Let's keep going, Pat," Dr. Lambert suggested, gentle as always. "I think this is helping you."

Dr. Lambert might have been the first man I ever trusted enough to believe him when he said what he thought was best for me. When men had told me that in the past, deep down, I'd felt that there was something they expected in return, that what they said was good for me was in fact good for them.

This was just one of the realizations that began to unfold about my so-called successful, well-adjusted life, and each one was painful, to be sure, but after each session, I felt a new kind of lightness, too, as layers of memories were recovered and replaced with a more integrated understanding of what I needed and how to find it. So much of my life, I realized, was driven by people pleasing. I didn't want to be disliked or rejected, so I wasn't as courageous as I could have been, going along when I shouldn't have.

I could have been a leader even earlier if I'd used my natural leadership attributes—but I was too busy testing people's feelings for me instead of saying, "This is who I am, with these imperfections." All along, there were good men who'd wanted to marry me, but I wouldn't even give them a shot; what if they found out my secret and learned I wasn't perfect? Of course, I was in a double bind; I couldn't be perfect because of the incest, yet I was constantly trying to be that way.

There were times I thought I was looking for forgiveness . . . for myself and, perhaps, even for my father. But I wasn't ready to even think about how to do that. Dr. Lambert encouraged me to stay focused on how to integrate the past with my present, how to take in the transformational changes I was going through and make them a part of my life, not to compartmentalize them again into a victimization or even to search for compassion or forgiveness. That might come later, he assured me, but for now, our work centered on recovery of memory and of the little girl I left behind with the past. She needed to be heard, seen, loved.

DURING ALL THIS time, I was in a loving and committed relationship with a man I thought I would marry. For the first time since my divorce, I came very close to making a lifetime commitment. But once I started therapy, we began to have trouble. I had to find ways to stuff it all back down into a dark secret place after each session because the truth of what I was remembering was too hard for him to hear. A father himself, he couldn't imagine the possibility of a father violating a young daughter this way, even though he knew that it happens to millions of girls around the world. Most are living and dying with this secret shame and pain. I didn't talk about the sessions, and we tried to go on with our life outside Dr. Lambert's office as if I weren't going into the hell of recovered abuse every Saturday.

I didn't know it at the time, but this was the beginning of the end for us, as I recognized that this was someone with whom I couldn't communicate my deepest secrets and pain. Being asked to remain complicit in keeping my silence was too great a burden. I realized that I still didn't have unconditional love, and I was ready to take another more holistic and emotionally healthy look at my relationships at work and in life.

I felt that I needed to acknowledge the little girl with big secrets, to remember her and honor her. I began to understand the connections between so much of who I was now and that little girl who had, in spite of what had happened to her, never given up—on herself or on men or even on unconditional love. I needed to offer myself more love and self-compassion. I began to try to appreciate myself more, seeing myself more fully instead of focusing on all the ways I wasn't measuring up. I'd never before looked at my life and said, "Well, this is pretty successful," instead always pushing forward to the next thing. Now I started to pause and appreciate my achievements. I could stop moving forward as a way to run away and instead construct the rest of my life as a way forward toward a more integrated life.

It would take a few months before I could make it through a day and night without a private episode of tears. I kept hosting and producing *Woman to Woman* throughout my therapy, and the work helped, not only as a distraction but also because I actually felt I was getting better. My therapy continued to make me an even better listener, more compassionate, and even more convinced of the positive effects of sharing stories.

Toward the end of our sessions, Dr. Lambert and I talked about the need to confront my father with the truth.

"You're doing pretty well, Pat," he told me, but he didn't think I could fully get rid of the shame, anger, and guilt if I didn't tell my father that I remembered. "You know, your father has had the luxury of either assuming you don't remember or believing that you maybe were more complicit—so he's relieving himself of the guilt in that delusion."

The matter had some urgency: my father was sick. A three-pack-a-day Camel smoker, he had cancer that was spreading quickly.

"He's going downhill fast. You need to come home," Mother called to say, unaware of course that I would be arriving with a different purpose than providing comfort to a dying man. All the way on the cross-country flight, I rehearsed what I would say, imagining his various responses. Was I seeking an apology? Would that seem so slight for such an injury? An explanation? That was what I really wanted, to understand how and why this otherwise decent man—a military officer who cared for his men, a deacon in the church, a kind grandfather to my son—could do what he did to his only daughter. No matter what I would hear for explanations or excuses, I told myself, I wasn't ready to forgive or forget again.

My father died before I could confront him, and at the funeral, I cried more than anyone . . . not from sadness but from anger. I had wanted and needed that moment of recognition. It didn't come, and I was once again stuck with my dark secret. I couldn't confront my mother now in this time of grief and loss, and it seemed insensitive, even selfish, to share such potentially devastating information with my brother, who adored my father, or my son, who idolized him.

So I returned to California, newly determined to move on past the memories, the therapy, to reclaim my active and accomplished life. But I did feel different inside. I had a new understanding about the lasting impact of the ultimate violation of trust: this theft of unconditional love from a child who needed it to be able to separate simply being loved from needing to do something to earn love. This was a critical understanding that I now intended to apply to all the rest of the choices I was making about my life and my work.

I never got to close the circle with my mother either. She developed Alzheimer's disease—the deepest kind of forgetting—and the one time I tried to tell her, the pain in her eyes alerted me to go no further. And until the writing of this book, I've never shared this with my brother or son. They both know now.

I'VE SHARED THIS personal story to raise awareness of the vast number of women carrying the lasting wounds and pain of incest, and coping with this violence and violation in their lives now.

I also hope to encourage any who have not dealt with their past or current abuse to do so. You may not know that the woman walking beside you as a friend or colleague or whose life you wish to emulate likewise survived incest to move forward to success and even happiness. Millions have survived and thrived and found their way to some kind of resolution. I'm one of them and I am grateful for being at a place in my life now where I am willing to risk the disbelief and even blame, which is possible when the perpetrator is family, because I believe my story might free others to break their silence and to survive the shadows.

DANGEROUS TIMES CALL FOR DANGEROUS WOMEN

In Conversation with Christine Schuler Deschryver

From my very first meeting with Christine Schuler Deschryver in Bukavu, Congo, I knew that I was in the presence of a tenacious woman who had survived more dangers and seen more violence than I could begin to comprehend.

Christine spent more than twenty years working for a non-profit in her beloved Congo, trying to help women who had been raped during the fifteen-year war fought there on the battlefields of women's bodies. She found herself at her lowest point when she held a nine-month-old baby who died in her arms following a gang rape. She despaired of ever making enough of a difference to the women who lined up by the dozens outside of Panzi Hospital, hoping for a spare bed so their insides could be put back together after horrific sexual violence.

Then she met Eve Ensler, who partnered with Christine to realize the dream of a community where the survivors of the epic sexual violence in Eastern Congo could be healed, physically and emotionally. Eve, with the support of V-Day activists and others, raised the funds to build a healing and leadership community center called City of Joy, a safe haven built brick by brick by the survivors themselves. More than 1,200 survivors have come to City of Joy since the opening in 2010 to receive skills and training that make it possible for them to transform their pain to power, to be prepared to become the leaders who can return to their villages and help build a far better future for the Congo. Time *magazine called City of Joy the single most effective healing and training for survivors of sexual violence they'd ever seen, and a very successful Netflix film documents the extraordinary work that Christine leads there.*

In a quiet moment of self-reflection during a recent visit, she answered my questions about how she became a dangerous woman.

What led you to become a dangerous woman?

Christine: I became a dangerous woman in 1998, during the [Congolese Rally for Democracy] rebellion, when a rebel group was fighting to overthrow President Kabila. I became dangerous for these rebels because I did not want to go along with their policies. I got involved in social mobilizations that we initiated in order to carry out citizen actions and civil disobedience against the rebellion. It was also the year they killed my best friend and her husband. I had felt danger on a daily basis and now I had to become dangerous myself.

What keeps you going in this work when you live with so much danger and violence?

Christine: Congolese women always have inspired me on my personal journey toward dangerousness. I always get encouragement from people who want things to change and who are willing to become a part of revolution to bring about change in the world. I have always been encouraged by people outside Congo who risk danger to come and support our work to heal and train women—people who know that in order for Congo to be free of violence and to have a future, women must be free to become leaders.

How does being considered a dangerous woman affect your work and life?

Christine: Being considered a dangerous woman is a huge challenge in my community because of the way our patriarchal Congolese society misunderstands the true meaning of dangerous woman. I constantly have to fight against the stereotypes and customs that degrade women. I sometimes frighten men—the officials and decision makers—because they know how committed I am to changing the lives of Congolese women; to fighting against the violence and abuse; to giving more women a chance to become dangerous enough to resist and to lead the change.

What advice do you give to other women confronting the dangers of violence in their lives, community, or country?

Christine: My best advice comes from Eve Ensler: "Focus only on what you can do and be the brightest light wherever you are, even in hell." I tell others that if they want to become dangerous women, they need to stride boldly beyond the shadow of fear, to persevere when they try to frighten us into submission, and to seek allies to take *action*!

Chapter 7

Going Global

"STEVE, THERE'S AN important story developing in Israel and I haven't seen anything about it on television."

It was always a good idea to emphasize the exclusive nature of a proposed story to the executive producer of NBC's *The Today Show.*

"It's a good story for a *Woman to Woman* segment—women on both sides, Israelis and Arabs, defying the blockade to work together. I'd like to go to Israel and meet them. I can use an NBC news crew in the region."

He stared at me incredulously. "What do *you* know about the Middle East?"

I had to admit, not much—but I continued to try to convince him to give me permission to go and report this story. It was a bold request, given that I had never reported an international story and never even traveled to the region, where there were news reports at the time of violence in the streets.

"No. Not a good idea," he said, standing to clearly end the meeting. "There's plenty of real news about Israel every night on the *Nightly News.* We have experienced foreign correspondents on the ground, and if these women are an important story, those guys will cover it."

Dismissed. In a toxic mixture of anger and disappointment, I called my producer, Coby Atlas, whom I had already convinced that this could be a compelling segment for *Woman to Woman* on *Today*, the weekly conversations I produced and hosted. "I'm going to pursue the story anyway," I heard myself saying. "I'm going to Israel."

I could make such a decision much more easily at this point in my life because Mark was away at school and my turbulent and unsatisfying personal relationship was on a hiatus. The appeal of an adventure that included faraway travel and new experiences was undeniable; I booked my first flight to Tel Aviv.

MY FIRST VIEW of Jerusalem will stay with me as a visual and emotional memory forever. Driving in at sunset is to witness the walls turn to a soft pink glow. Inside those walls, the sounds of prayers rise from the various synagogues, mosques, and Greek Orthodox and Catholic churches on nearly every narrow, crowded block.

I couldn't have been farther from my roots, but I felt a familiarity that didn't make sense, given that everything around this city, this country, this region of the world was a far distance from what I had known or ever experienced.

I had read a lot to prepare, of course. In particular, I had been captivated by Martha Gellhorn's *The View from the Ground*, a collection of her reports and stories from the front lines of many conflicts. As I walked into the bar of the American Colony Hotel on my first night in Jerusalem, I was trying to channel Gellhorn's confidence and even appearance, as I had actually purchased a sort of fatigue-looking jacket in an attempt to look the part of a war correspondent.

I had read in her reports and others' that this bar was the hookup place for news and connections, and it looked and sounded like that: voices spoke in various languages and accents and conspiratorial-looking conversations took place at small round tables. I could tell from inquisitive and somewhat dismissive glances toward me that my efforts to look the part had failed. Gratefully, I had planned to meet up there with my crew, who arrived and walked right toward me, another clear indication that I was the newbie in the bar.

I had been well advised to hire a mixed crew, meaning Israeli and Arab, and I had done that before arriving through the NBC bureau. They turned out to be experienced and prepared for anything, which was good because I was not. But I was eager to learn everything and to meet the women I had been reading about, and the Israeli cameraman and Palestinian sound guy—yes, we had two-man crews in those days . . . and yes, *man* crew is the accurate description of 99 percent of the television news crews working in conflict zones. A few years later, an extraordinarily brave and talented camerawoman named Margaret Moth, working for CNN, would break that barrier for women.

On my second day in Jerusalem, the camera crew and I found our way to the Mothers in Black, a group that stood on street corners every Friday to demonstrate a peaceful resolution to the occupation. They held signs that read "Mothers for Peace." I quickly recognized Anat Hoffman, founder of the group, from her pictures and approached her, explaining I was from the United States and making a documentary on the women in the region. That was the first time I had described what I was doing there in that way, but I thought *documentary* sounded more serious than a segment on a US morning show. Anat agreed that we could cover the demonstration; she would even give me an interview.

"We can't be a country obsessed with war and occupation," she told me when we sat down after the demonstration that she had organized in support of the uprising of Palestinian youth referred to as the intifada. "The intifada has led to the activation of women in my country. Women have a better understanding of the issues connected to oppression and inequality, and we are responding with peaceful demonstrations to raise awareness of the reasons for the violence."

Over the next few weeks, Anat opened both her home and her community of women to me, and the story I had come to tell was becoming more real—and to me, more important—with every encounter.

Because members of my crew had experience overseas, having worked for the BBC as well as US networks, and with support from my friend Carla Singer's high-level Israeli connections, I was able to travel the country with them. I listened to the stories of Israeli bombings and evacuations of people from their homes and met the Israeli survivors of Palestinian rockets that often struck civilian homes near the borders. I was realizing with each encounter and each story that this wasn't as simple as a story about women who wanted peace and men who wanted war. Or even a simple story of victims and oppressors. I met women in the Jewish settlements who told me that they carried guns in their purses and would shoot without hesitation to protect the land they felt was rightfully theirs. I met Palestinian women who were proud of their sons who led the violent protests.

And everywhere I traveled, I met women on both sides of the conflict who were willing to take enormous risks to their personal safety to reach across the divides to work together for peaceful solutions to long-held differences and deeply held opinions about what belonged to whom. In the weekly meetings I was privileged to attend at Anat's invitation, I observed the bonds between these women as examples of how women can navigate differences better when they have built foundations of shared experiences as mothers and community leaders, and share a commitment to creating a better future for their children.

Dr. Hanan Ashrawi was an important leader in this group and in the region. She would later serve as the official spokesperson for the Palestinian delegation to the Middle East peace process. In one of our interviews, she reflected a truth about women as peacemakers that I was witnessing and believing more every day.

"Women in both our communities (Jewish and Arab) have had to endure a lot," she told me, "and because of that, we are better suited and more prepared to negotiate peace."

Hanan had become good friends with an Israeli lawyer, Leah Tsemel, who had provided public-defender services for young Palestinian youth. During the long weeks of one of the trials, both Hanan and Leah were breastfeeding their babies, who often slept on the court benches. Whenever one cried from hunger, whichever of the two mothers wasn't otherwise engaged fed her. That made the two little girls, according to Arab culture, *milk sisters.* I got to meet the milk sisters on a visit to Hanan's home in Ramallah. The two girls, then nine years old, played and laughed together, connecting without a common language and in spite of a history intent on keeping them apart.

This is a story that stayed with me long after it was shared in one of the segments I produced for NBC's *Today* on this time in Israel. Over the years, I have shared the story of the milk sisters and their mothers as a model of the kinds of alliances we can, as women and mothers, form and sustain.

Hanan continues to dedicate her life to making peace. "It's not for the fainthearted," she told a reporter not long ago. "I started when I was a young undergraduate in hot pants, and now I'm a grandmother in a pantsuit." The Israeli/Palestinian divide, she said, isn't a religious conflict. "It is a man-made one, and definitely not a woman-made one." As for Leah Tsemel, she continues her fight for justice in Israeli courts, and her long-standing and tireless dedication has been recently documented in a 2019 film called, appropriately, *Advocate.*

I RETURNED FROM my first international reporting experiences with boxes of videotapes and a passion to share what I had seen and learned. Coby Atlas, *The Today Show* producer, got me an offer to broadcast segments under the terms of my contract, which gratefully she had kept NBC from canceling while I was in Israel learning on the job how to tell a story about conflict and deep-rooted differences and a new story about women's leadership.

I got a call to have lunch with a brilliant UCLA professor named Dr. Diana Meehan, who had been one of my guests on

Woman to Woman. She had written an excellent book about women's images in the media, *Ladies of the Evening: Women Characters of Prime-Time Television.* Diana was smart, provocative, funny. Her partner of many years, Gary David Goldberg, had created *Family Ties,* a comedy based in large part on Diana and Gary's own early hippie life together. Gary had a big deal at Paramount Studios, and together they had begun to explore good causes to fund.

I had an idea for her. As I started to describe what I had seen and the film I wanted to make about these women, Diana interrupted:

"What do you need?" she asked.

I hadn't thought about how much I would ask for, but I needed an answer now. "Fifty thousand dollars to get an edit process started."

"Is that all?" Diana asked. Then, to my astonishment, she took her checkbook out of her purse.

Just like that, I had $50,000—and a new producing partner. That was Diana's idea, and I loved it.

We edited a few of the interviews for *Today* and decided to use Diana's funds to continue filming, as the story was starting to become bigger.

Several of the women in the group I interviewed, plus other women leaders in the Knesset, Israel's elected representative body, decided to convene the first-ever international peace conference on the conflict, providing a forum for Israeli and Palestinian women from the West Bank and the Gaza Strip to negotiate a peace agreement.

"You keep documenting it," Diana told me, "and I'll keep funding it."

Along with nearly one thousand other women, leaders from the Middle East, Europe, and the United States, I traveled to Brussels in May of 1989. Proudly hanging on the front of the European Parliament building was a banner: "Women: GIVE PEACE A CHANCE."

Shulamit Aloni, a member of the Knesset, admonished the group at the opening plenary to remember that, "We only have a weekend. We have no time for speeches or long lists of grievances about which side did what to whom. We have to return home Monday to take care of children, husbands, our jobs, and our families and we are going to return with an agreement that will end the conflict destroying our communities."

And they did. With no loud voices or long speeches, they negotiated a one-page document with only seven paragraphs that could have gone a long way to ending the occupation. But when the Israeli delegation returned to Tel Aviv, the Knesset refused to review the document, saying it had been drafted at an unofficial, and therefore illegal, gathering; the Palestinian National Authority made the same judgment, and as far as I know, that document has never been officially considered.

It was also at that historic conference that a colorful congresswoman from New York, Bella Abzug, made a statement that has lived in my head and heart every day since. "In the twentieth century," she proclaimed, "women will change the nature of power, rather than power changing the nature of women."

In the second decade of the twenty-first century, there still aren't enough examples of this in the world, but I'm a believer in Bella's prediction because I have seen what can happen when women use their power, individually and collectively, taking big risks to get a seat at the table for themselves and others. And when there isn't a seat, remember the advice from Shirley Chisolm, an African American congresswoman from New York who was also a Presidential candidate in 1972: "Bring a folding chair." Being at the table, in the conversations that matter, *does* matter and is all part of changing the nature of power by how we use it for ourselves and for others.

DIANA AND I, who both have Irish roots, were closely following the eruptions again of The Troubles in Northern Ireland.

The Troubles had been roiling between the Catholics and Protestants since the British occupation in the late 1960s. Nearly 3,000 people had died, either in IRA bombings or through retaliation by the British forces. The women of Northern Ireland were, once again, on the front lines.

There had been a big peace movement in the mid-seventies. Mairead Corrigan Maguire, raised Catholic, and Betty Williams, raised by a Catholic mother and Protestant father, joined forces to gather as many of the women in Belfast as they could to march for peace. A gathering of a few hundred women for the first march swelled to more than 10,000 for the second, and soon the Women for Peace movement amassed more than 35,000 people demonstrating against the violence. Their efforts contributed to a peaceful end of that eruption of The Troubles, earning the two Irish women the Nobel Peace Prize in 1976.

Unfortunately, declarations of an absolute peace were premature, with bombings, hunger strikes, and paramilitary groups on the rise. That The Troubles were very much a presence was apparent the moment Mary Muldoon, my partner from *Woman to Woman*, and I arrived in Belfast in 1989 to produce a documentary. Soldiers carrying guns held in "ready to fire" positions were everywhere. Hotels were accessed behind sturdy barriers and locked gates. The tension was palpable. Everywhere we went, people asked us to repeat our surnames. Gratefully, Mary "Muldoon" passed muster with the Catholics; "Mitchell" was understood to be Protestant, so we got into the homes and meetings and hiding places we needed.

As I'd found in Israel, women were crossing the battle lines to keep lives and families together, not only parading and protesting, but organizing work groups. The Troubles were keeping a lot of men and women from getting jobs to support their families.

"Northern Ireland consists of open mouths and closed minds," one of the women in the group I interviewed told me. "When you are six feet under the soil, it doesn't matter who the soil belongs to."

Another said, "We must let ourselves feel the pain of every person still suffering and say to ourselves, we've not done enough."

"Religion doesn't come into it," another added to our conversation. "If there's poverty in my area, there's poverty in their area too. You can't blow up a factory and expect there to be jobs in the morning."

"Certainly the women couldn't do any worse than the men had done," yet another said. These working women were not politicians or even activists; they were wives and mothers and for them, the front line was economic survival. Their work helped bring about another uneasy peace.

Before Mary and I left Northern Ireland, we got to celebrate their victory and the election of the Republic of Ireland's first female president, Mary Robinson, who proved during her tenure that women can change the nature of power by the ways they use it for the good of others. In this case, President Robinson used her power to be an effective advocate for reproductive rights and protections for the environment, and she continues that work as a global advocate at the UN for human rights and the environment and as the chair of The Elders, a small group of wise and revered global leaders. Through her foundation, Climate Justice, she devotes her seemingly inexhaustible energies to alert the world to the urgency of response to the climate crisis, even cohosting a podcast, appropriately called *Mothers of Invention.*

"Receiving the Nobel Peace Prize is a lot of responsibility," Mairead Corrigan told me. "One day you're washing the dishes, and then suddenly, the world's media arrives and asks how you're solving world peace."

Mairead is one of only seventeen women who have ever been awarded a Nobel Peace Prize, and she decided to use her fame and global status and *become more dangerous*—those were her words! Every year since she won the Nobel, Mairead fasts the forty days of Lent to bring attention to the conflicts in the Middle East. At the end of the forty days, she travels to Jerusalem to break her fast in the chapel on the Mount of Olives, the ridge high above the Old City where Jesus is said to have prayed.

One year, Mairead invited me, Diana Meehan, and our crew to document the small ceremony. I was back in Jerusalem, this time with another peace warrior from another conflict. Once again, the city captured my heart and I remember every detail of this special day. As we drove up the winding road to the chapel, the sounds of Jerusalem became a glorious cacophony: the calls to prayer from the mosques, the bells ringing in the Catholic church towers, the choir sounds from Greek Orthodox churches, and the prayers in the synagogues and from the Wailing Wall. Diana and I rode in silence, giving ourselves over to the magic of the moment, feeling the privilege of being there.

A Catholic priest led a brief mass in the chapel as we knelt at the place named to honor the symbol of the olive branch, praying for a lasting peace to come inside the pink-washed walls of the Holy City.

"May all those who call Jerusalem their home and holy place live there peacefully together," he chanted. Diana, Mairead, and I prayed we would return to a more peaceful place one day together.

As we stood to leave, Mairead fainted, weak from the fast and the heat. But she recovered quickly, regaining strength with some holy water from the helpful chapel attendant. We decided to make one more stop before leaving. At the Wailing Wall, we found a place among the large numbers of people praying, folded up our tiny papers with our personal prayers written on them, and tucked the folded papers together into one small crevice.

As we walked away, with the sunset turning Jerusalem's walls to a rose color that I have never seen anywhere else, I realized that I had been on a profound learning journey. My view of the world and my connection to the women I now knew and so deeply admired had already set a new course forward.

BACK IN LOS Angeles, Mary Muldoon and I went to work in a small editing room. Within a few days, I had discovered a new love! Finding the way to weave together the personal stories of these amazing women while explaining the complex backgrounds of the conflicts was challenging but exhilarating. We didn't know the rules of documentary making—looking back on this effort, I cringe a bit at the narration and structure—but I'd discovered a medium that would be the right format for me to tell the stories that mattered, the stories that could compel social action.

A&E, then a new cable channel, liked what we created and broadcast the documentary, now called *Women in War: Voices from the Front Lines.* Mary and I were hooked on the subject and with Diana on board, too, proposed an additional story about the dual role of women in the civil war in El Salvador. Some were on the front lines in the rebel army known as the FMLN (Farabundo Martí National Liberation Front) and some were on the government side, advocating for a peace agreement.

Propaganda posters from the FMLN boasted several female *comandantes,* women carrying and using weapons, commanding troops, living in the forests where the rebels hid in camps. One story we read featured a *comandante* named Ana Guadalupe Martinez, who was shown with her companion, the leader of the FMLN, holding her baby on one hip and on the other, a rifle. Here was a women-in-war story not to be missed. A&E agreed.

We landed in San Salvador and headed for the American embassy to register that we were in the country. All of my news-correspondent friends had tried to talk me out of going: "too dangerous," they said. Nuns had been raped and killed a month or so earlier; the conflict was getting worse and moving closer to the capital; and besides, we didn't even speak the language! How did we plan to negotiate our way to the front lines to meet any of those women *comandantes*?

I admit to feeling a little scared as we approached the building with a small sign saying "American Consulate." Inside, there was no one in sight. Mary and I signed our names in the book that lay open on the front desk, then knocked on a closed office door. A middle-aged man emerged, looked us up and down, and barked, "Journalists?"

"Well, not exactly," I began. "We're here to get some stories for a documentary on women in conflict."

"Don't sign the book," he said, and seeing that we already had, he obliterated our names with a sharp black pen. "We don't want to know you're in the country. The American government has not approved your visit. You are in a war zone and we consider it unsafe for you and if anything happens, we won't bear any responsibility." With that, he closed the door.

We exchanged glances of concern. But it was too late—we were too committed to the story to return home. We met the BBC crew recommended by our Israeli cameraman, and we began to look for leads to get us to the women on the front lines. During our meetings at the hotel, I also noticed a couple of men, obviously American, whom we would see there and everywhere we went. CIA? Possibly, but we never found out. What we did discover was that it was harder than we thought to get connected to the women we came to interview, and days passed with lots of time in that hotel. Good thing we had come prepared with an entire locker full of snacks and food.

Yes, Mary and I were so sure that we would be in the mountains, trekking with the FMLN, that we brought our own food. How we expected to carry that heavy two-foot locker hadn't been calculated, and when we did get to the mountains, the locker was left behind.

One morning the headlines in the paper featured a big photograph of Febe Elizabeth Velasquez, leader of the activist labor movement in El Salvador, who had just been released from prison for protesting government policies. Through a translator/fixer that the crew found, she agreed to meet with us at a labor confederation headquarters outside San Salvador.

Febe was a powerful presence. A round-faced, smiling, almost angelic-looking woman, she was articulate, informed about labor movements around the world, and clearly a leader—no surprise that she was considered a threat by her government . . . and perhaps ours, too.

"Here thousands of women in different fields are giving their part to this struggle," she told us; she was convinced the FMLN would win and workers would have a better life. "What is missing is the real determination to make peace. Determination to finish this war. Determination to impel an economic program that will benefit everyone and get us out of this critical situation."

Not one moment of pessimism, no defeatist attitude; in our hour together that day, I saw Febe Velasquez as one of the most beautiful and inspiring women, inside and out, I'd ever met anywhere.

Febe's final words to us as we were packing up the equipment were, "I believe it's possible some of us will lose our lives along the way. We will not stop until we get a more just life. These are the hopes that we have especially for the children . . . we are doing it for them."

"We've got to build an entire segment around Febe, she's amazing!" I told Mary as we headed outside. Suddenly an enormous explosion threw us to the ground, debris raining over our heads. We staggered to our feet, raced to the van, and threw the equipment inside as people poured from the building we'd bolted from seconds before. "Get out of here—fast!" someone screamed and we did, shaking with disbelief at how close we had come to getting blown up—and worried about the fate of Febe.

Back at the hotel, we saw no sign that anyone knew (or cared) that just a few miles away, a bomb had destroyed a building and trapped or killed people inside. Later, on the local news, we saw Febe's photo and knew that she'd been the target of the bomb attack. She was dead. So were eight of her colleagues and dozens more injured by the bomb, which many believed had been planted by the government. It had been a close call for us, for sure, and we were shaken and decided it was best to return to the United States—after Febe's funeral, which we wanted to attend and film so that we could include her and her story in the documentary.

At Febe's burial, a man approached us and offered us the opportunity we had come to El Salvador for: to go to the front lines and interview Ana Guadalupe Martinez.

We took a helicopter part of the way, hovering low to avoid detection by the El Salvadoran military. We landed on a grassy knoll and hiked the rest of the way up the mountain to a small clearing where we met and talked with Ana Martinez. She was with one of her two children, both born since she'd become an FMLN *comandante,* and two other female rebel fighters. For the rest of this surreal afternoon in an idyllic forest setting, we sat in a circle with women dressed in camouflage uniforms with their rifles within easy reach.

It was a disconcerting image, and I was both awed by their bravery and courage and dismayed by their decision to take up arms. They had tried negotiations and talking, they said in answer to my questions about the decision to join the rebel forces, and after years of being unheard and policies not changing, they chose to change their tactics and become dangerous themselves—not only because they were now carrying guns and prepared to use them, but because they had a ferocious commitment to ending discrimination and oppression and shifting the power dynamic in their country.

Ana and the *comandantes* had created coalitions of village women who became their pipeline for shelters and supplies. Later we met with the so-called *conmadres,* fifty or so mothers marching for peace and social justice, all having lost loved ones. They were fighting for a better life for the majority of El Salvador's population—70 percent of the country's land was owned by only 10 percent of the people—but there were big questions about how they would implement the changes if they managed to oust the current regime.

A&E wanted to present both sides in this conflict, so we also interviewed the highest-ranking woman, the leader of the ruling party, about the role of women in government. She expressed some camaraderie with the FMLN and was prepared to meet with them once there was a peace agreement. That didn't look likely when Mary and I boarded our flight home, holding our breath as the plane made its way down the runway. We were feeling lucky to be alive, having come closer to danger than either of us had ever before, as well as incredibly fortunate to have had this experience. We had gained a deeper appreciation of the women and men who commit themselves to the urgent work of keeping the world informed about places most of us will never go but need to better understand.

SAFELY BACK IN the United Sates, Mary and I started the long process of viewing the hundreds of hours of footage, hiring translators for the interviews, and shaping a narrative for the documentary that would communicate our own great respect and admiration for women on the front lines of war and give context to their choices as well as to the conflicts in these countries.

Just as we were finishing the El Salvador segments, the FMLN declared a truce and peace talks were called by Costa Rican president Óscar Arias. The crew and I returned and were welcomed warmly by Ana and two other female *comandantes* who, it turned out, had led the FMLN to the peace table. We heard them offer terms for surrender of the FMLN along with their vision for a sustainable peace that could only be accomplished by including women in the decision-making positions and by extending education and health care as part of the agreement to end the fighting.

This was women using power differently. They were willing to lay down arms—but not willing to give up on their demands for greater economic opportunity and participation in government. It was clear to me that the negotiations would have ended without an agreement many times had the women not been present. With each point of blockage, they offered another perspective, a compromise or shift in language, and argued persuasively for guarantees about families and children of the FMLN that might not have been otherwise included.

Women at peace tables make a difference. Swanee Hunt, chair of the Institute for Inclusive Security, which includes the

Women Waging Peace Network, has supported women and their peacemaking contributions for more than two decades and documented the difference their presence at peace tables can make for a more sustainable peace and postconflict prosperity. This work is also a priority for the Carter Center, where Karin Ryan, director of the human-rights program, is an effective advocate for more women at every table where policies for enhancing human security, ending violence, shaping peace, and sharing prosperity are being negotiated.

Some of the FMLN leaders, including Ana Guadalupe Martinez, made a radical transition from leadership in a rebel army to government. She ran for and secured a seat in the next Congress and over the next few years, emerged as a peacetime leader in El Salvador's government. In fact, all of the women I met and interviewed, whose stories we told in a documentary, are models of what Bella Abzug (and I too) believes is possible: women using our power differently for different outcomes—to change the nature of power and shape a more peaceful and just world.

I RETURNED FROM my year of living dangerously with a much more informed worldview and greater confidence about what I could do, professionally and personally. I'd taken some risks and dared to do something I hadn't done before—and at an age when most war correspondents were retiring, not starting—and produced a two-hour documentary, having never produced one before. There was no going back, but what did moving forward look like?

My partner and original benefactor, Diana Meehan, was also gratefully hooked on the power of documentaries to inform, inspire, and shape opinions and even policy. We decided to form a production company, and since Paramount Studios had built a special office complex for her partner Gary and his talented team of writers and producers, we could set up shop there. Sherry Lansing, then Paramount CEO and the first woman to head a studio, referred to us as the studio's "good cause" group and gave us parking spaces and our own (very tiny) office suite next door to Gary Ubu Productions.

Diana and I decided to call our company VU Productions, which was both shorthand for "voice of Ubu" (Ubu was the name of Diana and Gary's beloved black Labrador) and also the name of an obscure French photojournalism magazine from the twenties. Explaining what VU Productions meant took the first ten minutes of every meeting. We added Diana's longtime friend Lynne Tuite and my former producer at *Today*, Coby Atlas, to the group, and declared ourselves ready to produce documentaries and specials on the critical issues of relevance to women and girls with the purpose of impacting policies and politics.

We had a lot of important subjects and some good ideas, but not many buyers. The donated funds from Diana and Gary split four ways didn't go far, and I explained that I needed to get more paying work. I called up Charles Kuralt, host and executive producer of CBS's *Sunday Morning*, one of the best programs on television for longer, more engaged storytelling. Fortunately, he was looking for an arts correspondent, and even though I had few credentials for that assignment, he assured me that "covering museum exhibitions and interviewing artists would be a lot safer than helicoptering into war zones."

Soon I was working seven days a week to juggle both documentary production and my CBS responsibilities, bouncing between LA, Santa Barbara (where I was living with a significant other), and New York, producing reports on artists like Eric Fischl, April Gornik, Robert Rauschenberg, and David Salle for *Sunday Morning*. "I can't believe you pay me to hang out with these talented people," I told Charles, with gratitude for one of the best gigs in television, then and now.

Coby took on freelance production work, and Lynne and Diana secured some funding for educational videos. We made films about infant-mortality rates and child labor, and we actually had some measurable impact on policies through congressional screenings and strategic advocacy work with the effective Kathy Bonk, founder of the Communications Consortium Media Center. Lifetime also commissioned us to do a series on women in politics during 1992, when so many more women were elected to Congress and as mayors and governors that it was actually called the "Year of the Woman in Politics." Finally, in 2018, those numbers, which had been until then our high point, grew, with more women running—and winning—elections than at any time in US history.

Women in history became our next big project: VU Productions proposed a ten-hour series documenting the stories of women's contributions to the twentieth century—a history largely untold in the history books. In 1992, we were already in the century's last decade.

I was thinking about how good my life was as that decade began—pulling into my special parking place on the Paramount lot; coming into our cramped but well-positioned offices to be greeted by friends, colleagues, and partners; truly enjoying again the experience of working with women; pursuing projects of passion and purpose; and lunching at the Commissary next to the fully costumed *Star Trek* cast. I was feeling more settled and satisfied with my life and work than I could remember ever being. I wasn't feeling that familiar urge to try something new, to push another door open or confront another challenge or chase another parade.

So why was I packing a bag to fly to Atlanta and meet Ted Turner?

DANGEROUS TIMES CALL FOR DANGEROUS WOMEN

In Conversation with Christiane Amanpour

Christiane and I were colleagues at CNN when she was becoming the network's most recognized face and most famous war reporter in the world. I have always admired her courage and her commit-

ment to doing what's right and not what's easy. We got to work together once, producing a documentary, Revolutionary Journey, *which chronicled her first return to Iran, where she'd lived as a child, to visit her family home with her father. Today, Christiane continues as the chief international anchor for CNN and host of its nightly* Amanpour, *as well as host of a new PBS program,* Amanpour and Company.

During a recent visit, I asked her whether she agreed that we are living in dangerous times and whether such times call for more women to become risk-takers.

Christiane: These times are dangerous because hard-won freedoms and rights that form our democratic world order are threatened from within, not from an external enemy. When the patriarchy challenges the basic concepts of truth, evidence, rule of law, and democracy itself, then it's time for women to rise up and reclaim the moral high ground, posing a real danger to the status quo.

Do you think of yourself as a dangerous woman?

Christiane: I do regard myself as a dangerous woman because I have always used my platform (at CNN and PBS) for something much bigger than myself, to speak truth to power and try to rebalance the global scales of justice.

Was there a specific time when you felt you were becoming more dangerous, and what was it that inspired or encouraged you?

Christiane: Covering the Bosnian War of the 1990s was when I first felt a sense of being dangerous. Firstly there was real physical danger, as it was the first war where journalists were deliberately targeted by armed groups. I have lost many friends in the line of fire on the front lines of truth-telling. But there was an almost greater moral and intellectual danger, in being conscious and daring enough to be truthful rather than neutral. In other words, that was where I learned that our profession's golden rule of objectivity did not mean drawing a false moral equivalence between aggressor and victim. I have applied this dangerous lesson learned to everything from war and peace to climate change, where there is no equivalence between the overwhelming weight of science and the tiny minority of deniers.

Who inspires you to be more dangerous?

Christiane: I've been inspired by many other dangerous women: women from the heights occupied by Gloria Steinem to ordinary but determined women in the trenches who have blasted tiny holes in the patriarchy that rules science, business, sports, media, and every other field! And especially I am inspired by the women who a hundred years ago fought bravely for some of us to get the right to vote!

What is the most important role for dangerous women today?

Christiane: Really dangerous women will vote and run for office! When you choose to be dangerous, you give up the right to be complacent and safe, but you gain the ability to change the world. There are too many danger zones worldwide for women to count, starting from the real and present dangers women face because of their bodies, from the external threats of terrible sexual and domestic violence to the cultural and legal threats that deny women basic rights over their own bodies. I do believe that "dangerous times call for dangerous women" because men have had the whole sweep of history to rule solo, so given these dangerous times, why not let the other half have a go? What have we got to lose?

Chapter 8

Taking My Shot

"YOU DON'T FIT the image of a Turner employee," said the president of Turner Broadcasting as he ushered me to the door of his impressively large office in Atlanta, the headquarters of this fast-expanding cable empire.

"What do you mean?" I asked, trying not to sound defensive.

"Well, you know," he stammered, "you look so . . . serious."

Serious? Did that mean *old*? I was clearly older than the youthful-looking executive interviewing me, Scott Sassa, and maybe I *had* looked a little too shocked at the rowdy stories about his boss, Ted Turner, that he'd just shared. Or maybe my formal tailored suit was a mistake; he was wearing jeans and a golf shirt.

After an awkward moment, I offered, "Well, I *am* serious about my work."

He laughed. "Enjoy your meeting with Ted. He's serious about his work, too."

I'd already heard my share of legendary Ted Turner stories—that he was a loud-talking, hard-driving, Southern good old boy who quite literally lived at the office, often sleeping there and appearing at early morning meetings in his jockey shorts (or less). Some of the stories probably were true, and many were part of the legend that had already developed around this visionary entrepreneur who was rapidly transforming the media landscape.

I didn't really want the job that I interviewed for—leading the documentary division of Turner Broadcasting—but I wanted a chance to pitch our documentary series on the history of women in America to Ted Turner. I had no reason to believe he'd go for the idea, but I was curious enough about the cable empire he had built in Atlanta to make the journey.

MOST OF THE media world—especially my colleagues in Los Angeles—were less than complimentary about the media entrepreneur, referring to him most often as "the Mouth of the South" because he publicly boasted about his company's successes. But Ted had a lot of reasons to boast: transforming a small, independent, money-losing Atlanta television station, TBS, into the first superstation by putting its signal on a satellite that delivered its programming nationwide. Genius idea—and no one had done it before Turner. Then he bought a losing baseball team, the Atlanta Braves, and turned them into America's team by putting their games on the superstation.

More recently, Turner had launched the first twenty-four-hour news channel, CNN, and even though NY and LA media circles dubbed it the "Chicken Noodle Network," by this time CNN had already revolutionized the news landscape. Its coverage from the front lines of the first Gulf War was a game changer, as was the whole idea of delivering news 24/7. As a news junkie, the chance for a closer look at that operation alone would have made the trip worthwhile for me.

Of course, Ted was married at this time to the legendary Jane Fonda, whom I knew, although we were not the friends we are today. I had interviewed her a few years before when she was still married to Tom Hayden. She had just launched the Jane Fonda Workout Studios. To be more specific, I'd sweated and strained through a conversation while we did leg lifts and tummy crunches. I had seen her a few times in LA at Hollywood women's gatherings, but I didn't feel close enough to let her know that I was coming to Atlanta to ask her husband to fund a documentary series on women and that my partners and I were also secretly hoping she would narrate. Getting the chance to pitch the idea to her, too, would be a bonus for this trip that was already going south, metaphorically as well as geographically.

As Sassa ushered me to the door with instructions to take a cab downtown to the CNN building where I'd find Ted, I wasn't feeling very optimistic about the outcomes of this quixotic return to the South.

THE SECURITY GUARD at the CNN entrance welcomed me with a big smile. "Take the elevator to the fourteenth floor. Can't miss Ted's office. Just follow the Oscars on the wall."

I'd already picked up that everyone seemed to call the boss "Ted" and never "Mr. Turner." As instructed, I followed the trail of Oscars, bathed in soft spotlights and placed strategically on pedestals in front of the posters of the corresponding Academy Award–winning films. The last one right before the big double doors that led to the chairman and founder's office was for *Gone with the Wind*, reportedly Ted's favorite and the reason he'd purchased the MGM movie library a few years before.

Dee Woods, Ted's clearly protective assistant, ushered me to a seat on one of the large leather sofas. "Ted will be with you in a few minutes," she said, giving me a quick head-to-toe appraisal much like the one I'd experienced from Sassa earlier. I assumed her intuitive radar was assessing whether I was a serious producer or one of the many wannabes known to make their way to Ted's office.

A booming voice from the other room broke the silence between us, and Dee motioned me toward the door just as it opened. There stood Ted, looking like the framed magazine covers papering the walls: *Time*'s Man of the Year (twice!); *Sports*

Illustrated featuring "Captain America," as he was dubbed, after winning the America's Cup yachting trophy; another photo showed him proudly wearing an Atlanta Braves cap, and others heralded the launch of TNT, the Cartoon Network, Turner Classic Movies, and, of course, CNN.

Ted shook my hand and thundered, "So you're a documentary producer from Hollywood." Another head-to-toe assessment. "Tell me what you've done."

I'd barely wedged in a couple of words before he started to pace the office, telling me what he had done, pointing to a long row of awards and plaques of every description covering the walls, talking fast and loud about the documentaries he'd funded: National Geographic specials, Jacques Cousteau's series, David Attenborough's nature series and others with environmental and conservation themes. I was surprised and impressed at the number and the scope of subjects, and Ted's enthusiasm for this work was clear.

"I started this documentary unit to be a force for social change," he told me. "That's why I called it the Better World Society. Had to change it to TBS Productions, though, because that's where most of the documentaries are seen. Have I seen any of yours?"

Finally, a question for me and a pause in what had been a nonstop monologue. I mumbled, "Some have been seen on Lifetime, A&E, and CBS."

Before I could continue, he began pacing again as he told me about his plan to make a movie about the Battle of Gettysburg during the Civil War. "I'm a real history buff," he said with a big smile, and I jumped into the pause.

"What about the history of women in America? That's a story that hasn't been told," I said in a voice much louder than before. Ted stopped pacing, and I knew to keep talking.

"It's almost the end of the twentieth century, and women in this country have done some amazing things, and yet there's never been a documentary about their accomplishments. A lot of the stories aren't even in the history books. Don't you think this is important history to document?"

"How many hours? What's the budget? Have you lined up any famous women to be in it?"

I answered in short spurts, trying to match his rhythm and volume (I later learned that Ted talks very loudly to compensate for a loss of hearing, caused by his love for duck and quail hunting and a few too many shotgun blasts).

I practically shouted my answers in short blasts—"Maybe ten hours . . . one for every decade . . . interviews with historians and yes, famous women . . . and, of course, a big name for the narrator."

"What about Jane Fonda?" he asked with a big smile.

"Well, she would be our first choice . . . and I could certainly ask her," I replied, trying not to look too pleased with how this was going.

"You know her? Did you tell her you were meeting with me?"

"No, I didn't, Mr. Turner. But we know each other and please tell her I said hello."

"Call me Ted," he said.

For the first time, there was silence. He was clearly making a mental calculation. He went to his desk, where my resume was in clear view, right beside a large plaque that read, "Lead, Follow, or Get Out of the Way." Clearly, Ted's approach to life, and at this point, after ten minutes in his office, I wasn't sure which approach was working best for me.

More questions came shooting from Ted. What was I doing now? What was VU Productions? Who were my partners? Had we won any awards?

Then: "How much money do you need?"

Was he asking about a salary for the job or the budget for the documentary? "Two million dollars," I replied, hoping I'd chosen the right question to answer.

"Sounds about right," he said. "Have you talked to my documentary team about this idea?"

I started to answer when Ted suddenly stood up and headed toward another door. "Just hitting the bathroom," he said. "I'll be right back."

A reprieve! This gave me some time to strategize, and when Ted returned, I addressed both issues—the job and the documentary. "I met with Scott Sassa this morning about the executive position at TBS productions, and I'm very interested," I told him, "but I'm also passionate about producing *A Century of Women*—"

"Why not do both?" Ted cut in. "Why can't you produce *A Century of Women* for Turner Broadcasting as the new head of the documentary team?" He gave me a wink and a Cheshire Cat grin, a look I soon learned meant "I win." Ted was seemingly offering me a job *and* funding for a ten-hour documentary series my partners and I had been pitching for two years!

Before I could say another word, Ted flung open the door and shouted to Dee. "Pat Mitchell here is going to be the new VP of TBS Productions. Take her to meet the right people."

One more handshake, one more head-to-toe appraisal, and "I'll tell Jane you said hello."

As the door closed behind him, Dee tried to suppress her amusement; this wasn't the first time someone emerged from Ted's office looking like they just got off the rocket-ship ride at Disneyland.

"Why don't you get back in touch with Scott Sassa and tell him Ted said to make a deal?" she prompted me. A loud "Dee, what's next?" from the inner office ended our exchange, and soon I was standing in front of the *Gone with the Wind* poster once again, trying to regain my balance from the whirlwind encounter with a man who looked and acted a bit like that movie's star—Clark Gable. (See the movie to fully appreciate the comparison!)

It took me fourteen floors on the elevator ride down to recover from what had just unfolded. I played it all over in my mind. What did Ted say and what did I say and what did it all mean?

My friend Glenda was waiting for me in the lobby. "Are you okay?" she asked. "What happened?" I stared at her, unsure how to reply. Had Ted Turner really offered me a job? Was he going to fund the documentary series? As I tried to reconstruct for Glenda what had happened, more questions floated in my mind: What would it be like to work for Ted? To live in Atlanta again? To tell my good friends and partners that I was leaving VU Productions? Was this a big opportunity that I couldn't turn down—and what was the offer, really?

An answer to the last question came the next day, when Scott Sassa called to offer me the job of executive vice president of TBS Productions at a more than respectable salary.

I was thrilled, but money wasn't the driver here; *A Century of Women* was. I was much more focused on getting that documentary series made than on becoming an executive at a dynamic and, as I was to discover, dysfunctional company that would upend my life just as surely as it was changing the media landscape.

BEFORE I BROKE the job news to Diana, Lynne, and Coby, I led with the good news that *A Century of Women* was going to be funded by TBS Productions. When I mentioned the job offer, their smiles faded quickly and the questions started coming fast and furious: What would happen to VU Productions, the commitment to each other?

I had a few sleepless nights and more than a little tension at home as I explained to the man I was living with and had talked about marrying that I would be commuting to Atlanta. "I will fly there every Sunday night," I told him, "stay in Glenda's guest room, then be back here by Friday night." He was skeptical about the plan but tried to be supportive. After a few months of increasingly jet-lagged weekends, the relationship was too strained to continue.

As an executive, I had a lot to learn . . . fast. TBS Productions in 1992 was a small unit with big personalities and big projects in full form when I arrived. Vivian Schiller, the interim leader until I arrived, joked that "she'd hired her boss," as she was the one who put my name forward to Scott Sassa for the open position that I'd accepted without knowing much about the team I would be leading or the company culture where I had a very high-profile position from day one. Vivian's insights about the company, her knowledge of documentary making, and her impressive diplomatic skills got me through those challenging early days.

When I asked her why she didn't pursue my position herself, she said, "I'm not ready to be the leader. But if I get to work with someone with your background and experience, I'll *get* ready." Her answer said everything about her self-awareness and strategic approach to her life and work. I had a trusted ally and she had a mentor, and we modeled another woman-to-woman working relationship that continued way past our days together at TBS Productions. She rose quickly to being ready for leadership, and when I left seven years later, she was promoted to lead the documentary unit, followed by executive positions at the *New York Times* and as president of NPR. She continues to be one of the industry's most respected and innovative leaders and one of the best examples of what I talk about later in Chapter 15, "Playing It Forward."

As I'd learned in that first pitch session, Ted responded quickly and positively to any opportunity to make history, document it, or change its course. He was a passionate student of history, and it didn't take me long to realize that whatever the subject, Ted knew a lot—often more than the producers, researchers, or experts working on the individual films. And he could be counted on to watch every film, start to finish, and often he had corrections or suggestions—and in every instance where he questioned a historical reference or fact, he was right.

Ted was also an environmental visionary, among the first to commit millions of dollars to make documentaries about conservation, climate change, and to support National Geographic, Jacques Cousteau, and even the BBC Natural History Unit. During my time with Turner Productions, we produced more than a hundred hours of documentaries with these partners and others on clear-cutting, natural resource depletion, population growth, family planning, even the practice of female genital mutilation (FGM). It didn't matter to him that sponsors pulled out and critics took issue with what they called *advocacy documentaries*.

Ted waved those concerns aside. "We're not making these documentaries to make money," he'd remind me, "but to make change!"

One of the first assignments Ted gave me was to produce a documentary series on Native Americans; he was deeply committed to raising awareness of American Indian rights. "I don't want the history of Native Americans to be told by white historians or filmmakers," he told me. "I want you to put together a team of American Indian storytellers to tell their stories. Robert Redford is doing a Native American filmmakers lab at that new institute he's running out there in Sundance. Go see him."

"Sure thing, Ted. Good idea." I practically flew to the Sundance Resort under my own power, fueled with fanciful imaginings about meeting one of the world's most famous actors. I knew nothing about Sundance or the labs Ted referred to, and in the pre-Google days, did as much research as I could find. I'd read that Redford bought a small ski resort near Park City, Utah, property he'd discovered on a motorcycle ride up Provo Canyon after finishing *Butch Cassidy and the Sundance Kid.* I was now being driven up that same canyon in a snowstorm.

"Mr. Redford will meet you tomorrow for lunch at the restaurant," the woman greeting me at the small registration office said as she handed me a key. I could see nothing but the outline of the Wasatch Mountains as I was dropped off at a charming wood-framed cottage decorated with artifacts and Native American rugs. I fell in love with the whole place and I hadn't even met the man who created it. I found out later that all the cottages at Sundance were designed by Redford to fit naturally into the environment and to honor the first people who lived on this land, the Ute nation.

Watching the snow fall from every window that night, I dreamed of calling a place like this home. In fact, a few years later, I did become a homeowner there, buying one of the small cottages like the one I slept in that first night.

THE NEXT MORNING, disoriented and in unfamiliar terrain, I flailed around in the snowstorm until someone redirected me to the only restaurant on the property at the time, the famous Tree Room, which Redford had built around a gigantic pine tree he didn't want to cut down. (The tree died the week the restaurant opened.) It's filled with Redford's personal collection of Native American art, pottery, rugs, and kachina dolls, and as I waited for him in this beautiful space, I fell more deeply in love with this place called Sundance.

And I waited. And waited. The woman who had checked me in stopped by to reassure me that waiting for Redford was expected—and yes, I had already read that part of the many legends surrounding him. I didn't mind waiting, of course, but I was getting more and more nervous. When he arrived, he gave me that heart-melting smile and said, "Call me Bob." My head was spinning. In less than eighteen months, two of the world's biggest names had shaken my hand and said, "Call me Ted" and now "Call me Bob."

I struggled to stay present as one dreamy movie scene after another passed through my head. I felt like I was having an out-of-body experience while Bob talked, sharing the story of Sundance, and in my head, scenes from *The Way We Were* had me longing to brush his hair off of his forehead and say, "Come back, Hubbell." How many women in the world have had that dream? But no time for daydreaming here. I had an important mission and I told myself to stay present and focus on the purpose of being there.

Bob listened intently to Ted's plans for a multiyear, Native American–focused initiative, one that would feature a documentary series as well as television movies from Native American authors and producers and CNN reports on current issues and challenges for American Indian communities—in total, a four-year project for which Ted had allocated $20 million.

Bob had some important questions, including one that Ted had asked too: How would we find and hire Native Americans to lead the creative teams for all these projects? After more conversation, he offered to introduce me to the person running the lab he had created to mentor, nurture, and support emerging writers and filmmakers from the Native communities in the United States and around the world. This Native lab continues today and has nurtured many successful projects and elevated the ideas and voices of many indigenous storytellers.

"Would you consider co–executive producing?" I asked, tentatively.

"I might," he said. "I'd really like to see this done well."

I couldn't wait to share the good news with Ted, trying to refrain from gushing about "Bob." "How much money is he gonna want to do this?" Ted asked. I hadn't even thought to ask—so I called Bob's office. "Oh, no, he doesn't want any money," I was told, "but he would appreciate a contribution to the Native American lab." Done! Ted committed to three years of support.

I began to assemble the creative teams to tell the stories of more than five hundred American Indian nations in six hours of television. It wasn't easy then to find experienced directors and producers in all the Native communities, but through the contacts from the Sundance lab, we did fulfill our promise that Native voices and filmmakers would tell their own stories.

Bob and I would meet every few months to view the rough cuts. Every time I sat in that editing room with him, I was amazed by how incisive Bob's insights were; he'd make one small suggestion for an edit or a script change, and the impact was transformative. Always careful to listen and to honor our creative teams, he also used every opportunity to mentor, to share what he knew or had experienced.

It was a master class in documentary filmmaking and in observing close-up the model of creative mentorship that Redford initiated in all the lab programs of the Sundance Institute, the nonprofit he'd established in 1983 to lead this work for emerging screenwriters, directors, and producers at the Sundance resort. I learned so much from these occasional sessions with Redford, a consummate storyteller, and from working with these creative collaborators as the stories of *The Native Americans* were told by and with them in this six-hour documentary series that was broadcast on TBS and is still shown from time to time around the world.

For me, the learning journey of documenting this history with teams of American Indian historians and filmmakers and spending time with many of the diverse and resilient communities across the country deepened my personal advocacy for righting the many wrongs perpetuated against America's indigenous people. As tribal attorney and leading activist, Tara Houska (Couchiching First Nation) reminds us in her powerful TED Talk that I invited her to give at TEDWomen 2015, "We're still here!"

The documentary series also yielded a lasting friendship with Robert Redford . . . yes, "Bob" to me and all his friends. Two years after the documentary aired, he invited me to join the board of Sundance Institute, which I did with true joy. I've been a trustee since, and for the past several years, I have served as chair of the board. Bob and his talented artist wife, Bylle Szaggars Redford, are beloved and much valued friends.

I often reflect upon the fact that Redford could have turned this property into a beautiful private reserve for himself and his family, but from his initial purchase of the land until now, he has sustained his commitment to protect the land and its natural beauty, assigning much of the property to a conservation trust and using the facilities that he personally funded to be built to create a home for the Sundance Institute's programs. Today, nearly forty years after he held the first director's lab at the Sundance resort, artists from nearly every country in the world find inspiration for their work in the natural surroundings and in the lab programs now designed for writers, producers, screenwriters, playwrights, and film composers as well as directors. Stories from Sundance continue to benefit from the creative alchemy of nature and art, inspired by the artist-founder who saw the need and responded.

OVER THE YEARS, I've also seen up close the difference Bob has made in the lives of so many independent storytellers who might not have told their stories without all the mentoring, nurturing, and personal support that they received in the institute's lab programs. In the early years, Bob financed the institute's labs with very little funding from other sources. Even after the Sundance Film Festival became recognized as the most important festival for independent films and Hollywood studios benefitted greatly from the movies and talent they discovered there, very little financial support for the institute's work has come from that community. But Bob, like Ted, stays the course of his passions and convictions; both men's lives are great examples of what it means to engage with passion and purpose, to embrace great risk, to go against the mainstream, to achieve measurable change. It's no surprise that these two men, so different in styles and approaches to their work, share a deep passion for nature and are lifetime advocates for the environment and conservation of our natural resources, and that both of them have used their personal resources to impact the lives of so many other people all over the world. How lucky am I to have worked with them and to know and admire them as friends and mentors.

Working for Ted gave me the opportunity to tell so many important stories that I wouldn't have been able to without his total commitment to the issues that mattered. The first documentary, *Avoiding Armageddon*, was on the nuclear threat. One of the first series we produced was about epidemics, *The Virus Hunters*, and it presciently documented the six CDC doctors who went to Africa to track the Ebola crisis. We made *Moon Shot*, featuring the astronauts who walked on the moon, and *Chasing the Dream*, a biopic on Hank Aaron, which was nominated for an Academy Award. Another nomination followed for a collaboration with Steven Spielberg called *Survivors of the Shoah* and ultimately, a twenty-four-hour documentary series on the Cold War.

We won lots of awards for all the documentary work, but we didn't get big ratings, and I still had to remind people from time to time that the National Geographic series and many other historical series they loved were on TBS, not PBS. I had a big budget, and once Ted believed in an idea or the value of an untold story, we were never questioned about how much we spent—only whether we got it right!

Working for Ted Turner in the 1990s, when he was shaking up the media world, was being in the game with the big boys—and yes, with one exception, executives whose offices lined the fourteenth floor at Turner Broadcasting in those days were men. Luckily, I was a fast learner. I needed to be. We were working for the ultimate entrepreneur who had a big new idea every day, and there were no barriers to his implementing them.

Since Ted owned the Atlanta Braves, and later the Atlanta Hawks basketball team, going to games was almost as important as showing up for staff meetings. I became a big baseball fan and admit to loving the executive privilege of sitting in the owner's box next to another big Braves fan, former president Jimmy Carter. Along with the other Turner executives, I learned how to use a well-placed sports metaphor in nearly every sentence, especially when pitching a project to Ted. "It's our turn up to bat." "Well, we're only on second base with this one." "This one was nothing but net." No touchdowns, only home runs, because Ted didn't own a football team.

TWO LESSONS ABOUT how to win the game with Ted—or with any hard-charging boss—came early on.

The first was in my first week. There was a regular Monday morning 8 a.m. staff meeting for senior executives. Glenda drove me to work that morning in her son's stick shift Mustang. About a half mile from CNN headquarters, the car began to smoke and stall. We pulled into a gas station. I jumped out of the Mustang, grabbed the arm of a pickup driver about to pull out, and asked for a ride to CNN. "I'm going to be late for a meeting with Ted!"

We arrived at the CNN door at 7:55, and I flew toward the elevators, pushing aside a few people to get into the first door that opened. Stepping out on the fourteenth floor, I practically collided with Ted coming into the elevator. "You're late. Meeting is over."

It was 8:05.

That's when I learned that an 8 a.m. meeting for Ted was really ten minutes to eight, and that the meetings rarely lasted longer than five minutes.

That was true of the pitch meetings, too. I'd go in with my suggestions for documentaries, and if I couldn't convince Ted with one or two sentences that this was a good idea, the answer was always no.

"If you can't tell me in less than ninety seconds what the film is about and why we should make it, then you haven't figured it out yet, and I'm not wasting my money while you do," he said, and he was right.

Early on, every single idea I presented got a quick no and at the end of four or five of them, Ted got up, announced, "Meeting over," and left the room.

I shook with anger as I strode past Dee (whose knowing smile made me all the madder) and slammed my office door like a child. A second later my assistant called out, "Mr. Turner is on the phone."

"What's wrong with you?" Ted bellowed.

"Nothing's wrong, Ted, but no one since my father has ever said no to me so many times without an explanation."

"Well, I'm not your father," Ted replied, "and I will tell you no until you are prepared for a yes and that's your job."

With that, he hung up, and I started thinking about packing up and heading back to California and partners who never said no.

I calmed down, of course, and took the instruction seriously. It wasn't that I hadn't been prepared to answer any and all questions about the project; I just wasn't prepared to condense all I knew into three sentences or fewer.

But I learned to do just that, and the yeses started to come. This ability to be brief and clear has served me well. It's essentially composing a compelling theme sentence. I encourage everyone to develop this skill. If you can't figure out how to say it in under thirty seconds, go edit yourself until you can. I'm a far more effective change-maker because I've followed that advice!

HAVING COME FROM nearly a decade of working mostly with women—women producers and partners and with *Woman to Woman*, an entire production team of women—it was strange and slightly disorienting to be back in a big company where most of the people in charge were men. The only woman on the executive floor was the EVP of communications and community relations, Julia Sprunt. Everything about her communicated efficiency and effectiveness.

I asked Julia to have breakfast a few months after my arrival, hoping for some insights about how to navigate this highly charged, macho-driven corporate structure. I'd already figured out that whoever got to Ted last would win the point, whatever the point was, and that Ted played the power game by the Machiavellian rules of survival of the fittest.

Julia was wary at first, but pretty soon we were sharing war stories, and by the end, we committed to creating a more supportive environment for women at the company. We both had one powerful ally and advocate for this idea, Gail Evans, already a force at CNN, and who, later, wrote a best-selling book, *Play Like a Man, Win Like a Woman.* The three of us decided to host a breakfast and invite all the women.

About two hundred showed up at a club named after some pioneer women pilots. For the first few minutes, it felt like any other company gathering, with polite chitchat. But when Julia, Gail, and I spoke about our careers, focusing on the failures, mistakes, and times we could have used more friends and allies, the mood quickly shifted.

"You're not going to make this a feminist thing, are you?" one of the more junior staff asked. "Because if that's the agenda, I'm out of here." Here we were, twenty years after the women's movement, seventy years after women died getting that young woman the right to vote, and we were still being challenged about a "feminist" agenda!

It was disheartening but not unexpected, so Julia, Gail, and I put on our widest smiles and explained patiently that a feminist agenda was at its core a belief that women and men deserved equal protections, rights, and opportunities. Not special attention or favors—not women win; men lose—a win-win, full equality for all.

Suddenly Ted bounded into the room.

"Good morning!" he shouted. "Just thought I'd drop by and see what you girls were up to." Ted was staring at me; clearly I was the most likely instigator of this rebellion.

"Just getting to know each other a little better, Ted," Julia said smoothly. "What a great group of women work at this company!" She made a sweeping gesture to the room as we all smiled for the boss.

"Okay, that's good," Ted said, "but next time, invite a few men. We have good men working here, too!" And then, flashing that Cheshire Cat grin, he added, "And I'm the best, so invite me!"

What could we do but laugh, knowing that underneath the calculated charm was the challenge of finding our way to influence and power in a company that was run by an alpha male, albeit one committed to doing good work. How would we, as women with big jobs but little influence in the big decisions, get the respect that was directly linked to power and, in this case, to Ted? How could we become truly influential?

We started slowly with the monthly breakfasts, executing a mentoring strategy to help our colleagues find the support they needed. One that was particularly effective, in a company where the loudest voices tended to get heard and promoted, was to train our younger, less experienced colleagues to speak up in staff meetings, to ask the first question, to get used to hearing their own voices, getting their opinions heard and their talents recognized. I told everybody how empowered I'd felt at the White House press briefings when I challenged myself to ask questions early and often.

How to encourage what felt like risky behavior? In the beginning, we offered to buy a drink for the first woman to ask a question in a big meeting. A small step with a silly reward, perhaps, but it worked—and slowly, more women spoke up, their ideas were heard and adopted and, yes, during those years, more women were promoted too. Think about it: How many times has your hand been the first to go up at a meeting? What kind of encouragement do you need to change that?

And as more women became managers, the rule was *play it forward*, an adaptation of the *pay it forward* I'd heard before. *Play it forward* meant that if you've got the ball, pass it to someone else on the court and open the opportunities for them to score. Each step up the corporate ladder came with an opportunity, indeed a responsibility, to drop the ladder behind you and offer a hand to the women coming behind you. And to use Ted's sports lingo: take your shot, and then make sure you make it easier for other women to take theirs.

That's my number one rule for changing the power dynamic: one woman at a time, helping another take a step up. We've got to advocate for each other, support and promote each other, replacing ourselves with other women as we move up. It was the single best strategy for achieving greater equity, and at Turner, I watched it in real time, including my own succession.

When I chose to leave my job, I advocated for the promotion of Vivian Schiller, the young woman who had first recommended me to get the job. When I left, there was a woman running the news operation of CNN International and one running The Cartoon Network—and women all through the ranks, standing up for themselves, using their voices. You could see the difference in the newsroom and at staff meetings.

You have to be intentional and strategic about it, and I have been in every position and with every board appointment since my Turner tenure—playing it forward, preparing for succession by preparing another woman to take my place—passing the ball because it's going to take more women leading to level the playing field so that all women can take their shot.

DANGEROUS TIMES CALL FOR DANGEROUS WOMEN

In Conversation with Kimberlé Crenshaw

Kimberlé Crenshaw has been making a difference as a lawyer, professor, author, and activist. She is perhaps best known for putting forward the theory of intersectionality—a construct that cuts across the many divides of gender, race, sexual orientation, physical abilities, and economic status to view through a broader lens all the ways those differences impact social-justice issues of oppression or discrimination. Kim has built connections across these divides to make the often invisible, more visible—through her Say Her Name initiative, which reminds us of the many black women dying from violence whose stories and names are often not known and through her leadership of the African American Policy Institute.

I have worked closely with Kimberlé as a colleague on the V-Day board, and I know her to have a bold, brave voice. But did she think of herself as dangerous? I wanted to know.

Do you describe yourself as a dangerous woman?

Kimberlé: Well I certainly want to be *dangerous*—I want to be a threat to a status quo that is savagely unequal and to a feminism that doesn't include antiracism or to an antiracism that doesn't value feminism. But having named a concept that disrupts conventional thinking about a lot of things, I've been called *dangerous* by people who probably don't agree about a lot beyond that. I've read critics who report that intersectionality is a dangerous idea that undermines our ability to find common cause with each other. I've also read the opposite claim—that intersectionality is dangerous because it conflates what ought to be seen as distinct movements and populations into one unruly mass of grievance. If merely uttering a word can leave so many ordinarily confident people apoplectically discombobulated and breathless, then yes, I suppose I am discovering that I'm dangerous in a way that I've not fully appreciated.

Was there an age at which you began to feel more dangerous?

Kimberlé: During my twenties and thirties, my goal was to explain the many injustices that were created by overlapping inequalities like sexism and racism. I thought I could make my case with better analysis, more facts, or a more persuasively articulated moral imperative. Years of playing out this script have clarified for me that my dangerousness can't be mediated through softer, gentler discourse. I've come to realize that I am seeking to disrupt habits of thought and action that are in fact dangerous to those invested in keeping things pretty much the way they are. With maturity comes acceptance that being true to who we are will inevitably mean that we all are dangerous as against the proscribed ways of being a woman—either by choice or by birth.

Was there a specific incident or a person who inspired you to become more dangerous?

Kimberlé: The first time I felt dangerous was probably in my late twenties. I was hitting my stride career-wise, and dating one of those guys your mom likes—one who looks good on paper but you've got to lower your expectations to make it work. I came to visit him once—we lived in different cities—and he told me over dinner that he had something very serious to discuss with me. He'd heard something about me from one of his buddies that was very upsetting. He was sure it wasn't true, but he needed to bring it to me so I could set the record straight. I leaned in to hear what this disturbing allegation might be. After a few false starts, he finally came out with it: "I heard you were a feminist!" he said, pain breaking out across his face. I paused a second to hit instant replay—did he say what I thought he did? Then I guffawed, which turned his hurt to fear, which made me laugh even more. Holding my sides, I said "Boo!" since he had clearly just seen a ghost. Dabbing my eyes with the napkin, I'm like, "You have no idea who I am!" He'd never taken any interest in my work—my intersectionality article had been published by then—but only after a friend's complaint did he really see me. And what he saw felt threatening to him. Once he finally realized that who and what I was had a name—one that he and his friends didn't approve of—I became a dangerous woman. I thought it was hilarious. I was still laughing when the cab arrived to take me to a hotel. And that was certainly the end of that. I still chuckle about that one.

How does being dangerous play out in your life and work?

Kimberlé: A dangerous woman gives up the starring role in fairy tales, the happily-ever-after endings, and all the accoutrements of being valued for "best performance inside the patriarchal box." It's not always easy, since so much of what we learned growing up teaches us how to perform the role of "girl" in a way that ensures we will be liked, valued, and loved unconditionally. I was disabused of those notions when I was only in kindergarten and it was made clear to me that I couldn't be the princess in a Cinderella–Snow White kind of game. Being dangerous isn't just accepting that you won't be part of that precious girl club, but challenging the idea that anyone should be valued for these things in the first place.

The way men and women who are dangerous are framed is often different, and that makes a difference. Men with committed agendas are celebrated as determined and focused; women are disciplined as stubborn and inflexible. Men fight hard for their vision; women are argumentative. Men who are uncompromising are great leaders; women who stay the course are obsessed. The very concept of danger plays out differently for men and women. Male leadership that endangers the status quo is bold, creative, a breath of fresh air. Women who become captured by that label are borderline characters, admired but conditionally so; the support they receive almost always is subject to renegotiation. I live unapologetically within that contradiction. I work transgressively, push boundaries, question assumptions, expose gaps in our coalitional commitments, and refuse to go to the back of any bus, whether it is bound for a feminist, antiracist, or some other destination. I don't do trickle down, we'll-get-to-you-later kind of politics. I don't settle and I don't give up. And for some, this is a kind of danger that courts trouble. I'm good with that.

Chapter 9

Making History

"YOU HAVEN'T LIVED until you've danced on a rooftop in Havana at 2 a.m., and not so sure how you got there or why you're there, but you're feeling fully alive!"

So said my friend, Harry Belafonte, as we prepared to travel to Cuba together in the early nineties—my first time and on a special State Department permit, as there was a travel ban in place. This had never stopped Harry, a frequent visitor in those days.

Driving into the city from the small airport, I was struck by how familiar Havana seemed, like looking at a faded postcard of a place visited long ago. With the fifties cars (including the highly dented and bright red Chevy Impala we were being driven in) to the old buildings in need of a fresh coat of paint and repairs, everything I was seeing felt familiar but from another time and place.

As we pulled up in front of the historic Hotel Nacional, I felt so strongly that I had been here before. "You have been," Harry reminded me, "in the movies!" The Nacional, built as a luxury hotel in 1930, was an imposing mash-up of Art Deco, Greco-Roman, and other styles. In the heyday before Castro's revolution, it had been *the* place for movie stars from Marlene Dietrich and Errol Flynn to Gary Cooper and Marlon Brando. Mafia kingpins had brought high-stakes gamblers there. Titans of industry strolled the elegant halls. Then Castro had commandeered it to serve as headquarters for his revolution. It wasn't until the seventies that the hotel began to recapture its earlier glory.

As soon as Harry stepped across the portal, a Hollywood-type scene unfolded: lots of familiar hugs and air kisses with what I assumed were staff and friends, all gathered to greet him and his wife at that time, Julie. Within minutes, we were holding freshly made mojitos. My Spanish wasn't good enough to follow this conversation, but I felt included and welcome.

I was introduced as a filmmaker who'd be showing the *Women in War* documentary at the Havana Film Festival. It's a big deal to get invited to show your film at this international film festival, run at that time by the charismatic Tomás Gutiérrez Alea, who appeared as if on cue with his black leather jacket topping well-cut jeans and t-shirt. He and Harry seemed to be easy friends.

I added to Harry's generous introduction that I would also be visiting the Cuban Film Institute in Santiago to observe a Sundance lab program. The institute had been founded by Gabriel Garcia Marquez, and was a real magnet for film students from all over the world—except, of course, the United States. Despite the strictly enforced embargo between the United States and Cuba, exceptions had always been made for artists, provided you were willing to jump through some diplomatic hoops.

I got two sets of kisses from Tomás, apparently in recognition of my knowing two men he greatly admired, Redford and Belafonte. It was still unclear how official or unofficial the visit was, even then, because we'd been instructed not to get our passports stamped so there would be no evidence of a visit to a country where the United States had no diplomatic ties. We wouldn't be able to use American money or even make a phone call. Cuba might be only ninety miles away, but it was a world apart in every way at this time.

And I was loving it.

After another mojito, I was shown to my room. As we passed through the lobby and down the dimly lit hallways, the lack of funds to keep up appearances following the withdrawal of Russian support was evident. The cushions on couches were a bit frayed; the white linens on tabletops in the dining room yellowed at the corners. With encouragement from others, I peeked beneath the buffet tables to discover a second set of tables used by gamblers for blackjack and roulette during Cuba's more celebrated past. These tables, I was assured, were ready to be flipped over with the return of diplomatic relations.

Harry, Julie, and I met for a walk through Havana. Walking through the streets full of potholes and broken pavement, we saw the crowds of young people gathering in front of the small theatre marquees and ticket sellers pushing tickets to the film-festival screenings.

I watched my documentary that evening with a mostly Cuban audience who didn't need the subtitles to understand that the leaders of the FMLN were fighting for the same principles that Fidel and his band of revolutionaries had fought for years before and that had fueled the Sandinistas' struggle in Nicaragua, too. They wanted what all free people want: greater economic opportunity and a more equitable distribution of wealth. Sadly, these values were not sustained in the policies that followed these revolutions.

The Cuban audience cheered at the conclusion of the film, which ended with Sting's song, "They Dance Alone," playing over the final credits. Sting had written it to honor the thousands of women in Chile and so many other countries, including El Salvador and Nicaragua, who had lost their husbands, sons, and daughters in violent conflict.

No one referenced Cuba's revolution in the Q&A following, and I was happy not to have too many questions. I was too tired and emotionally spent when I returned to the Hotel Nacional to notice that the bed, like Cuba, had seen better days.

HARRY, JULIE, AND I joined the Sundance group the next day to travel to the film school, where Harry hinted that there might be a special surprise after lunch. Would *el comandante* himself be paying a visit?

Harry talked about Castro's love of music and poetry, his family life with his wife and daughter, and his nocturnal habits; it wasn't unusual for him to hold meetings at midnight and continue well into the night. Clearly, they had spent a lot of time with him, although they neither denied nor downplayed the reported human-rights abuses during his long period of leadership. They both seemed to believe in some of the principles of Castro's revolution, particularly the equality of education and health care. To some extent, they also defended his choice of an alliance with Russia to sustain his idealistic revolution. They were confident he would come to visit us, but finally, at almost midnight, I was falling asleep sitting up.

I dragged myself back to the Nacional, only to be dragooned by a group of film-festival celebrants back into Havana for a night of dancing. Somehow I found myself inside a rickety elevator in an abandoned building. When it shuddered to a halt, the door opened and I found a crowd already dancing to a local band. Within minutes, my exhaustion forgotten, I'd kicked off my shoes, my hands wrapped around yet another mojito, and was doing the salsa and merengue. Here I was at 2 a.m. dancing on a rooftop in Cuba, feeling fully alive just as Harry had predicted. I was feeling something else, too.

I feel there is purpose every time that music and dancing bring me together with people I may not know or ever see again but with whom I feel a heightened sense of shared humanity. Music and movement diminish the boundaries, differences, and inhibitions that separate and divide. It's no secret to anyone who knows me that I love to dance, so little wonder I could be persuaded to join the dancing that night on a rooftop.

Later I would learn that at that same moment, Castro was indeed visiting Harry and Julie. This ever-curious, "get the story" journalist regretted missing the chance to meet *el comandante*, but somehow I knew even then that this would not be my last opportunity.

MY NEXT VISIT to Cuba actually started early one morning when Ted Turner slammed his cup of coffee on the table in the hotel cafeteria and asked, “Pat, what about the Cold War?”

Given that it was 1994, we were in St. Petersburg, Russia, and I was incredibly jet-lagged from an overnight flight from Atlanta, I answered with my own question: “It *is* over, isn’t it?”

“Of course it’s over,” Ted boomed, in a voice loud enough to be heard across the vast cafeteria where a large crowd of athletes, officials, and international visitors were having breakfast and preparing for the opening day of the Goodwill Games, an international athletic competition Ted had created as a response to the United States’ boycott of the 1980 Olympics in Moscow. “That’s why we’ve got to tell the story!” he said. “Pretty soon, everyone will have forgotten why there was an East and a West and why for forty years, we got up every day worried about which country would hit the red button and set off a nuclear war. How many know even now that millions died to keep the Cold War from becoming a hot one? I want to make a documentary about this . . . now!”

“Sure,” I said, without a clue what I was agreeing to, “but Ted, isn’t that why we’re here for the Goodwill Games—to show that the post–Cold War world can be a more peaceful one?”

Ted had almost singlehandedly initiated the Goodwill Games with Russia (then the Cold War enemy, the Soviet Union) as his partner, first in Moscow in 1986, then Seattle in 1990, and now in St. Petersburg in 1994. The Goodwill Games were global athletic competitions with all the pomp and circumstance of the Olympics but none of the politics.

At the start of these third games, we might once again be in “enemy” territory, if leaders Mikhail Gorbachev and Boris Yeltsin had not entered into a competition for power that led to the assertion of sovereignty by the constituent republics of the

Soviet Union and the dissolution of the USSR. The man who would open the games with Ted by his side was the mayor of St. Petersburg, Vladimir Putin.

Ted gave me that wide grin that usually came right before he said something unexpected or outrageous, often both. "All the leaders could be dead soon, too, and the whole thing will be a paragraph in our grandchildren's history books."

"I'm sure you're right, Ted. What did you have in mind?"

"Forty hours! One hour of documentary for every year of the Cold War."

I nearly choked on my coffee, but tried to keep my voice level. "*Forty hours*? Well, that could take some time to produce . . . and would be pretty costly, too."

Ted wasn't the slightest bit perturbed. "Money isn't the issue; time is, and we have to get started right away. That's why I wanted to talk about it this morning. You're here in Russia. Get started on the research." With that, he took a final gulp of his coffee and got up from the table. "Oh, and I already decided who should help you produce this series . . . Jeremy Irons. Give him a call and offer him the job of executive producer."

I assumed he didn't mean Jeremy Irons, the actor, but I didn't have a clue who he did mean.

Back in my room, I called Vivian Schiller and recounted the conversation. She laughed. "I'm pretty sure Ted meant Jeremy Isaacs," she told me. "He produced the longest documentary series ever, *The World at War.* It was twenty-two hours for the BBC."

After two failed attempts to convince Sir Jeremy to leave his lofty position at Covent Garden and produce a television documentary series for an American cable network, I did persuade him to come to Atlanta to hear about the project directly from the visionary media executive himself. We finally connected at Ted's private hangar in Atlanta, where Ted was flying in from his son Rhett's wedding ceremony in South Carolina.

For the first few minutes, Sir Jeremy looked like a man caught in a wind tunnel as Ted talked nonstop, loudly and passionately, about his big idea. Jane and I were mostly silent, taking in this historic exchange or, to be more accurate, monologue, as Jeremy never finished a sentence or question. But he understood what Ted wanted—the most comprehensive documentation of this forty years of global history ever produced. Within a half hour, the two titans shook hands, and with that "I win" grin, Ted and Jane headed back to the waiting Gulfstream.

As I drove him back for his return flight to London, Sir Jeremy was already musing about which historians should be brought on board. "But we have to talk Ted out of that forty hours bit," he told me. "I won't live long enough to produce them."

With Sir Jeremy's leadership, we assembled a group of historians—Americans, Brits, Germans, and Russians—to fulfill Ted's mantra: "This is the global story of the Cold War; not the US version or the Russian version, but the whole story."

On the Good Friday before Easter in 1995, I delivered Ted the book, which laid out, hour by hour, the way we would tell the global story, proposing a twenty-hour series.

My phone rang on Easter Sunday morning at 8 a.m. "This is great stuff," Ted boomed. "But you and the team didn't include enough on spies, China, Cuba, Africa. So it can't be twenty hours; it's got to be at least twenty-four hours."

Before I could respond, he hung up. When I gave the Ted report to the team, the historians were silent for a few minutes, considering this quick assessment of eighteen months of research and writing, but soon all agreed that Ted was, once again, right.

THREE YEARS LATER, we had interviewed nearly all of the leading players in the Cold War—Helmut Schmidt, Margaret Thatcher, Mikhail Gorbachev, Robert McNamara, Henry Kissinger, plus five hundred others. These interviews, over 1,000 hours, are an invaluable source of history and lessons in leadership, but sadly, this content has not been optimized for its value as history or education. After Turner Broadcasting was sold, first to

Time Warner, now AT&T, no one even seems to know where this valuable archive is and CNN has not programmed it again since the premiere. Four years of work, history documented by the leaders who lived it and the people who survived it. History too important not to be remembered . . . so as not to be repeated.

Two of the Cold War interviews led to personal stories too good not to share with you: Fidel Castro and Mikhail Gorbachev.

Cuba was a satellite country for Russia's communist expansion, and the placement of Soviet missiles there, within easy range of US territory, brought the three countries to the threshold of war during the period known as the Cuban Missile Crisis.

Were those missiles in Cuba armed with nuclear warheads—and would Fidel Castro have fired them at us? In three trips to Cuba, Martin Smith, the series producer, had not succeeded in getting an interview with Castro. The deadline for completing the documentary was bearing down on us.

"You go to Havana, Pat," Ted told me. "Fidel will talk to you. He knows me and he's happy about CNN setting up a bureau there. I'll call him myself and tell him this is the last time; if he doesn't do this interview, he'll be left out of the Cold War story."

I went and waited for an entire week, mostly hanging out at the Nacional and seeing friends I'd met on the previous visit, but never venturing far from the phone, which didn't ring until our last night in Havana. My crew and I had gone for a great dinner at one of our favorite *paladores*, the restaurants that many Cubans were opening surreptitiously in their homes and on their rooftops. And yes, there was dancing, too. I was packing up back at the hotel when Castro's chief of staff called. "*El presidente* will see you now."

"Now" was around 2 a.m. by the time we got to the palace, went through the intensive searches, and set up our cameras. I reviewed the twelve questions we knew we needed answers to with Castro's longtime translator, a friendly woman named Eleanor. She would translate my English into Spanish for him, which was not really necessary because Castro spoke and understood English, though he spoke publicly only in Spanish.

I would have his answers simultaneously translated into my earpiece. We were ready to go when he walked in without any fanfare and strode toward me, hand extended.

He was tall. Unlike many movie stars and bigger-than-life personalities, Castro was taller, not shorter, than you expect. He was wearing the familiar green military fatigues, popularized in all the photographs of the revolution and in most of his public appearances since, but his uniform was starched. He looked fresh and alert despite the late hour.

"You look like my friend Jane Fonda," he said to me in Spanish. The translation flowed into my earpiece.

"Thank you," I replied, then hesitated, realizing I hadn't asked what to call him—so I mumbled, "*el presidente*. Thank you for agreeing to this interview, which we feel is very important for the documentary series we are producing for CNN on the Cold War."

Castro sat down, took the small clip-on microphone from the audio technician, clipped it on like a professional journalist, and gave me that look that said, "Okay, I'm here. Let's get started."

I asked my first questions about the original values of the revolution, and how the leader of that revolution evaluated the status of their accomplishments so far. Castro's answers were well framed, even erudite sounding as he quoted interspersed passages from Plato and Aristotle, and even quoted a poem from memory . . . and every answer included a lengthy lecture on democracy. Ten to fifteen minutes later (the average time of his answers), I managed to squeeze in another question, and so it went for the next three hours. I had asked twelve questions but not yet the most critical one, to set the record straight, hopefully, on what actually happened during the Cuban Missile Crisis.

As soon as I spoke those words, Castro got more animated and more agitated. At one point, he began to describe a telex exchange he had had with Nikita Khrushchev, the Soviet leader at that time, and suddenly he jumped up, nearly pulling the audio deck with him, and disappeared. Was the interview over?

"No, no," his translator assured me, "he's just gone to his office to retrieve something."

Castro returned with the actual telex he'd written to Khrushchev on the night of the deadline that the United States had imposed to release the ship Cuba had seized in the waters off their coast. The standoff that resulted when the Soviet Union threatened to launch missiles from Cuba in retaliation for any aggressive move from the United States had put all three countries—the United States, Cuba, and the Soviet Union—on high alert for potential nuclear conflict.

In his message to the Soviet leader, Castro pointed out, translating the Spanish into English by himself (which reminded us that he spoke and understood English quite well in spite of insisting on a translator for the interview), that he had asked Khrushchev for permission to launch the missiles, saying that Cuba would take the consequences if there was a counterattack.

I knew I was looking at one of the most important documents of the Cold War, a document that made it quite clear that Castro himself was prepared to take the action that would have created *mutually assured destruction*—MAD—as strategists often referred to such crises during the Cold War. And most agreed that the Cuban Missile Crisis was one of the times when we were closest to MAD. I had a flashback to the absolute fear I felt as a college freshman, sure that the world would be ending just as my new life was getting started.

Castro pointed, with some pride, to Cuba's willingness—or at least Cuba's leader's willingness—to launch the missiles aimed at the United Sates, and most assuredly launch another world war. Then he revealed Khrushchev's response, which was essentially to stand down—to not use the missiles. That response, according to Castro's account now, reached him only twenty minutes before the deadline.

"Were the missiles armed and ready to go within that twenty minutes had the instructions been to fire them?" I asked. This had always been the central point on which Cold War historians differed, as did the intelligence reports. I held my breath for his response.

"Yes," Castro answered. "Armed and ready to go."

Had he ever admitted that before? I glanced over at my producer, whose look communicated what I was realizing: we had a big story! Before I could ask anything else, Castro stood up again and announced, "Excuse me, but I have to go."

I quickly stood to thank him, knowing we had the answer for which we'd come to Cuba.

"I'm only going to the men's room," he told me with a big laugh. "I'll return in ten minutes. Do you have to go, too?" he asked with a wink.

I didn't dare move out of that room. The crew, who had been documenting this story for three years, had asked about the Cuban Missile Crisis in every interview from Robert McNamara, Kennedy's secretary of defense, to press secretary Pierre Salinger, to the Soviet Union's current leader Mikhail Gorbachev and his minister of defense Andrei Gromyko. No one had admitted that those missiles were armed and could have been fired and hit their target within the half hour or so between that telex and the deadline!

I knew we had to push for more on this, and I did when Castro returned. We went over every detail of the telexes between him and Khrushchev. Had he been aware that if he had fired those missiles, the United States stood ready to retaliate in kind? "Yes, absolutely," he said. "I was prepared to accept the consequences." He never backed down from this position or his opinion that it would have been a necessary sacrifice for the ideals of the communist revolution he had led and that at the time was still being supported, financially and with other resources, by the Soviet Union.

When he stood the next time, he announced it was time for dinner, even though the sun was rising. We went to a small adjoining dining room, and for the next couple of hours, Castro entertained us with songs and stories of the revolution. The crew and I were still trying to make sense of what we had heard from Castro and had observed in the country that he ruled with absolute power for more than fifty years. "I've outlived more than ten American presidents," he boasted as we said our goodbyes and headed directly to the airport.

I WANTED TO return to the United States quickly before anyone changed their mind about letting us leave with this momentous, five-hour interview. Back on home soil, Jeremy and the experienced team, headed up by Martin Smith and Taylor Downing, with whom Jeremy was writing a companion book, *Cold War* (published in 1998 and released in 2008 in paperback), included some of the best archivists and researchers working anywhere in television. They rushed to translate and integrate the interview into our Cold War documentary series in time for the CNN broadcast. In the middle of editing, we got a call from the National Security Archive advisor who had been working with us on validating archives, photographs, and interviews. Since some of what Castro had said in the interview contradicted some official interviews in the National Security Archive, a closer review was called for to ensure that the evidence from our interview and the telex met CNN's standards for accuracy.

Our translation team rushed to get the transcript done. "I'm going to put some of Castro's use of the familiar Spanish back into the more expected and respectful formal Spanish," one of the translators told me. "He is far too familiar in his language. People may think you know him or something."

I wondered whether the translator would have made that comment if Castro had used the familiar form of *you* with a male reporter, but even so, I didn't like the implication that being a woman reporter had elicited the familiar tone or the newsworthy confession from a dictator who was rumored to have had many affairs during his long tenure at the top. Ted dismissed my concerns: "If feeling more comfortable with a female reporter got him to tell the truth about the Cuban Missile Crisis," he said, "then so be it. We have a war to document."

In the fall of 1998, CNN released a special called "Castro in His Own Words," which covered this revelation and included more of my interview than could be used in the twenty-four-hour documentary series that was broadcast on CNN in the fall of 1998—to great acclaim and some controversy.

Some conservative critics accused the series of being biased toward Russia by not giving Ronald Reagan enough credit for ending the global East-West standoff, while others questioned the choice of historians; but even the critics acknowledged that this series, the longest television documentary series to be broadcast up to that point, was a monumental achievement, one that only a visionary leader like Ted would have seen the need for and would have supported doing the right way.

He had instructed us to tell the whole story—not the US story or the Soviet story but how this war impacted lives on every continent, how it was the ninth deadliest war in history, one in which 10 to 25 million people died in related civil wars, interventions, and genocides, which were the so-called surrogate wars for the superpowers that drew the lines, built the walls, and diverted resources to create the weapons that could, then and now, create mutually assured destruction. MAD, indeed.

For all of us, the presence of nuclear weapons in the world is a primal concern. Recent estimates are that the United States will spend nearly $500 billion on modernizing and building nuclear weapons, and in the budget passed in 2018, Congress boosted the annual commitment for weapons activities within the nuclear sector to $11.1 billion. MAD, mutually assured destruction, as a foreign policy strategy, still exists, not only here but in many other countries now boasting nuclear weapons capabilities.

Imagine what we could do if we redeployed those billions into education, or to fund the sustainable solutions to the climate crisis, or to ensure access to affordable health care for all! We need some dangerous women to raise their voices of concern and activate their networks of support to demand the end of nuclear weapons and of MAD once and for all.

TWO MONTHS AFTER the series aired, I was back in Cuba. This time, I was traveling with my boyfriend (now husband) Scott Seydel. We were taking a short trip to meet with the new CNN bureau chief there, and to show the Cuban Missile Crisis segment of the Cold War documentary at the Havana Film Festival.

Since I had no reason to request another audience with *el presidente*, I hadn't informed Castro's office that I would be in the country. Nevertheless, the moment we arrived at Havana Airport, my mobile phone rang, a new phenomenon in Cuba. Mobile technologies had connected the two countries in ways politics and diplomacy had failed; American dollars had radically changed the economy top to bottom. The call was from a man in Castro's inner circle.

"Welcome back to Cuba," he told me jovially. "What are your plans?"

"Oh, it's mostly personal," I told him. "I'm going to visit the beaches and hotels and meet some artists."

"You're staying at the Nacional?" he asked. "Wonderful. I'll be in touch later."

Patty Villa, our CNN bureau chief who had met us at the airport, looked at me. "You know what this means, Pat, right? We're going to be followed for sure, and I wouldn't be surprised if Castro springs a meeting on us."

We struck up a conversation with the driver taking us from the airport to our hotel. A former physician, he'd quit his practice to become a driver because he got paid in American dollars. The same professional exit into service jobs was evident with the waiters, private restaurateurs, tour guides, and interpreters we met. The educated class in Cuba was moving down the economic scale in order to move up in American cash.

Felipe's call came, two days later, just as Patty, Scott, and I emerged from the beautiful waters of Varadaro Beach. "*El presidente* will see you now."

My voice went up an octave. "Felipe, that is not possible. We're in Varadaro and just came from a swim. We're wet and have no clothes with us!"

Felipe was firm. "Patricia, you are expected. Begin the drive back and we will send an escort." He hung up.

We climbed in the car, Patty got behind the wheel of the CNN Jeep, and she started to drive—fast.

"Wait a minute," I said. "We can't go to the palace like this! We have to go to the hotel and change!"

An official government Range Rover flashed its lights and pulled onto the road in front of us: our escort back to Havana. Suddenly, we were flying down the road as Patty tried to keep up, veering to avoid hitting chickens and children along the winding, bumpy road.

"Stop, Patty!" I begged. "We have to go to the hotel first!" I had no intention of seeing Castro with wet, drippy hair, no makeup, and only a dirty serape covering my soaking bathing suit!

Patty wholeheartedly agreed. "Look at me! I'm in nothing but a bikini with cutoff shorts. I'm CNN in Havana and I *can't* meet Castro looking like this!"

Scott, in wet trunks and a dirty t-shirt, eyed our presidential escort up ahead and laughed. "Sorry, ladies. It looks like we're going straight to the palace. You can forget changing clothes."

He was right. Less than an hour later, we were pulling up at the guard gate. Two gun-toting guards waved us through.

Once inside, the guards tried not to laugh as they searched our sparsely clothed bodies. Barefoot, wet, and bedraggled, I considered making a run for it, but the armed guards surrounding us reminded me that we were more like prisoners than guests.

After a few minutes of standing—we didn't dare sit down on the chairs for fear of leaving big wet spots—*el presidente* appeared, in the same green fatigues. Without a smile, Castro walked directly over to Scott, extended his hand, and said in perfect English, "Welcome to Cuba. I heard you were here."

Then he looked at me, again without a smile, and said, "Welcome back, Patricia. I didn't expect you to return so soon after our conversation. Did you have any more questions?"

Before I could answer, he stepped back to give us another once-over. His gaze lingered on Patty. How could he not have noticed this beautiful young woman in that tiny bikini top and cutoffs? To her he said, "I am sorry we have not welcomed you to the palace before, Señorita Villa. Can I offer you some tea?"

With that, he summoned the official photographer and translator and never spoke to us in English again. We posed for a number of photographs, only one of which was sent to us, a degraded digital image showing the three of us at our most bedraggled. Who knows what happened to the rest?

We were escorted to Castro's office and told to sit down on the brown leather sofa. We did so, wet butts or no wet butts. For the next half hour or so, Castro entertained us with stories about the pope's recent visit, holding court with his three visitors who looked more like beach bums than the CNN bureau chief, president of CNN Productions, and her new boyfriend.

He finally bid us adios with one last good laugh and we were hastily hustled out a secret exit. The passageway was surreal: a large, dark tunnel with soldiers hefting machine guns as they sat in makeshift nests. I assumed this would be Castro's escape route in the event of a palace coup. It was one of the most unsettling walks I've ever made. I didn't really breathe easily until we were out of the gates of the palace and on our way back to the hotel.

During another, later visit to the Havana Film Festival, I was allowed to screen the hour of the Cold War documentary series that included this interview with Castro and the revelation about the Cuban Missile Crisis. Because of the news blackout, most of the Cuban people were unaware that nuclear missiles on their soil had been aimed at America and that the United States stood poised to annihilate them should nuclear war break out.

The documentary was showing them their own history—including possibly the most alarming moment for them since the revolution—for the very first time. US secretary of defense Robert McNamara was up on the screen saying, "I never expected to live another Saturday night." The people in the theatre were seeing evidence that their own leader was willing to make that their reality, too, by launching the armed missiles at the United States. I expected a spirited Q/A session at the end, but instead, there was silence. "Remember," the festival director whispered to me, "we are living in a dictatorship and you don't ask too many questions."

To a much lesser extent, I had also learned not to ask too many questions when Ted Turner gave me an assignment. So when he said, "Fly to Moscow and find out what Gorbachev is planning to do now that he's dissolved the Soviet Union," off to Moscow I went, with Diane Meyer Simon, philanthropist and environmental leader, who had more information about Gorbachev's plans and had agreed to support them. Together, in Moscow for the first time, we found our way, with much difficulty as no one wanted to share information about Gorbachev, to a tiny, well-hidden office in the Kremlin where he had been exiled without his papers or any staff other than his faithful and ever-present translator, Pavel. As we waited outside, devouring the muffins we had picked up after our four-hour interrogation at the airport about our "intentions" in Russia, Gorbachev appeared, laughing at our muffin-filled mouths as he extended his hand, saying "bon appetite!" We began to talk rapidly to cover our embarrassment only to discover that those words, plus a few he knew from Frank Sinatra songs, were all the English he spoke.

Describing his plans for a new global environmental movement he called Green Cross International to restore the natural resource depletion and devastation from the Cold War, he asked Diane and through me, Ted, to fund the movement in the United States.

I became the first chair of Global Green USA, and—along with my soon-to-be husband, who would follow me as the board chair—formed a strong personal bond with Gorbachev, traveling the world with him to convene forums on the environmental threats that remain his focus. At eighty-eight, he is less active, but in my opinion, never acknowledged for his important environmental leadership and his role in ending the Cold War.

I also became close to his wife, Raisa—a truly dangerous woman who spoke her mind, no matter whom she alienated—and when she died in 1999, Gorbachev asked me to speak at her funeral, alongside world leaders and ambassadors.

All of this happened, and more than I have space to share, in my seven years of working with Ted Turner—he made media history, and what I learned about leadership and power would shape, in large measure, my forward journey.

DANGEROUS TIMES CALL FOR DANGEROUS WOMEN

In Conversation with Zoya

Zoya—not her real name, as printing that would put her in danger—is a member of RAWA, the Revolutionary Association of the Women of Afghanistan, an underground organization dedicated to helping Afghan women fight for social justice and human rights. When the mujahideen killed her parents, a teenage Zoya and her grandmother fled to neighboring Pakistan, but Zoya made the decision to forsake personal safety and return to her home country to document the full story of how women are suffering under the harsh Taliban regime and tribal factionalism as well as the fallout from the presence of US and NATO troops.

Despite the fact that she's witnessed such horrors as amputations and public executions, she remains hopeful about the coura-

geous women dedicated to education and to improving their lives. Her life and work have been profiled in Zoya's Story: An Afghan Woman's Struggle for Freedom. *I have known her for nearly two decades as one of the activists supported by V-Day. She is one of the most quietly courageous and committed women I have ever met.*

How do you begin to become a dangerous woman when you live with such grave dangers every day?

Zoya: Breaking the chains of patriarchy, religious restrictions, traditions, customs, and social norms can make any woman a dangerous woman. A woman who swims against the tide that oppresses, deprives, tortures, takes their lives, and brings about extraordinary inequality is a dangerous woman. She is dangerous because she challenges the status quo and wants to be part of the equation for any social and political change and reshuffling.

This woman can be anyone. A woman who, despite her family's objections, makes endless excuses at home to secretly go to the nearest place that offers to teach her something; a woman who wakes up in the morning with a battered body and bruised face after being hit by her husband the previous night, but still looks at herself in the mirror with the hope that things will change and she will get her freedom; a woman who will jump off her balcony so she can escape being gang-raped by a group of *jihadi* fundamentalist brutes; a woman who risks being stoned to death by the Taliban, and runs away with the love of her life instead of marrying an old man who has paid her father a big sum of money in exchange for her; a woman who refuses to be silenced by the threats of fundamentalist criminals and their foreign master, and ends up paying for this resilience with her life.

These women fight to unwrap the grip of the bloodied talons of the cruel society and its merciless rulers to change their lives for the better, and the lives of others. These are the dangerous women of Afghanistan.

At what point did you feel you had to become dangerous to survive?

Zoya: I didn't choose to become a dangerous woman. I was born into a dangerous country, at a time when the Soviets had invaded my country. My mother remained in Afghanistan to fight against the invaders and the dangerous internal enemies. She sacrificed her life, her family, and her children to struggle for her people's rights and freedom. After her death, I could have fled to the United States or Europe to lead a normal life. Instead, I've tried to make a difference the way my mother did. Change is a long and difficult road, and needs generations of struggle and sacrifice.

Who influenced or inspired you or gave you the strength and courage to continue your work?

Zoya: My grandmother taught me to follow my heart in everything that I did in life. She told me that I should not chain myself to my father, brother, or husband, and follow their orders; that I should not bow down to the oppressive customs, traditions, and practices of the Afghan society; and that I should not stop moving forward in life simply because I have to step out of the line that the society has drawn for me. But if someday I meet a doctor, a lawyer, a teacher, an engineer, a journalist, a political or social activist, an artist, or a writer that I have somehow helped in achieving their dreams, it will be my biggest reward.

What advice do you give other women about how to survive dangerous times?

Zoya: Women should not be afraid to raise their voice, even if they have to pay a high price for it, because they should know that their actions and sacrifices, from the smallest act of defiance to the biggest social or political activities, contribute to the struggle of women everywhere. Challenging the norms and the status quo makes them, more than anything else, dangerous.

Chapter 10

Rising to the Challenge

"GLENN CLOSE IS on the phone!" my assistant shouted from her desk outside my office at Turner Broadcasting.

Glenn was also on the board of the Sundance Institute, and we'd become friends. I reached for the phone.

"Pat, you have to come see this play I'm in," Glenn began immediately.

"Love to, Glenn. Where is it and when?"

"It's Saturday night"—she paused dramatically—"in Sarajevo!"

Racing ahead, she said, "Pat, you won't believe what's going on here. It's a big story. Women from the refugee camps, hundreds of them, are expected to be here. It's about them."

I heard the *big story* comment and my journalist instincts kicked in.

"What's the story?" I asked.

"The war may be over, but these women are still in those rape camps . . . that's what they call them, you know," Glenn continued, her voice rising in urgency. "So many thousands of women lost their homes and families and most of them were raped. People need to know this and that's what the play is about. Their lives during and after the war."

"Who wrote it?"

"Eve Ensler," Glenn replied. "You know, the woman who wrote *The Vagina Monologues.*"

I didn't know, but right away, I knew I *should* have known.

Glenn continued, "Eve spent months in the camps and wrote a play based on their personal stories. CNN should do a story about this, don't you think?"

"Yes," I said, "of course we should. I'll track down Christiane Amanpour. No one knows more about the Bosnian War than her. Can I call you back?"

"You won't be able to reach me," Glenn replied. "This is the first call I've been able to make the whole week. Please, try to make this happen. It's important." With that, the connection died.

My mind was already racing with *how* to make this happen in four days. I was dying to book a flight to Sarajevo myself, but in my current position, leading Turner's original production team, I was more a desk-bound executive who sent *other* reporters and producers to the front lines to get the stories.

I called Christiane Amanpour, whose reporting on Bosnia had rocketed her to international fame as CNN's most recognizable face. Who doesn't remember her standing in her flak jacket, so close to the conflicts that we could sometimes hear the shots and bombs in the background?

Of course Christiane was interested. She, more than almost anyone in the news business, understood how this war had torn apart families and communities before ending with an uneasy peace and Yugoslavia divided into Serbian Bosnia and Muslim Croatia.

"I can't go, Pat, I'm getting married! But why don't *you* go?" Christiane asked. "You've reported war stories before, and this one seems right up your alley."

Minutes later, I went to Ted's office and before he could control the conversation I said, "Ted, there's a great story happening in Sarajevo tomorrow. Glenn Close . . . you know her . . . the actress from *Fatal Attraction*"—this made him look up—"Well, she's acting in a play by the author of *The Vagina Monologues*"—this secured his focus for another few, critical seconds. "She's written a play about the rape victims of the Bosnian War, and in four days, Glenn and some other well-known actresses"—I was stretching the truth at this point—"are performing it. CNN's got the exclusive."

I had Ted's full attention. "Who's going? Christiane?"

"She can't. She suggested I go."

Ted raised an eyebrow. "You? You're not a reporter."

"I was for a lot of years, Ted. I've reported from war zones and I can produce too, so you get two for one. This is our story. The other networks won't even know it's happening."

"Okay. Go for it." He liked the sound of exclusivity.

Permission granted. Now, how to do it?

My assistant booked the flights while I rushed home to pack, calling Scott on the way.

"I can't go to dinner Saturday night, I'm going to Sarajevo to report a story."

Instead of asking me sixteen questions designed to get me to change my plans, Scott said, "That's fabulous! What can I do to help?"

LANDING AT THE Sarajevo airport, which looked more like a military barracks, many hours and two connections later, I struggled to find the CNN crew in the crowd. Then, when I finally found them, I tried not to look surprised when they asked, "Okay, where are we going?" I didn't know!

I hadn't been able to reach Glenn again by phone and decided to trust that the crew would be able to find out where someone as well-known as Glenn was performing. Luckily, the crew assured me that there weren't that many theatres still standing, so it should be easy enough to track down a group of famous American actresses, especially in a city with half the population it had before the war.

The evidence that this had been a war zone was visible everywhere: unoccupied buildings, some half standing, with missing walls; most shops boarded up; and very few people on the streets. Within a half hour, we stood in front of a large brick building with a sign propped up against the double doors saying "National Theatre." On an outside wall, next to a huge hole where an artillery shell had made a direct hit, a brightly colored poster read: "*Necessary Targets,* a play by Eve Ensler." The poster listed Glenn Close, Marisa Tomei, and names of Bosnian actresses in the cast.

We walked quietly inside the darkened theatre. Way down at the bottom of rows and rows of seats was a big stage. I spotted Glenn, who stood near the stage's footlights. She squatted down, shielding her eyes to see who was emerging from the shadows. When she saw me, she threw her arms in the air and shouted, "Pat Mitchell, you cunt!"

Well, that stopped all movement . . . onstage and off. The CNN camera crew stood very still, staring at me for a response. I was speechless as Glenn jumped down from the stage and wrapped me in a bear hug, repeating over and over, "You came! What a great cunt you are!" Now in the light, she could see the dumbstruck reactions on my face and the crew's.

Glenn laughed. "That's a term of endearment and empowerment! You'd know that if you'd read *The Vagina Monologues*!" Which I should have done.

Just then, the playwright, Eve Ensler, approached, looking just like Louise Brooks, with her dark hair parted in the middle and full-forehead bangs. Eve shook my hand and gave me a look that didn't transmit a feeling of gratitude as much as it seemed to acknowledge that I had done the right thing. "Thanks for coming. Listen, I can't talk now; we're going on for the first time in about three hours, and the Bosnian actors are backstage still learning their lines in English. Why don't you take your seats in the theatre and we'll talk later."

The crew and I found our places in the cavernous dark theatre and watched Glenn and Marisa rehearse. Glenn was playing the role of an American psychiatrist and Marisa, a young journalist. Both had come to a Bosnian rape camp to offer group therapy for the women being played by Bosnian actresses as well as a few local activists.

Later, when I interviewed the women backstage, I learned that all of the Bosnian women in the play had been, in one way or another, victims of the war. They were the "necessary targets" in a war that was, to a large extent, fought on women's bodies. Eve's purpose in telling their stories and performing it in the city where so much of the violence had happened made the whole evening so electric and emotional. I knew for sure that Glenn had spoken a profound truth when she called me. This was an important story.

Watching Eve's work as playwright and director, I fell deeply into awe for the small woman with the big presence. She was an undeniable force field of energy and passion, coaxing and coaching the actors trying to deliver phonetically learned lines in a language they didn't speak and managing more than one complete breakdown when the stories being acted were too close to the real memories of pain and violence.

Clearly the actors didn't seem really ready to perform, but soon the doors were opening and the VIPs—the US ambassador and other high-ranking representatives of the international community working in Sarajevo on postwar recovery efforts—were ushered to their seats. But the audience that mattered most to Eve was the women from the camps.

The crew and I went outside as their buses arrived. Hundreds of women of all ages poured into the area in front of the National Theatre. Their faces reflected their suffering; even though the war had ended, these women couldn't come back to Sarajevo because they no longer had homes or families to return to.

As the women filed into the theatre, they looked both apprehensive and excited as they greeted old friends from other camps or demolished neighborhoods. When the play began, there was scattered applause as the audience recognized the local actresses and activists who appeared on stage—and there was a big applause for Glenn and Marisa.

From the very first scene, the wails began—not quiet tears or gentle sobs, but heart-rending wails, loud and unlike anything I'd heard before. The sound swept through the parts of the theatre where the women from camps were sitting, waves of pain spreading from row to row. Onstage, the play continued as if these sounds were part of the performance, and in a way, they were. It was impossible not to be swept up in this collective experience of recalled pain.

Near the end of the second act, a large group of the women sitting in a bloc behind me stood up and filed out, still crying audibly. Had the pain of remembering become too much? I had to know, so I followed them out. As they were boarding one of the buses, I approached the driver and, through an interpreter, asked why they were leaving before the play was over: "Curfew!" he answered, adding, "It's time to return to the camps." A painful reminder that the war wasn't over—not for the women still living in forced isolation in camps, many without homes or families to return to, the war's forgotten "necessary targets" that Eve's play had documented.

Back inside, the play continued. At the end, the remaining audience showed their gratitude with endless rounds of applause and standing ovations.

I found Eve backstage and told her about the women forced to leave because of camp curfews. "I want to talk to you more about that," she told me. "Let's meet up tomorrow at the hotel."

Hotel? In all the rush to get to the story, I hadn't made any sleeping arrangements for myself or the crew!

"Don't worry," Glenn told me. "It won't be a problem for you to stay with us." The crew and I followed her back to the hotel, where no rooms were available. Beth Dozoretz, an American friend of Glenn's who came with her to Sarajevo, quickly offered to share hers with me, and our crew bunked in with another crew in town. That's how it always happens with journalists or activists with passion but very little planning; details like where you'll sleep or eat just work out. No hot water? Skip the shower. No extra bed? Share with someone you just met.

The next day, Eve explained her vision to raise awareness of the global epidemic of violence against women and girls. "I don't want to create another nonprofit organization," she said. "I want to use art—my plays and whatever else I create—to support the work already being done on the ground by local activists and organizations. My work begins with asking women what they need to heal and restore their lives."

Less than a year later, Eve launched a global movement with a star-studded Broadway performance of *The Vagina Monologues* on Valentine's Day, which she proclaimed to be V-Day. What followed was a movement built on the rights to perform *The Vagina Monologues* anywhere by any group for no fee beyond a commitment to use the funds raised to support groups in the community or country working to end gender-based violence. For more than twenty years, there have been tens of thousands of productions in 140 countries—from Pakistan to the United States—in more than forty-five languages, raising $100 million to support locally led antiviolence work.

MY FRIENDSHIP WITH Eve Ensler, which began in that theatre in Sarajevo, is one of the most important friendships in my life. Working with her, supporting V-Day's programs and activities, has taken me to places I might never have gone, from Juarez to Eastern Congo. Through this work, I have met women who have transformed pain into power, who have survived unspeakable violence to rebuild families and hold communities together.

Many times, as I've traveled to South Africa, Kenya, and Congo with Eve to support the work of V-Day activists on the ground, friends have asked, "Aren't there dangers in traveling to some of these places?" There are dangers in all places for women and girls, but what really frightens me is what I've witnessed in Bukavu in Eastern Congo, for example, where a war is being fought, like the one in Bosnia, on the bodies of the women. When one of the leaders of the militia groups that ravage the countryside was arrested, he said, "Raping a woman is a lot cheaper and a lot more effective than a SCUD missile."

And he's right. When you rape a woman in front of her husband and children, you essentially destroy the fabric of the family, which is the fabric of the community, the village, the country. That's what fills me with fear and rage—witnessing the evidence of human beings committing inhuman acts of violence on other human beings—in most cases, the most vulnerable populations of women and girls.

Stories of what's going on in these war zones around the world should be big stories in the news all the time, but as I found out when I returned with the story of the survivors of the Bosnian conflict and an interview with the playwright and the actresses, CNN gave me a mere five minutes for the whole story. Another challenge was that I wasn't allowed to say the word *vagina*, which made it difficult to talk about the playwright's seminal work and her plans to use that play, *The Vagina Monologues*, to launch a global movement. It would take a couple more years and a certain incident with a Clinton White House intern, whose testimony included the word *vagina* as part of a public record, for naming this important part of a woman's anatomy to be permissible on CNN and every other television network.

As for *cunt*, that four-letter word hasn't yet passed the censors for television. Many years later, when Jane Fonda was asked on *The Today Show* about her involvement in an upcoming *The Vagina Monologues* production, she answered, "I'm doing the *cunt* monologue." The horrified producer ran toward the control booth, yelling, "Bleep that and go to commercial!" Jane seemed oblivious to the panic, accustomed as she is, and all the rest of us vagina warriors are, to the responses evoked by the words that Eve's taboo-breaking play redefines—her intention, in part, to take the power out of the words for denigration or abuse and restore it to women. Traveling the world with Eve, from churches in Atlanta, Georgia, to villages in Kenya, I've felt the power when women "say it," "own it," "love it."

BEING A PART of the global V-Day movement has been a defining factor in my journey to becoming a dangerous woman. I have stepped more fully into my own willingness to take risks by observing and learning and working alongside my V-Day sisters, in this country and around the world. With them, and with Eve as our inspiration, I've learned to wail, to be in touch with my own pain, and to feel the healing that comes with sharing stories and being together. I have danced with women who have no reason to dance or laugh or smile but do so anyway, pushing past fear to feel their own power and strength. I've seen communities change one warrior at a time, and I've watched with admiration and awe as Eve's vision for what is possible and what must be done to bring attention to the epidemic of violence, gets bigger and more audacious.

"We're calling it One Billion Rising," Eve announced at our summer board meeting in 2011. "We're going to get one billion people all over the world to dance together to end violence."

The women in the room exchanged looks that said we weren't sure we heard her right.

"You meant to say one *million*, right?" asked Carole Black, the former president of Lifetime who I had persuaded to see *The Vagina Monologues* with Eve performing and had immediately become one of V-Day's most effective supporters.

"No, I mean one *billion*. That's with a *b*. Think about it! The largest demonstration ever to end violence, and we can do this by asking all the local V-Day activists to organize their own risings."

And that's what happened. The next February 14, risings in nearly every country, all organized and coordinated by Eve and Monique Wilson, an actor/activist from the Philippines, created a movement the world had never seen before. Women, men, boys, girls dancing—yes, dancing. There was a One Billion Rising anthem, "Break the Chain," written by songwriter/producer Tena Clark, and each community created its own dance and actions.

An event this global was covered widely by media, but some reporters were skeptical. "What can dancing do?" they'd ask. "In dancing," Eve explained, "we liberate our bodies, give them freedom to move and to take up space, together, to put aside differences in race, age, culture, religion, if only for a dance or a day. And yes, to make a difference, too."

Every year since, millions have danced in the streets of thousands of towns and villages in two hundred countries, in the halls of parliaments, in schools and churches, in prisons and large public squares, in private rooms and with thousands in the streets—dancing, sometimes marching, too, and always rising, moving together.

"What can dancing do?" Dancing insists we take up space. Dance is joyous, sexual, radical, disruptive, and dangerous. It breaks the rules. Dance connects us and pushes us further and that is why it's at the center of One Billion Rising.

I've seen the difference dancing with purpose can make—as I danced on those Havana rooftops, with Shangaan women around a fire in the Sabi Sands, with survivors of the violence in Eastern Congo, with Syrian women in the Zaatari refugee camp, with V-day sisters in Atlanta, New York City, Sundance, and so many other places. Women and the men who stand and dance with them can come together with passion and purpose. Whenever I'm in these dancing circles, I feel freer, more purposeful, and yes, I feel more dangerous, too—more ready to engage fully in the work that follows the dancing.

Vaginas united and dancing together, working together, supporting each other, and rising to the challenge is a dangerous act of disruption that will continue going global until the violence ends.

DANGEROUS TIMES CALL FOR DANGEROUS WOMEN

In Conversation with Monique Wilson

Monique Wilson has spent her life blending acting with activism. Born in the Philippines, she started her professional acting career when she was only nine years old (in the musical Annie, *of course!). By the time she was eighteen, she was performing the lead in the West End's production of* Miss Saigon. *When she returned to the Philippines and started her own acting company, the New Voice Company, she produced and acted in* The Vagina Monologues, *and became a member of GABRIELA, a national alliance of grassroots Filipina women's organizations.*

Monique has used her talents as an actor, organizer, and passionate advocate to lead changes in the Philippines, and now, as director of One Billion Rising, organizes activists and risings around the world. I wondered what had sparked her willingness to engage with risk, and asked her to tell me how it began.

When did you become such a dangerous woman?

Monique: There was no particular incident or moment that inspired me to become a dangerous woman. For me, I believe, the seed is certainly what we have carried as a colonized people—and particularly as colonized women. And even as a child, I've never accepted the double standard between men and women and always fought against the norm of unfaithful and abusive husbands/fathers, the wives always doing the coping and adjusting, the children living in a culture of silence. I remember being as young as three and thinking that life was never fair for the women in my family. And because of that I became a fighter, a rebel.

How does being considered a dangerous woman impact your life and work?

Monique: The greatest reward of being a dangerous woman is that it brought me to GABRIELA, to V-Day and One Billion Rising—which then brought me closer and deeper into revolutionary and visionary work. And all these brought me back to the heart and core of my own fierce warrior women ancestors: the Babaylan women, our priestess-warrior-healer-teacher-protectors. Filipina women have the "dangerous collective subversive memory" of her equality and strength—and this lives in us today.

How do you think about the role of dangerous women in such dangerous times?

Monique: I have learned what it is to be a revolutionary: somebody who is guided by a fierce, passionate love. A deep, deep love of others, of fellow women, of community, of country. Who is willing to take risks and live on the edge. Who doesn't just believe in change, but is willing to *live it*—to be wild in possibility,

> to live in every breath,
>
> to be magic.
>
> And remind us of what we have always been . . .
>
> Radical.
>
> Courageous.
>
> Rebellious.
>
> Unafraid of the wild heart beating inside each of us.
>
> ALIVE.

Chapter 11

Protecting "Viewers Like You"

"I'VE BEEN ASKED to become the president of PBS," I told my significant other, Scott, as we prepared dinner together in the small kitchen of my Atlanta home.

"Well, that's wonderful!" he said. Then he looked up and stopped cutting the onions. "So why aren't we celebrating?"

"PBS headquarters are in Washington," I said, expecting his big smile to fade. He was a lifetime resident of Atlanta and loved it.

"That's terrific! I always wanted to live in the nation's capital," Scott responded with the biggest smile yet.

"Then you'll come with me?"

Instead of answering the question, Scott dropped to one knee right there in the kitchen, took my hand, and asked, "Will you marry me?"

My first response was to laugh. Not appropriate, of course, but we'd been happily together, unmarried, for nearly seven years. "Why now?" I heard myself saying.

Still on his knees, Scott said, "You're not going without me."

"But you've got a business to run!"

"I'll figure that out. Say *yes,* and start this job as a married woman."

Now we were both laughing and deciding the order in which to share the news with the children—the new job, the move to Washington, or the upcoming wedding?

Within a few weeks, we were off to DC. I would be the first woman president of PBS and the first producer to take the reins of this country's only public media broadcasting service.

IT WAS FEBRUARY of 2000. I'd already decided I was leaving Turner Broadcasting after Ted got fired and the disastrous AOL/Time Warner merger. I'd been asked to become the dean of a journalism school, an offer that I was considering seriously, when I received the call to interview with the PBS search committee. I'd never worked for public television; I was just another "viewer like you." But after I met with the search committee and spent some time with its esteemed chair, Colin Campbell, I became more interested in this unexpected opportunity.

Joan Ganz Cooney, the cocreator of *Sesame Street,* who was on that committee, called me after my interview. "Pat, why would you want to do this job?"

"What do you mean?" Who wouldn't want to work for the network that gives viewers choices like *Sesame Street, Masterpiece Theatre, Frontline,* and *American Masters*?

"It's a really tough job!" she said. "PBS is not really a network. Not in the way you're thinking it is. You'll be spending more time herding cats, trying to get 349 public television stations to agree on anything!"

I didn't fully understand the warning, and even if I had, I would probably have said yes anyway, believing, as I did and still do, that public broadcasting is a national treasure, an essential media enterprise in a landscape that even in 2000 was changing at cyberspeed with the internet emerging as a force and commercial media merging, acquiring, and being driven to deliver bigger returns to investors.

In fact, it was those same forces that motivated a small but committed group of concerned citizens to begin to petition Congress to put aside some of the public spectrum, the airwaves that belong to the public, for noncommercial television and radio. Their efforts eventually led to the passage of the Public Broadcasting Act, which provided for some federal funding for the television and radio stations already operating locally with educational or public-broadcast licenses and created the national organization PBS, the Public Broadcasting Service.

Service is the operative word in the name. PBS is not a network or even a system, but a service organization created to serve its members, the local public broadcasting stations. At the national level, television stations joined PBS, and public radio stations joined together as members of NPR, National Public Radio. Some local stations have both radio and television licenses, but at the national level, the services are separate. I admit to being disappointed when I learned that NPR was not part of my responsibilities, as I came into this new position with a huge admiration for public radio, which has only continued to strengthen since my PBS tenure.

Importantly, in the legislation that formalized our public media service, Congress also set up the Corporation for Public Broadcasting (CPB) to distribute government funds to the local public television and radio stations. This system ensured that federal taxpayer dollars would be handled by a bipartisan group, with a presidentially appointed board. This led to some unintended consequences from time to time.

A paranoid Richard Nixon, who believed *public* meant *progressive*, tried to use the nine-member board of CPB to influence programming decisions and, failing that, to cut federal funding. Since the membership tilts with whichever governing party is in power, I inherited the more conservative Bush-appointed board when I started in March of 2000. George Bush, like many detractors, had characterized PBS as a luxury at best and at worst a megaphone for public opinions that might not concur with current administration policies.

As Joan Ganz Cooney had predicted, I had underestimated the challenges as president of PBS of keeping 349 stations happy, and I had overestimated the extent of the power of the position. I did have the "power of the pulpit," as we used to refer to it in the South, and I was the public face and the national advocate and voice for funding and support, but the power of public media is local and each station has its own president and its own board of trustees.

To be effective, I had to try to accommodate vastly different needs for vastly different communities. I made it my business to travel to almost every one of those 349 stations, from Biloxi to Bozeman. What I discovered was, as former Speaker of the House Tip O'Neill famously declared, "All politics is local." In those individual communities, there wasn't a strict division between Republican and Democrat; what they cared about was "our public TV." My brief was to protect those individual stations' interests and to help them raise funds from "viewers like you," who are the primary source of nearly every public station's support.

During my tenure, PBS's congressional funding was often in peril. But time and time again, the funding would survive the efforts to keep public media weak and dependent entirely on pledge drives, primarily due to a reluctance of any member of Congress to vote against Mr. Rogers or Big Bird. But it was a pretty constant fight with Congress, and every day I felt as if I was putting on my boxing gloves. In fact, I literally got to put on a boxing robe and gloves for a special appearance on the *Sesame Street* set after I secured appropriations for them in my first year.

I also had to navigate a very fragile line between wanting to be a different kind of leader as a woman, but not being so different that I was defined solely as a woman. In making the first seven hires for senior executives, I reported to the board on my choices: five extremely qualified women and two men. A board member challenged me, "What are you doing, running an affirmative action program for women?"

"No, I'm just running an effective search process to find the most qualified candidates." I'd told the search firm that I wouldn't even consider a list of candidates that didn't have people of color and women represented after they'd brought me list after list of the same names—all men, all white, usually similar backgrounds, too. We were public television and we needed to look more like the public we served.

What I realized then—and in every leadership position since—is that becoming more representative of the communities we serve, with greater diversity of backgrounds, experiences, ages, and gender, doesn't happen because it's the right thing to do, or even because it leads to better performance and more public or consumer support. It happens when the leader takes whatever steps are necessary to make it happen. It's not hard. It just means being committed to making it so. At PBS and every other organization I've engaged with, being more inclusive and representative has *always* meant better outcomes—from every perspective and by every measurement!

I made some changes that I felt were important for better management of limited resources: reducing the size of the board and enlarging the number of public trustees; making the PBS greenlighting process more inclusive and collaborative; setting up regular consultations with the stations, and transitioning from analog to digital delivery of broadcast signals, which was developing faster than any of us predicted or could have anticipated—and required us to raise an additional $2 billion. But we couldn't move as fast and as far as others did, which meant we began losing support from the generation growing up with the internet.

That was the first year's big challenge, and then 9/11 shifted everyone's perspective and priorities.

I was at a breakfast meeting near PBS when the first plane crashed into the World Trade Center towers in New York. Rushing to my office, I arrived as another plane crashed into the

Pentagon, a mere quarter mile away. The panic was palpable as the call came from some government office that media companies were the next target, and PBS was immediately put on lockdown. We waited for explanations and focused on what PBS needed to do for a country reeling from this first major terrorist attack at home.

I called the producing stations to confer. With their support, I made the decision to bring back the retired, award-winning journalist Bill Moyers, whose interviews and documentaries defined the best of PBS for many years. *Now with Bill Moyers* went live on PBS at 11 p.m. just days after 9/11, and as Bill said in his opening statement, it was "intended to be a nightly conversation to help the nation heal."

Very soon after the launch and an outpouring of gratitude from viewers for Moyers's insights, I began to hear complaints about Bill's editorial slant, which some leading Republicans characterized as antigovernment and anti-Bush. Bill had previously enraged some conservative leaders with his investigations into campaign financing; long before Citizens United, he had highlighted money in politics as the real threat to democracy. On *Now*, every week, he openly shared his concerns in the aftermath of 9/11 including the Iraq invasion and the bombing of Afghanistan.

It was no surprise that Bill became a target for a lot of political firepower, and as the executive who put his program on PBS, I also wore a bull's-eye. At first, the pushback was subtle, with thinly veiled threats about PBS being *unpatriotic* at a time when patriotism was defined as unquestioning support for the Bush administration's policies, including declaring war. Then the pressure became overt: "Take him off the air or your appropriations are going to be struck from the national budget." I'm proud to say that the majority of stations supported Bill, and us. We all knew that the responsibility of PBS was to be a platform for the full spectrum of public opinion.

More upsetting was the friendly fire and those unintended consequences of having a presidentially appointed board governing the CPB. I was summoned to a CPB board meeting where Ken Tomlinson, its chairman, pushed me to cancel Bill's weekly broadcast. I declined to do so, and after the meeting, Tomlinson asked me to stay behind, and then turned to me in fury, jabbing a pudgy finger in my face. "You better do what I say or I'll take you down—and Bill Moyers with you."

I was speechless. The CPB chairman was threatening me with personal repercussions for doing my job? Was this some cheesy gangster movie?

I took a breath. "Ken, I'm going to do what I think is right for the PBS board and 349 public television stations. You do whatever you feel you have to do. I'm going to put aside that threat, but I'm not going to forget it."

I walked out of the room deeply shaken. I didn't tell Bill Moyers what was going on because he'd already offered to resign several times, knowing he'd become a flashpoint for attacking PBS.

Next, I was summoned to testify before a committee headed by Republican senator Ted Stevens, never a supporter of public media.

"You put your *Democrats* on the air," he thundered, and "especially that well-known liberal commentator Bill Moyers!"

In fact, a newly commissioned study had concluded that the public didn't believe there was liberal bias in PBS programming. "Senator, actually, that's not true, I have the numbers right here—"

"Don't you speak unless you're called on!" Stevens roared, cutting me off. And so went that hearing and the ones that followed—one-sided attacks by the Republican leaders of the committees.

I recognized the need for restraint, staying focused on the ultimate outcome of keeping our funding, so I resisted the urge to further defend or correct. I couldn't call on Mr. Rogers, whom we had sadly lost—and what a loss that was, as Fred Rogers was one of the most admirable people I have ever had the privilege to know. I did bring Big Bird once again to Capitol

Hill along with a few other PBS icons, and visited nearly every Senate office, asking for help and listening patiently to many attacks. But I also found support with people like Senator John McCain and Congressman (now Senator) Ed Markey. In spite of heavy lobbying against us, we got the funding renewed and *Now with Bill Moyers* stayed on the air.

When you're successful at keeping your appropriations before a bipartisan committee, the press describes you as *solicitous* or *compromised*; if you lose appropriations, *too confrontational* or *liberal*. I just had to take the press hits and stay quiet. Soon after, of his own accord, Moyers decided to end his show. The program had served its purpose, and Bill had proven once again that speaking the truth, standing up for American values and democracy, is one of the strongest arguments for a media enterprise beholden only to the public it serves.

AT PBS, I often felt more like a firefighter than a CEO—trying to douse the flames of some controversy or crisis. And the next fire was started by a bunny named Buster who sent video postcards from his travels around the United States—the premise of *Postcards from Buster*, a popular children's program series designed to teach four- to eight-year-olds about cultural diversity. In one episode, this adorable oversized talking bunny, Buster, visits a family in Vermont and learns how maple syrup is made. Buster is greeted by two moms and their daughter, who lovingly show off family photos. Buster exclaims, "Gee, you sure have a lotta moms!"

Yes, that was the offending line. The Department of Education secretary Margaret Spellings dispatched a letter asking me not to broadcast the program.

"Many parents would not want their young children exposed to the lifestyles portrayed in this episode," Secretary Spellings wrote. I didn't agree and gave the episode the go-ahead. Most stations supported the decision. Unfortunately, Spellings rallied support for her position on Capitol Hill, and the episode became another flashpoint in the war for editorial freedom and independence.

Peggy Charren, the founder of Action for Children's Television, one of the first advocacy groups for positive role models and storylines in children's programming, weighed in publicly. "Are you sure this is what all the fuss is about? The amount of information about lesbian families in the program is zero. I learned more about cows—that all cows are female—than I did about lesbians." After a flood of threats and complaints in an organized campaign reached the local stations, about half announced they wouldn't broadcast it. I didn't have the power to make any station play any program, but PBS always took the heat for all such decisions, and I took a hit in the press again. Even today, when you google me, the articles about me and a bunny named Buster still pop up.

How irrelevant and downright silly it seems now to have had all that sound and fury about an episode with two moms who today can legally marry in every state. At the very time of Buster's busted episode, my goddaughter Maddie and her two moms were staying at our home. Now *that* would have caused a stutter or two—and probably a call for my resignation.

DO I BELIEVE that there could be a better organizing principle for public media than PBS as it's currently configured? I do. Just look at BBC Worldwide and other public-service media around the world, an analysis I took on when it looked like there might be an opportunity to redesign the whole structure, at least of public television, which would be strengthened, in my opinion, by a different governance and funding model. In a media ecosystem where PBS is being outspent and outpaced in innovation by streaming services like Netflix and Amazon with billions of dollars to spend on content, being nimble and able to make quick and unified decisions about everything from programming to rights management is necessary.

The good news is that we can find some of PBS's best programming on demand, and that outstanding series like *Downton Abbey* can still break through the clutter of choices. Hats off to my successor, Paula Kerger, for keeping the standards high on programming and keeping PBS as current as limited funding for innovation allows. I remain an advocate and a loyal viewer, especially of *NewsHour,* anchored by one of the best journalists in media, Judy Woodruff. And I'm devoted to the news and podcasts from NPR.

In 2017, when President Trump tried to cut the funding once again for public broadcasting, Ken Burns, PBS's leading documentarian, testified before Congress: "While we count on the marketplace to do lots of things in our lives . . . the marketplace doesn't come to your house at 3 a.m. when it's on fire. The marketplace does not have boots on the ground in Afghanistan at this moment. And while I wouldn't ever suggest that public broadcasting has anything to do with the defense of the country, I think with every fiber of my being that it makes our country worth defending by what it has added to our national conversation."

Keeping the threats to public-service media at bay is not only the responsibility of PBS and all the local public media leaders; it's on each and every one of us, too, to let our voices be heard that we value the voice, content, and local community connection as well as the national programming that PBS and NPR provide. I considered it a privilege to fight for a vibrant and sustainable public-media enterprise because it is critical, in my opinion, to serving and sustaining a thriving democracy.

AFTER SEVEN YEARS, I'd made as many changes as I was going to be able to make as PBS's leader. I stayed about another year to help identify my successor. I'd grown enormously as an executive and as a leader. I'd certainly improved my consensus-building and negotiating skills and was better able to cope with criticism—because I got a lot of it. Being a transformative change leader during a time of great change will test your appetite for risk and commitment to the way forward.

In 2007, I wanted to take what I had learned at the PBS helm and lead a global discussion about the undeniable power of media and the impact of the enormous changes happening at cyberspeed across the global media landscape. I accepted a position as president and CEO of the Museum of Television and Radio in New York City and LA, an institution created by CBS founder Bill Paley to be the largest archive of television and radio programming in the world, open for public viewing and a convener of programs focused on the impact of media in our lives and culture.

Once again, I was going to be the first woman and only the second president in its history. Why did I keep finding myself the first, the only, or one of the few, and it seemed, stepping in at a time of major transition? It's worth noting here that many women leaders find themselves in similar situations—taking over a business or a global NGO or even a country just when the profits are declining and competition is growing or there's a transition from war to reconstruction or the other way around.

I think of Ellen Johnson Sirleaf, who became president of Liberia at the end of a ten-year civil war and faced the challenge of rebuilding a country. Or the dozen or so women who were promoted to CEO just as their companies were on a downward trajectory. There are many examples of times when women are brought in (or promoted or elected) just as everything hangs on a precipice. And often, these leaders end up like the sacrificial virgins of long-ago cultures—tossed off the precipice. This has led to a new expression about women's advancement—forget the glass ceiling, look out for the glass cliff!

I'm not sure I considered whether my next CEO position was a ceiling breaker or stepping off a glass cliff, but I knew within weeks of moving into my office next door to the historic

21 restaurant in midtown Manhattan that I was once again on a steep learning curve, and I would have to take some early risks to make some big changes.

Within the first eighteen months, I proposed a radical move: changing the name of the institution. Being the Museum of Television and Radio just didn't sound relevant, and the institution was losing ground with visitors and supporters. The board agreed to a process to find a better name, and after months of consultations and board discussions, we landed on the Paley Center for Media, a name that honored the founder. Losing the *museum* moniker was important if we were going to have relevance to media consumers who had no doubt felt a disconnect between *museum* and *media*, and whose media worlds went way beyond television and radio.

Given the history and the culture and the fact that many of the staff had been in their jobs for two decades, these moves could have put me on a precipice for a short tenure and dramatic fall. That didn't happen, though, because I had important support. Frank Bennack, board chair for more than twenty years and still, at this time, CEO of the Hearst Corporation, wasn't an easy man to convince of anything. He was too wise and too experienced to go along with change without being fully convinced that it was the right move. I could not have been successful with this change or any other without Frank's wise counsel and support.

There were some outsized ego battles in the boardroom; with Frank's experienced guidance, I learned to choose my battles very carefully. To change the culture of the board and increase the relevancy quotient of our programming, we decided to invite technology CEOs to join the prestigious board, which had always included the CEOs of major media companies.

"We're not a media company" was why Larry Page and Sergey Brin turned down my original invitation to join the board when I met them at the World Economic Forum in Davos. They had just launched this start-up called Google. Eventually, Google joined the board when Eric Schmidt became CEO, and so did

Yahoo and AOL and Verizon and most of the rest of the big players—bigger today in terms of consumers, users, reach, and impact than any television or radio network.

Shaping programs that had value for all these leaders of media and curating programs that brought the public back into our museum-like buildings in Manhattan and Beverly Hills was a challenge—but also an opportunity to use my almost-retired talents of moderating, hosting, and interviewing. I was once again on television, too, broadcasting a series of interviews on PBS with well-known women, called *She's Making Media,* filmed on the Paley theatre stage.

I had, once again, landed in a job that optimized all previous work experiences and connections and opened up new worlds to explore, discover, and disrupt. Arguably, there has never been a bigger disruption in the media landscape than the launch of what we quaintly called *new media* in the beginning and now refer to as *social media.* The Paley Center for Media was a platform for me to observe the enormous transformations taking place within the media industry worldwide, as we convened annual global gatherings of media executives and top leaders for the purpose of exploring media and technology's ever-growing power in our lives, cultures, and even government.

At one of our first international meetings in Istanbul, where we partnered with Doğan Media, Turkey's leading media company at that time, the newly elected president, Recep Erdoğan, lectured a hundred media CEOs about the "damaging and dangerous" power of media. (He later jabbed "Know your place!" to the *New York Times* when it offered an editorial critical of his regime.) He also made it clear that he planned to take down independent media in his country—and he did, allowing a pro-government conglomerate to buy out Doğan Media.

He also refused to have me—a woman—in a photograph with him and my board. Diminishing and disappearing women comes with diminishing, silencing, and attempting to shut down all independent media, which Erdoğan has done during his tenure. We have witnessed similar events across Europe, in

China, and certainly in Russia, as power-driven leaders dismantle the power of media in order to rule without dissent, which can arise when viewers and readers and listeners like us know the truth.

IN THIS NEW media space, I believe women are in a very strong position to influence media's power. Women are the number one users of social media; but men, mostly very young men, built and still own the platforms and run the companies that use them. In 2019, the numbers tell the story of the potential power women can and should leverage when it comes to social media: 89 percent of women online use Facebook and 73 percent of women use social networks, and among younger women, the numbers are even more dominant.

I confess to resisting the urge to start my day on my Facebook page and with visits to the Facebook pages of friends and family. It's a time suck that I can rarely afford, but it's also supporting a company that allowed, unwittingly or not—and that's still debatable—a foreign government's use of the platform to influence the US elections.

When I think of the dark power of Facebook and other social media companies to manipulate and misuse data, and when I am reminded of the bullying, the misogynistic content on many pages, the outsized influence of Twitter as a national policy forum, I'm tempted to forgo the instant connections and communications of social media altogether.

In 2019, the thirtieth anniversary of the internet, the debate rages about the right use of the technological innovations that have transformed our ability to communicate, to share knowledge, to be connected. Even the web's founder, Dr. Timothy Berners-Lee, has been speaking out with clarity and concern about the corporate control of the World Wide Web, which he and others envisioned in 1989 as a free and open space for global connectivity. What has evolved instead are a few dominant players collecting and monetizing our personal data.

It feels like we are at a tipping point in the future of the internet, and certainly I can't predict which direction we will take as media consumers and as citizens. When I watch the faces of my youngest grandchildren, transfixed by a screen, I know why some of the very people who created the addictive platforms are restricting their own children's use of them—this, according to a recent report on Thrive Global.

My husband and I sometimes have caught each other texting or emailing under the covers after lights out. And I further confess that, some days, when I'm tweeting rather than listening in a forum, when I'm sending Instagram photos of boots that I know my granddaughter would love instead of looking at a glorious sunset, or when I'm working on a blog post instead of this book, I remember my father's explanation of why he wouldn't allow us to have a TV set in our home when he sold them to other people in his appliance store—"too distracting." I also remember my Garth Associates colleague, Jeff Greenfield, who said my decision to take a job in television "will ruin your life!" The question for all of us is whether the World Wide Web is ultimately a force for good or evil, and the answer is most likely "it's up to us and how we use it."

BEING A FRONTLINE participant in at least three media revolutions: the early 1970s for women, the 1990s for cable, and the 2000s at the helm of the country's only public-media enterprise during the digital revolution, I've had a privileged front-row seat to transformative change and media's power, and I believe that there is no single bigger power than media, collectively, to both distract and detract, to amuse and offend, to inform and misinform, to entertain and inspire; and now, with all that power and more consolidated at one end in the hands of less than a dozen corporations and at the other end in our hands through social media—we must use that power for good.

In my more radical state of mind, I think a lot about whether I should jump back into the media parade and launch an idea that

I had in 1999, which was all set to become a new cable network. Ted Turner and I had named it WIN, Women's Information Network, and the concept was to deliver global news and information that women want and need, using a similar format to CNN—news through a woman's lens. We believed that WIN, like its older sibling, CNN, would connect the world's women by sharing stories of what women were doing everywhere to meet challenges and shape solutions. Since women then and now are responsible for 85 percent of purchases in the home and are the number one consumers of online merchandise, women are the best customers for purpose-driven products. We were sure we would have the financial support through sponsorships to sustain a new global cable network that would also be launched online.

In 1999, this was in our plan, and I had hired a team, produced sample programs, arranged to have a studio allocated in Atlanta's Turner headquarters, and was ready to launch when Ted decided to sell his cable empire to Time Warner.

I was flying to meet the family for a vacation when I heard my name called over the intercom at the airport. I found a phone, and the voice of Ted Turner boomed into my ear: "Pat, WIN is dead. Jerry Levin [the CEO of Time Warner at the time] killed it. He says there's already one women's channel and there's going to be another one—something called Oxygen. So you better come back and tell the team."

I was devastated. The same feelings I had when I got a similar call about *Woman to Woman* came rushing back—mostly rage and helplessness. I knew how different WIN would be from Lifetime and the not-yet-launched Oxygen, and when I got the chance to meet Levin, I tried to argue the case for reinstating the idea.

"There are 114 sports channels on every cable system," I reminded him, "and WIN is nothing like Lifetime"—which was doing very well, by the way! Lifetime was the number one cable network in ratings and revenues, being led by my friend and extraordinary media executive, Carole Black. But Levin was not persuaded that there could be room for a second women's network, and WIN was dead.

Every year since, I have thought about bringing back the concept to take full advantage of the technology that would make it so much easier and cost-effective to build an online communications network focused on news for and about women. There are many good online news services that offer information and stories about women. I value them all and still believe there is a place, in fact, a need, for a women's news and information network.

Women could be the big shift needed in today's media environment to ensure that we're ready and well armed with the one weapon against tyranny and against loss of personal freedoms and for a more equitable and sustainable world: a trusted source of information.

With or without a WIN, I'm urging us to be active media consumers and support important initiatives like the Representation Project, founded by Jennifer Siebel Newsom, and the work of the Sundance Institute, the research from USC's Annenberg School, and the Women's Media Center; to use the on/off switch when media misrepresents us and to raise our voices when it underrepresents us and our stories; to vote with every Instagram or Facebook posting or tweet, every video or podcast, every film or meme viewed; to keep public media public with our support and independent local media vital and reliable with our engagement; and to keep in mind the need for a better balance between "always on" and fully present, so that we can optimize the power in our hands and on all our screens for good.

DANGEROUS TIMES CALL FOR DANGEROUS WOMEN

In Conversation with Laura Flanders

Laura Flanders has her own network: she created it, and with a small team and a modest budget but a big vision, she has produced and hosted her own weekly online news program, The Laura Flanders Show, *and managed a business she calls Grit TV for a decade. She describes the purpose of her media enterprise, a nonprofit that is supported by individuals and foundations, as "to raise radical spirits by interviewing forward-thinking people who have real experience of shifting power, from the few to the many, in the world of arts, entrepreneurship, and politics."*

Deeply involved with the media watchdog FAIR (Fairness and Accuracy in Reporting), she's also contributed to The Nation, Ms., The Progressive, *and* Yes! Magazine. *Her latest book is* Blue Grit: Making Impossible, Improbable, and Inspirational Political Change in America. *Laura and I are working together on an initiative we launched with Jane Fonda and Kat Taylor, an initiative that began at that meeting, organized by Eve Ensler, where I first declared myself to be a dangerous woman. Would Laura say the same of herself? I asked her.*

Do you consider yourself a dangerous woman?

Laura: I do consider myself a dangerous woman, although I am nowhere near as dangerous as I'd like to be, which is to say, as dangerous as reality itself. I'm still working on it. Choosing the unofficial briefing over the official one, going where the cameras aren't, not worrying too much about my future and myself: all of that helps. There is no more pernicious lie than the one that tells us to fear the stranger. Settling for the devil we know is the route to a deadly life.

Is age a factor in how dangerous you feel?

Laura: Young or old, inoculating oneself against the toxin of tolerance requires daily practice. Let up for a moment and the crimes and cruelties that outraged us yesterday become conventional today. Early on, when the bloodstream's fresher, one rejects guff and poison naturally. It's in the middle that you can find yourself succumbing to the noxious notion that (as that dangerous woman, Margaret Thatcher, put it) "there is no alternative."

Years later, if you've stuck at it, experience builds resistance. It's in the middle that can get you: the temptation to accept that there is no alternative. As journalists, it is our responsibility to hold a line against that normalizing of inhumanity. Our job, it seems to me, is to do what we can to un-bland life at every age.

Who inspires you to be more dangerous?

Laura: I live with an action hero, choreographer Elizabeth Streb, who inspires me to be more dangerous. She walks down tall buildings and dives through glass. In contrast to her, my risk taking is purely pedestrian. I risk security, which, as Buckminster Fuller reminded us, is nothing but a fiction. We are all just matter, hurtling through space.

What are the challenges for many women in becoming risk-takers and more dangerous?

Laura: To paraphrase Susan Sontag, society's kiss is overrated. Who wouldn't give up a side seat in the status quo for a perch on the prow of possibility?

For women, especially those with the least proximity to power, the times have always been dangerous. Chattel, scullion, trophy, threat: women didn't set things up this way, but we have become experts at gathering information and pulling off improbable shifts. As Arundhati Roy says, "A new world is not only possible, she's coming, and women are leading: leap!"

Chapter 12

Investing in What Matters

"CHANGE DIRECTION," MY instructor slurred, barely able to stay upright.

She was standing in the middle of the ring, shouting directions to us riders while she clutched a huge cup of coffee. "Wrong lead. You're posting on the wrong leg." I looked around at the other riders; they were clueless that our teacher was, once again, visibly hungover. That should have been the first indication that I had no business being in that equestrian ring. The second was that my fellow riders were all about nine years old; I was closing in on forty.

I had invested $50,000 in two Andalusian stallions, Spanish horses known for their high, arching necks; gorgeous, flowing manes; high-stepping gait; and calm demeanor. Mine came with a fancy name: Destinado. Destined to change my life.

My significant other at the time and I stabled these expensive horses at the equestrian training center in Burbank, which cost almost as much as the rent on our West Hollywood condo. We paid extra for riders to exercise them daily, of course, and for grooming too—had to keep those manes gleaming!

Next came outfitting the horses and ourselves: saddles, halters, bridles for them and for us, handmade Dehner riding boots and top-of-the-line jodhpurs. Why couldn't I just put on battered cowboy boots and go on a trail ride?

I was hosting *Woman to Woman*, employing eighty people in a production company that had my name on the door and the checks; I didn't have time for such an ill-advised investment of money and time. And when the alcoholic instructor suggested I learn dressage—a series of complicated maneuvers in which rider and horse move in sync—any reasonable woman just learning to ride would have laughed and continued posting on the wrong lead.

But I said, "Why not?" I was a good dancer, I thought foolishly, and had already been told by that same instructor that I was a natural in the saddle: surely, I could learn the Olympic-level moves in a couple of extra lessons.

One morning, I climbed onto the stiff new saddle, half asleep from another long night of preparing for the three *Woman to Woman* programs I was scheduled to host that day. My expensive stallion sensed my mind wasn't on him and suddenly began to canter sideways across the ring. I was easily dislodged and fell to the ground.

I woke up in the emergency room as they were cutting off my Dehner boots and protested to the attending physician: "Don't cut them off! Do you know how much they cost?" What cost more, of course, was the diagnosis. "Looks like you've broken your pelvis. We're sending you for X-rays."

"But I have three shows to do!" I explained from the non-negotiating position of flat on my back on a hospital bed. "Guests have been flown in and we have to go live at noon. I *have* to get to the studio!"

"You won't be going anywhere today," the doctor said as he gave me a shot for the pain, which I was just beginning to feel, along with the panic of not being able to move. I can only imagine the panic—and anger—that my producer and partner, Mary

Muldoon, experienced when she got the call from the hospital. She'd warned me about doing something as chancy, expensive, time-consuming, and, in her opinion, silly, as learning to ride in the middle of producing a hit series. She didn't rub it in, and she sent the guests home.

X-rays revealed the pelvis was cracked but not broken, and I was sent home two days later strapped into a special wheelchair designed for lower-body injuries. First challenge: I lived in a small house with twenty-two steps to the front door. I had to be carried up the steps while strapped into that wheelchair. Inside, the chair wouldn't fit through a single doorway. Carpenters were called and doorframes removed. I needed full-time assistance at home and at the studio. Expenses were piling up and I didn't even know what my insurance covered.

THE FULL WEIGHT of what this accident meant, physically, financially, emotionally, and professionally, would come to me over the next six months as I returned to the studio, which didn't have an entrance for a wheelchair. That got fixed quickly with a temporary ramp, but then of course the chair wouldn't fit into a bathroom stall. The studio responded quickly to accommodate my situation, and every day I got a new appreciation for how many barriers there are for people with physical challenges. At least my situation led to our studio being more accessible to all.

After a month in my wheelchair on set, I got the doctor to agree that I could be transferred in the arms of our production manager to a regular chair, strapped in to keep my lower body immobile. Happily, our living-room set with its sofas and chairs where the guests and I sat in a semicircle accommodated the setup. It was awkward, to say the least, not to be able to move at all from the waist down.

And then there was the challenge of the pain pills, which were necessary for quite some time. Honestly, there were some shows where it took very judicious editing to cover up my mistakes—from forgetting guests' names to even dropping an expletive or two when a wince of extreme pain followed an inadvertent movement. Not my finest hours on television.

And certainly not my easiest time financially either. Thanks to the extra costs of help at home and in the studio, physical therapy, medications, and the expenses of missed programs, I wasn't as financially secure as I should have been. I sold the expensive horse (at a great discount) to my trainer, and one year later received a nice photo from her in the winner's circle—she and Destinado won the regional dressage championship.

I now think of this episode as my "Carrie Bradshaw" *Sex and the City* moment: Remember the time Carrie can't muster the $40,000 down payment to buy her Upper West Side brownstone? She later realizes that the row upon row of Manolo Blahniks in her brownstone's closet is the equivalent of that down payment! "I will literally be the old woman who lived in her shoes," Carrie moans. At least Carrie had that—shoes to walk and dance in. I could do neither for a long time, and I needed to rethink how I was spending my money.

I was a forty-year-old single mother with a son in college, still renting rather than owning. Making a good salary but with the ever-constant fear that the series could get canceled, I wasn't financially secure, and I didn't seek out financial advice. Essentially, I was spending what I made and had no investments beyond the equestrian gear that I ended up giving away.

Consider this chapter a cautionary tale! I believe, as many women who understood far earlier than I did, that the final frontier of feminism is financial independence. If we want to reach our potential as agents in the world, we have to understand the role of money in our lives—its potential power and impact—and use it well. I have no excuses and a lot of regrets when I review this aspect of my life. I could have done better for myself and my son had I made it a priority to learn more about money earlier.

MONEY HAS ALWAYS been a difficult subject for me. As a child, I would watch the unpaid bills pile up and up and up, and not once did my parents ever discuss money with me, except to deny nearly every request to do or buy something: "We can't afford it." But no one ever took the time to explain our financial situation. I didn't have a clue what my father made as an appliance salesman or what Mother made at the local drugstore and later, as a clerk in a women's clothing store. I would overhear my parents' raised voices in arguments around how to pay the bills. We weren't poor; we had enough to eat and a house and a car. But when I started talking about college, it was clear that I'd need a full scholarship to fund such a dream.

I did get a scholarship to the University of Georgia and took out student loans (which I was still paying back well into my thirties), while working part-time at a local clothing store (of course) so I could shop at a discount. Most of my earnings went toward clothes, too. During my three years as an undergraduate and my two years of graduate school, lack of money was baked into my nervous system. Every time a new bill arrived, I'd have a stress attack.

But that didn't stop my spending. During the years of on-camera work, a lot of money went for trying to find the right look. (It's a myth that local news people have wardrobe budgets.) I also spent too much buying Mark clothes, which I mistakenly thought might help him fit in. He'd then cut the little logos off his shirts because he didn't want to look like anyone else! Even as a child, he was a nonconformist.

"You know, you really ought to have a will," my lawyer in Boston told me.

"But I'm only thirty-five!" I said.

"Well, if something happens to you," he told me, "Mark will be left a closet full of women's clothes and not much else."

My fears about money were a kind of silent shame; I never felt it was something I could talk about, or ask about. I don't remember one discussion in my consciousness-raising groups or among my feminist friends about who made what, who did what with their money—no talk then about connecting our incomes to our power or our value in the marketplace or our ability to support each other.

Clearly, a few of the leaders of the movement did make the connection and enterprises like *Ms.* magazine got launched, in part because smart women made the necessary investments and women's donor funds got started, too, but I confess that this part of the liberation movement hadn't hit home for me. As a result, I lost time and money—and both are critical to full empowerment and necessary ingredients for becoming a fully realized woman.

I KNOW MANY women with money, and I've learned so much by observing how they use their financial resources. I've read that more than half of the world's wealth will be in the hands of women in the next twenty to thirty years. Talk about power and impact!

A few years ago, I attended one of the first meetings of Women Moving Millions, an organization started by sisters Helen LaKelly Hunt and Swanee Hunt to recognize women who give away more than $1 million a year to causes supporting women and girls. I was being interviewed by one of the founding board members and later chair of WMM, my friend Jacki Zehner, about the women's organizations I was involved in and passionate about supporting.

Later that night, I woke up with a start and asked myself the big question: Why wasn't *I* one of the women in the room able to give more generously to causes I care about? Many probably assumed I *did* have that money—after all, I'd had some pretty high-profile jobs. I'd certainly raised over a million dollars for women and girls and other causes over my lifetime. But I didn't have the financial security I should have had or the financial acumen to invest or advise other women.

As I've moved into leadership positions on boards that govern nonprofits and taken on personal donation commitments,

I've deeply regretted that I didn't start earlier both investing and focusing on my potential to be a better manager of money so that I could make a bigger contribution to the work I want to support both financially and with time and talent. It's a regret I can blame on no one but myself.

MONEY MATTERS, OF course, and to act as if it doesn't—whether negotiating a salary or reviewing an investment—is leaving more than money on the table. It's also leaving power and the ability to make change and the possibility of making bold moves just when there's a greater need than ever for more funds to elevate, leverage, and strengthen solutions to global challenges.

Of course, having money or even giving it away doesn't necessarily translate to greater impact, or to feeling more freedom or power. Money isn't an end but a means. Because I'm not ever going to be one who starts her day reviewing her stocks or slavishly following the markets or worrying about the costs of everything I do, I've taken some steps to make money less of a stressor and more of a means to invest in what matters.

I've hired a financial manager to handle payments and whatever investments of capital made sense. I've agreed to a budget with allocations for personal expenses and set aside a percentage no matter my income for donations and contributions because this use of money gives me the greatest satisfaction. I understand that, for many, seeing the ROI on invested capital increase is the joystick, but this isn't what motivates me. I get quarterly reports to track my spending and investments and most important to me, to determine how much I can give away. It never feels like enough to me.

ONE OF THE ways I have leveraged investing in what matters is through my nonprofit board work. This means supporting V-Day activists and organizations, an annual commitment to the Sundance Institute, and more recently, my board work for the Skoll Foundation as a trustee of the Skoll Fund and the Acumen fund, both of which invest in social entrepreneurs who are innovating new solutions to the world's biggest problems.

Sitting on those boards, reviewing the work of the enterprising global entrepreneurial community, has opened my eyes to how much still remains to be done to equalize the opportunities for women entrepreneurs to have the same access to capital as their male counterparts. From the beginning in both boardrooms, I heard over and over again how difficult it is to find women entrepreneurs working at scale and who manage to get their enterprises to what investors call the *mezzanine level*, meaning they have proven they can attract investments for seed funding and early rounds of investments.

This way of assessing who gets foundation funding or capital investments perpetuates the barriers to equal access and equal opportunity that women have experienced across every sector of life and work. It's the same argument you hear about why there are fewer women in C-suites in business—lack of experience or perhaps sponsorship, meaning someone advocating for them with the same impact as the effective networks among men.

I just don't buy the scarcity argument or the "hard to find eligible women" excuse . . . and I certainly don't accept that in the world of social entrepreneurship, there are fewer women entrepreneurs deserving of funding or capital investment. So I consider it a privilege and a responsibility to keep the gender lens focused when it comes to selecting social entrepreneurs for investment or grants and when it comes to choices about philanthropic giving.

Another aspect of my financial history I'll share without recommending: I've never relied on a man for money. Even when I got married, it never occurred to me that my husband would support me. I worked while pregnant and going to graduate school; I've always worked to have my own money. In every relationship with men of varying means, I was always financially independent. To a large extent, I equated financial independence with emotional independence. The downside was that keeping my finances separate, paying my half of everything, helped me avoid important conversations about money.

When a longtime partner and I finally decided to buy a house and live together, I paid half the down payment and half the mortgage every month, and even though I had the right to be on the title as one of the two purchasers of the residence, I never checked to be sure that my name was on it. Years later, when we parted company and I moved to another state, I discovered I had no legal means to force a sale of the property that he had chosen to keep as his residence. I chose not to try the legal options that were open to me, and instead lost the investment I had made over the years with my portion of the mortgage payments.

I was also embarrassed, as I should have been. A forty-year-old woman with her own income and professional accomplishments not knowing she wasn't on the deed of the house she paid for in equal parts! Here was another painful lesson: there is no glory in being financially independent in a relationship if you're going to lose money because you don't like to talk about financial issues or diminish intimacy by cordoning off an important area of all partnerships.

Ironically, I'd always understood budgets because as a producer and running my own production company, I had to allocate funds and balance expenses with revenue. I had to meet payrolls and pay taxes. But investing time and attention to my personal budgets and investments wasn't a priority—until I moved back to Atlanta.

Shortly into my tenure at Turner Broadcasting, I had another one of those financially opportune moments that turned out to be a game changer. I received a very tempting job offer to become president of ABC daytime entertainment, and it was clearly going to double or even triple my salary at Turner.

Thankfully, Ted's ultra-competitiveness—and my own intuition—convinced me to stay at Turner when Ted matched the

ABC offer and made me a stockholder in TBS, Inc., along with giving me much more responsibility. My TBS, Inc. stock was going to fund my retirement until a certain media merger—the worst in media history, according to many—rendered the stock pretty much useless. However, there's a better ending to that story that I'll get to in a few pages.

The point is that it took other people's serious investment in me, my skills, and my talents for me to take investing in myself as seriously as I should have. Buying a home instead of renting; buying stocks instead of shoes. Asking for a raise even when I didn't have another job offer because I believed in my own value in the marketplace. All things I should have done earlier and share now in the hopes that money matters will matter sooner for you.

PERHAPS THE MOST important financial shift in my money matters came through my service on corporate boards—something I couldn't do as a journalist but was allowed to pursue when I became president of PBS. My marketplace had been the media landscape, and then with the boards I was asked to join, I received a global economic education.

Bank of America was the first to approach me to join their board. I thought it was quite ironic that I, whose relationship with banks as a customer was pretty much limited to student loans, would be asked to essentially oversee the finances of a multibillion-dollar company.

I told the CEO, "If I'm going to do this, you're going to have to get me a financial tutor."

"Oh, we'll do that because the first committee you're on is the audit committee." Wait, I was now on the *audit* committee of one of the largest financial institutions in the world? That financial tutor was an enormous help, explaining every line item on the budget and the accounting ledgers: where the money goes, how it's spent, and how it comes back; lots of complicated financial instruments. Through the next eight years while I was a Bank of America director, the board helped guide major acquisitions and big changes in the business itself, and I moved from audit to compensation to the nominating committee, where I felt my contributions and relevant experiences were most valuable.

I advocated for additional women on the board and more were elected. Colleagues on the board, women as well as men, cautioned me not to play the *women's card*—nominating other women directors or paying too much attention to issues regarding gender or equality. I ignored the advice; following it locks in the status quo, and means most corporate boards will be predominantly white men. That's not good for business . . . or for customers or for women or people of color. I want all women to play the women's card or the race card at every opportunity to shift the power dynamic everywhere—especially in boardrooms where more than money matters.

I left the board in early 2008, concerned, like so many, about "bigger is better" and all those subprime mortgages and credit-default swaps. We all know how that story ended.

"YOU'RE DOING WHAT?" Ted Turner yelled into the phone. "You're going on the board of a company responsible for me losing *$2 billion* and your losing your entire retirement fund!"

"Well, yes, Ted, I've been invited to be a director of the new AOL company, and I believe it's going to work," I answered. "You should buy some stock."

Ted and I . . . and a whole lot of other people . . . were losers in the worst media deal in history, as *Time* magazine called the AOL/Time Warner merger. Ted had asked all of us to hold onto our stock; smart people sold immediately after the deal closed. I dutifully held onto stock that evaporated into nothing. Ted indeed lost $2 *billion* dollars. I lost a lot less, but for me, it meant a lot more.

So when I got the call several years later from Tim Armstrong, who was now running the new AOL (the old one was essentially absorbed into Time Warner and then spun out as an independent company again), asking me to come see him, I initially hesitated. I had a negative reflex reaction to the name AOL and what it conjured up for me in terms of personal loss. Ultimately, I decided to go because I knew Tim from his days as Google's president and admired him.

I'd just come back from Kenya where I'd been visiting V-Day activist Agnes Pareyio's school for girls who were escaping female genital mutilation, a practice in some cultures and communities. Agnes, newly appointed by the Kenyan government to a commission to end the practice in Kenya, is one of the dangerous women who risked alienation and even exile from her Masai community when she started this work. While visiting some villages where the girls had been reunited with their families, I fell forward on some wet stone steps and broke off my four front teeth. (I don't think this is what my grandmother had in mind when she encouraged me to fall forward!) There were no dentists within reach, so I stayed and continued our work and even went on a safari with Carole Black, V-Day colleague and close friend. We shared a lot of laughs about my appearance, and while not at all comfortable, some of the Masai warriors we met—warriors often pull their own teeth to show courage and signal their status as a warrior—gave me high fives and even danced with me around the fire one evening.

I got a quick fix of the teeth in Nairobi from an Indian dentist who shaped beautiful temporaries, which he warned would last less than a month. The dental restoration was still in progress when I met Tim.

I arrived at the meeting sporting some other funky temporary front teeth and told him the story of losing my real teeth to which he replied, "Anybody brave enough to come to a meeting with those teeth has to be on my board. You clearly show up, no matter what."

I did show up, as did the other directors Tim invited onto the new AOL board. This ended up being the best board experience of all—in every way. Our group of experienced directors worked well together, and with Tim and his young team, rebuilt the company.

But in today's media landscape, it's get big or die, and it became clear after four years that AOL needed to be bigger to compete in the ever-transforming technology space. The decision was made to sell the company to Verizon for a healthy return to shareholders. Maybe Ted didn't recoup his $2 billion, and for me, at seventy, this was the final opportunity to make a difference in a place where all the decisions matter greatly: not only the ones about money and profits, but also those about culture and gender and corporate responsibility.

And in all those decisions in all boardrooms, women need to be willing to show up and make a difference.

It's important for more women to be on boards; research has shown conclusively that diversity on boards and in management *always* produces better results. For example, according to the Harvard School of Public Health, Fortune 500 companies with the highest numbers of women directors on their boards had a 42 percent greater return on sales and a 53 percent higher return on equity than the others. Good governance has been directly linked to the presence of women on boards in terms of better compliance and less corruption and misuse of funds.

In September 2018, then California governor Jerry Brown signed a bill requiring all publicly traded corporations in California to have at least one woman on their board of directors by the end of 2019 as part of a larger effort to narrow the gender gap. By July of 2021, the bill states, at least two women must be on boards with five members, and at least three women on boards with six or more members. The bill might have "potentially fatal legal problems," Brown says, but "given all the special privileges that corporations have enjoyed for so long, it's high time corporate boards include the people who constitute more than half the 'persons' in America."

In Norway, where the first quotas were enforced requiring companies working there to have at least 40 percent women on their boards, the initial pushback was significant. "We'll never find qualified women directors in the eighteen-month time line," said more than one CEO. But they did find them, and four years later, every company in Norway has at least 40 percent women; research demonstrates that every aspect of business has improved.

Now almost every country in the EU has some form of incentive or quota around representation in boardrooms—but not the United States. "I don't want quotas," the young woman attending my forum on board service blurted out after I shared the Norway story. "I don't want to be forced on some company because the government says it has to have women. I will get there on merit."

I've heard this over and over, and while I'm sympathetic to the "merit, not numbers" defense, I also believe that without quotas or incentives or regulations, the numbers won't get better. As a famous leader once observed and the current representation in most corporate boardrooms exemplifies, "no one ever gave up power voluntarily." The power that exists inside corporate boardrooms is significant, and if the opportunity arises to serve on a corporate board, be prepared for consideration.

There are downsides, certainly. It can be challenging to attend all the board meetings (which always exceed the number expected or on the calendar) and to be prepared for the responsibilities that are real and sometimes exceed expectations; and being put up for a shareholder vote every year can be humbling, too. I remember one Bank of America shareholder meeting when a well-known shareholder activist took the mic to demand of the CEO that he "fire the two blondes on his board." The two blondes were me and Jacki Ward, one of the smartest women I know, and we had just received the highest shareholder votes. All in all, I learned a lot from my corporate-board experiences—about money and the global economy, and a lot about human nature, too.

I'M STILL LEARNING more about how to have a healthy relationship with money. I'm proud of how much money I've given to causes about which I'm passionate. But I'm not so proud of how long I waited before paying attention to my own money matters. I don't want other women to make the same mistakes.

I'd advise any woman to hire an investment counselor, someone to sit down and help her plan for savings and investment strategies. If I had the chance to do it again, I would definitely learn more about personal finance and discuss it more. Even now, my closest women friends and I rarely talk about money unless we're raising money for a cause together.

My mother often said that the way I liked to spend money, I was going to end up as an old woman alone "in the home." Now those old folks' homes are called *assisted living* and my mom ended up in one, alone and with not enough insurance money or savings to pay for her care. Every time I visited her, I thought about the fact that she had worked her entire life, but when my father died, she had no savings, no assets, no credit, and now at the end, she had to rely entirely on my brother and me, who could gratefully afford to pay.

This fear is irrational. I am a white, healthy, and privileged woman, and I am financially secure—not rich by any means, but if I stay on budget, I will have enough. I'm in a marriage that is secure, and while we don't mingle our finances, we use the same financial advisor, have no money secrets, and share equally in our big expenses. Finally, I feel financially independent and emotionally interdependent, which makes me feel incredibly rich in all the ways that matter.

At seventy-six, I'm still working, sometimes for money as a paid curator or speaker or conference organizer, but I still don't value my time in terms of money and probably never will. The return on investment for me is knowing that whatever I invest—time, money, information, connections—the value will be measured in change: positive social change, positive personal interactions, and positive experiences that add value to my life and to the lives of others. As I said at the beginning of this chapter, this is a cautionary tale that began with an expensive horse, a big fall, and the forward movement that followed. Becoming a dangerous woman for me means discovering more ways to make my money matter and to advocate for all women to know more about money, to make more money, and when we have it, to be motivated to use it well to open access to what money can mean to others. Money matters for everyone.

DANGEROUS TIMES CALL FOR DANGEROUS WOMEN

In Conversation with Jacqueline Novogratz

As I mentioned earlier in this chapter, I'm proud to serve on the Acumen Board, a nonprofit capital fund that supports entrepreneurs offering products and services for the world's extremely poor populations. Acumen was the vision of Jacqueline Novogratz, an entrepreneur, author, and former banker. I admire her passion and commitment to changing the way the world thinks about the poor and about money. She is the author of The Blue Sweater: Bridging the Gap Between Rich and Poor in an Interconnected World, *based on the moment when she spotted a young boy wearing one of her own sweaters, which her mother had donated to Goodwill years earlier. That put her on a lifelong path to changing the way the world views the poor and the ways we address their needs. Acumen has invested more than $115 million in social enterprises providing products and services to the consumers at the bottom of the economic pyramids in Pakistan, India, East and West Africa, Latin America, and the United States. Her organization also developed and manages KawiSafi Ventures, Ltd, a $70 million off-grid energy impact fund designed to prove that clean off-grid solutions to electricity are the best way to solve energy poverty in Africa. I recently sat down with my good friend Jacqueline to talk about her journey to becoming a dangerous woman.*

When and where did your journey to becoming a dangerous woman begin?

Jacqueline: As a young banker, I loved the power of investing in an entrepreneur or idea and seeing the investment translate into jobs or new ways of doing things. What I didn't love was how the poor were excluded from the banks, often fearing even walking through the bank doors. I left Wall Street and went on to cofound a microfinance bank in Rwanda, learning both the potential and limitations of markets to solve problems of poverty. Yet, when I shared my dream of using philanthropy to back "patient capital" and invest where both markets and government had failed the poor, a number of Wall Street titans said to me, "You obviously don't understand business." I was a forty-year-old woman who had already built a bank, yet something gave them permission to question whether I even understood business, let alone what it took to create a business serving people earning just a couple dollars a day in places with limited infrastructure and skills but abundant with bureaucracy and corruption.

You make a connection between business and power and money that many of us don't make until later. What did you do next?

Jacqueline: Through Acumen, we've invested nearly $120 million in companies that have served more than 270 million low-income people. The experience has taught me the potential of redefining investment and the purpose of business, of seeing money simply as a means to doing something else—not as the end in itself. Too many see capitalism as a religion, rather than keeping capital in its place—as a tool to enable us to solve our greatest problems. Markets have extraordinary power—and limitations. At the end of the day, we can't take money with us. Think of how much would change if we measured success not based on how much money we earned but on how we used that money to release the energies of other human beings?

Too often we think of financial success as the last frontier, our single definition of success. It's more powerful to control money, to move other people's money, if you will, toward a greater good. I didn't have financial assets when I created Acumen; I built it in partnership with a lot of wealthy individuals who made our work possible by giving money and so much more.

What is the connection between money and power that relates specifically to women?

Jacqueline: The question isn't, "Do we have our own financial security?" because without the freedom and strength to use it, the money is for naught. "Do we have the confidence to put money in its place?" If you have wealth, use it. But wealth isn't the only means to create change. We all have the chance to make a difference. Like MLK, I dream of a world in which we judge each other by the content of our character, because I've learned that just as the word *poverty* doesn't tell you anything about a person's character, neither does the word *wealth*. I think that's why I'm so hell-bent on the work that we do for character and moral leadership.

What do you say to other women about the need to embrace our financial power, to become more dangerous in this part of our lives?

Jacqueline: Money, power, technology, information. . . . If we saw these as tools and not as what defines us, we could create a world in which every one of us were enabled to flourish. That's where I see a huge opportunity for women. If we could get together and start the conversation about the world we seek to create, then we could take a clear-eyed view of where markets work and whether they fail. Markets are a powerful listening device: people don't necessarily tell you the truth if you offer them a gift; but they walk with their feet if they have to make decisions about whether to purchase something, even at a highly subsidized price. We also must understand the role of government, which has a responsibility to care for the most vulnerable, and the role of philanthropy as a de-risking mechanism, to enable intrepid individuals to build solutions to poverty. We can solve our biggest problems. What gets in our way is power unbridled, pushed by ego, and the rest of the world bowing to it. They're false idols.

How do we get to this world where the power of money and power of women come together for positive change?

Jacqueline: We need a new moral framework that measures success not by how the wealthy are treated, but how the poor, the vulnerable of the earth fare. A framework that recognizes that we are not only part of each other, we *are* each other. I exist because you exist. If we dare to get close enough to see each other, then it becomes impossible to exploit each other. It becomes impossible for us to live in a world where my winning necessarily implies your losing, but rather one where I can only have the full dignity of what it means to be a human being if I afford that full dignity to you and every other person on the planet.

Chapter 13

Being in the Rooms Where It Happens

"WHY AREN'T THERE more women on the TED stage?" I asked Chris Anderson, chief curator of the TED conferences. We were taking a Sunday afternoon walk in 2009, basking in the aftermath of yet another awesome TED conference. "I've been a TEDster for years, and value the TED Talks I hear at the conferences and watch online, but I've noticed that most of them are given by men. Surely, there are women with 'ideas worth spreading,'" I said, quoting TED's famous tagline.

"I'm sure there are," Chris answered. "We just have a bit more difficulty finding them. I was looking for a woman rocket scientist this year, but just didn't find one."

"I'll find one for you," I heard myself offering, "and I'll also send you a list of tech entrepreneurs, physicians, architects, artists. You name the sector, I'll find a woman for it." And with that offer accepted, I began to send him names of women for the TED stage.

THAT'S ESSENTIALLY THE origin story of how TEDWomen came into being. Chris recommended I meet with the smart women on TED's leadership team at this time, and after several brainstorming sessions, we proposed a new TED conference dedicated to TED Talks by women. Chris agreed that the timing was right and we put together a team that was led by June Cohen, then editorial director, and included Lara Stein, who was leading the burgeoning TEDx movement; Ronda Carnegie, who headed up partnerships; and Kelly Stoetzel, one of the leading curators and now head of conferences at TED. I signed on as editorial director, continuing my responsibilities as CEO of the Paley Center for Media. We had no sooner announced the first TEDWomen conference for 2010 when the avalanche of criticism began:

"Don't create a pink TED!"

"Women shouldn't be put into the TEDWomen ghetto!"

"You're going to lower the standard of a TED Talk."

And perhaps the unkindest cut of all: "Women want to be on the *real* TED stage, not some feminist sideshow."

Some charges of gender washing came from women who were already longtime "TEDsters" and either wanted to keep their privileged places inside that mostly male-dominated culture and community at the time, or perhaps were honestly concerned that TEDWomen might be viewed as a "lesser" option for speakers.

I shouldn't have been surprised or even disappointed by the criticism, but I was. Most of these hostile tweets and Facebook posts were from women, and that's always the hard part for me—women not supporting other women. Some see this as internalized self-hatred; I think of it as part of cultural conditioning to compete and compare, leading us to sometimes vote against our own best interests or to buy into a scarcity ideology that there are only a few places at the top and it's best to protect that turf rather than try to share it or to advocate for another woman to get her own turf.

The press fanned the flames of the burgeoning controversy, but Chris and the TED team didn't back off their support. Instead, we decided to embrace the criticisms as the theme for the first TEDWomen conference.

On December 5, 2010, in the nation's capital, TEDWomen 2010 welcomed a sellout audience of more than one thousand attendees, and as the lights went down in the theatre at the International Trade Center, the opening video posed the same question we had been hearing for months: "Why a TEDWomen?"

The screen at the front of the theatre flashed with a single, incomplete sentence: "Talking about women's ideas in 2010 is ________."

One by one, the blank was replaced with words we'd heard from critics in the previous year.

Not necessary. Irrelevant. Gender ghettoizing. Dated. Risky.

Then the video offered some alternative opinions:

Important for progress. Bold. Worthwhile. A game changer.

Moans, then laughter, then cheers rose from the audience as we collectively acknowledged the skeptics and then used the moment to highlight the profound potential of TEDWomen.

That week, we broke new ground with the world-changing ideas of forty-two women and eight men (we were clear that this wasn't a women-only conference or program, just one that reversed the ratio of gender voices on the main TED stage or seen on TED.com in 2010).

That first program had its share of marquee names, such as Hillary Clinton, who was secretary of state at the time, and former secretary of state Madeleine Albright. Ted Turner appeared, too—and joked in an onstage interview that he thought the conference was named after him! Sorry, Ted—but TED actually stands for technology, entertainment, and design, even though that program definition expanded long ago and TED is just TED, recognized and respected as a breakthrough idea that well-prepared and well-presented talks about ideas would find an online audience. Indeed, TED Talks are available in nearly every country, translated by volunteer translators into multiple languages and viewed by hundreds of millions of people.

It's a pretty impressive reach for an organization that began in Monterey, California, with a few hundred mostly male technologists, engineers, and scientists.

In our first year, we also featured TED Talks by not one but two rocket scientists, as well as two robotics engineers! Cynthia Breazeal, founder and director of the Personal Robots group at MIT's Media Lab, explored the conundrum that we use robots on Mars but not in our living rooms and argued that we need robots to be socialized. Heather Knight, who runs Marilyn Monrobot, a robot theatre company with comedy performances, shared some of the work she'd done to help integrate socially interactive robots into the world, where they could be of value in areas like education and medical care.

Featuring women from other countries was a focus, too, and Dr. Annet Namayanja, a farmer from Uganda, got a standing ovation when she shared a new process for producing a bean that had more protein and nutrients for a population that relies on them for sustenance.

Eve Ensler brought the audience to its feet—again—with an impassioned plea for a global community of women to be more aware of the violence threatening one out of three women in the world.

Buddhist leader Joan Halifax took up the difficult subject of death and coping with grief.

Omega Institute for Holistic Studies founder Elizabeth Lesser issued a caution about *otherizing* and suggested that we all take someone we considered *the other* to lunch.

There were talks and conversations during meals and breaks, and at one of the community dinners, Arianna Huffington held us rapt with her convincing argument that we all need more sleep. It turned out that Arianna had taken a red-eye to give that talk, which she sandwiched between two conference commitments in the same day. I don't know when she sleeps, but I have loved watching her thrive as a visionary entrepreneur and good friend.

We also introduced a new kind of TED session: *duets,* two people giving one TED Talk together. A Masai father, Lemeria Ole Leperes, and his daughter, Jacklyne Mantaine Lemeria, traveled for the first time out of their village to stand in their traditional dress and talk about their family's decision to join a movement to end the practice of female genital mutilation in their region. Wildlife filmmakers and conservationists Beverly and Dereck Joubert spoke about the threat to the big cats, elephants, and rhinos, subjects of their award-winning documentaries and critical to the survival of the fragile African ecosystems in which these two remarkable human beings, National Geographic explorers for two decades, live and work.

Over the years, these duets have included mothers and sons, husbands and wives, business partners, and in one especially memorable talk, a young woman from Iceland stood with the young Australian man who had sexually assaulted her when they were both teenagers. There were tears, disbelief, even anger in that room that day, but also admiration for the courage it took Thordis Elva and Tom Stranger to go public with their story of healing and reconciliation. For me, it was a brave step forward that helped many people view their own experiences with sexual assault through a different lens and perhaps find a new path to understanding and even forgiveness. Theirs was a very brave talk and a somewhat controversial experience for the TEDWomen audience, but Chris supported us in tackling tough subjects.

Also at this first TEDWomen, a then little-known Google executive named Sheryl Sandberg took the stage to talk about a phenomenon she was witnessing in the tech industry—young women "taking their foot off the pedal just as they should be accelerating in their careers." She called for women to *lean in* to opportunity. She had planned to talk about technology, but right before she went onstage, Sheryl told me how hard it had been to say good-bye to her daughter—again—to fly to Washington, DC, for this conference. "Tell that story!" I urged, and she did! The talk was well received but none of us, including Sheryl, had any idea what a phenomenon *Lean In*, the book based on the idea of her TED Talk, would become: it launched a global movement, landing Sheryl on the cover of *Time* magazine. More recently, her position as COO of Facebook put her on the front-page news again, but this time for allegations of the company's role in the 2016 presidential election.

From that first TEDWomen to the present, the TED team has always been clear that TEDWomen isn't a "women's conference" as such, but rather a TED conference with a central narrative about women's ideas and accomplishments. Unlike TED, which convenes in the same venue in Vancouver every spring, TEDWomen has moved every year, tapping into new communities while sustaining a large group of TEDWomen who return time and again.

Another objective of TEDWomen was to connect and build a global community through the TEDx organizers. We have accomplished that beyond our expectations. In 2010, more than two hundred TEDxWomen licensees organized convenings all over the world and in hundreds of US cities, taking a live feed of the TEDWomen program and adding their own on the same theme. Every year the size of these simultaneous conferences has grown, and we have, in fact, built and sustained a global community of women and men coming together to hear TED Talks at TEDWomen and curating their own TEDxWomen conferences.

The responses over the years from these gatherings are reminders of how many remaining barriers to women's voices and ideas still exist. Consider the TEDxWomen convening that takes place in Saudi Arabia. The TEDxWomen organizer wrote me that she has to take extra precautions to convene somewhere where doors can be locked, so that the women students can learn from the diversity of subjects and themes of a TEDWomen conference without the content being censored.

OVER THE YEARS, I've noticed that a narrative will sometimes emerge that was unplanned in our curatorial meetings—as a number of talks will reference a common idea and lift it into a meme. *Spatial justice* was one such idea that evolved at TEDWomen 2017 in New Orleans. Harvard-trained architect Liz Ogbu, a woman of color, introduced the term to explain why design needs to be looked at through lenses of equality, fairness, and justice. Liz invited us to look at how architecture can thoughtlessly perpetuate systemic injustices dividing communities and isolating individuals.

In a later session, another architect and woman of color, Deanna Van Buren, talked about how she's been designing restorative-justice centers instead of prisons. If we're looking at prisons simply as a place to imprison instead of rehabilitate, she told us, we're not looking at how design can foster justice; we're just perpetuating mass incarceration, a problem that disproportionately affects African American men. "You can't just go in and create a new space until you go through a process of truth and reconciliation; you need to first understand everything that's been lost in that community so you can rebuild it," Deanna told us.

In another session, John Cary, also an architect, demonstrated how most buildings, designed by men, reflect a gender lens—for example, ladies' bathrooms never have enough stalls! The novel theme of spatial justice, which crossed all lines of community and environment, emerged as one of the most talked about of the entire conference. Many came up to me and said, "That idea of spatial justice shifted the way I think about everything now."

That's the point, actually, and the satisfaction of curating TEDWomen—to shift perspectives through new ideas and powerful personal stories and experiences. We've made it possible for more than three hundred women—scientists, architects, artists, activists, and writers; leaders from government, civil society, and social enterprises—to give their TED Talks and to see their ideas spread to the world. So rather than creating a *pink ghetto,* as some feared, TEDWomen has made TED a more inclusive community, too. The numbers of women at the big

TED have grown substantially, as have the numbers of talks by women on TED.com.

THERE IS NO question that TED has set new standards for all conferences. A TED Talk may be a life-defining invitation, a singular opportunity to have your talk captured with multiple cameras and by the most experienced production team, on a well-designed set and with months of preparation. More and more, I observe that in every forum that features talks, the influence of TED Talks is clear. What makes a successful TED Talk? TED's curator, Chris Anderson, answers that question in his book, *TED Talks: The Official TED Guide to Public Speaking*. I recommend it for everyone, and we send a copy to every potential TED speaker.

Of course, being a good storyteller is key and women are, in my experience, innately good storytellers. But what many have to overcome are self-imposed barriers, such as the fear of sounding *braggy*, a feeling I experienced writing this very book! Even the most accomplished female scientists and technologists or physicians worry about being good enough to give a TED Talk—a response that I've never heard from any man I've coached!

There is also a very particular alchemy that happens when women gather together, which is one of the benefits of TEDWomen that I value most. I hear from women in the audience about a talk or a conversation that ignited something new for them—a new direction, passion, purpose. Or how they met someone they later collaborated with, or formed a deep friendship during dinner. I think some women come more for the community than the talks! I noted a group of about twenty women sitting together during lunch at a recent TEDWomen, talking, laughing, and listening intently to one another.

"How do you all think the conference is going so far?" I asked them. "Did you all come together?"

"Never met before!" one volunteered. Another added, "We're all search executives on this side of the table," and from the other side, another said, "And on this side, we're all therapists of one sort or another."

I had to smile. "This is an interesting combo; maybe your connection will lead to better-adjusted women getting bigger and better jobs."

That got a laugh, but I heard the following week that one of the search executives at the table did, in fact, put forward one of the family therapists across the table for a major executive position in a pharmaceutical company. Such outcomes are not our intention, but it's part of being in the rooms where this and so much more can happen.

One clear intention for me in curating TEDWomen and other conferences is that often there is an opportunity to showcase some of the awesome women I am lucky enough to know as friends. In one particularly memorable interview on a TEDWomen stage, I talked more about female friendships with two such friends, Jane Fonda and Lily Tomlin, whose friendship is the frame for their series, *Grace and Frankie.*

"I don't even know what I would do without my women friends," Jane said onstage. "They make me stronger."

Lily added, "Recent research points out that not having close female friendships is as detrimental to your health as smoking or being overweight."

"Our friendships are full disclosure, we go deep, we risk vulnerability, that's something that men don't do," Jane agreed. "Women's friendships are like a renewable source of power."

For me, that interview summed up why it matters for us to be in these rooms together—tapping into that renewable source of power!

We've done some reframing about age, too, at TEDWomen. Every year, we've invited girls to give TED Talks, showcasing the smart young women of tomorrow whose ideas are worth knowing and spreading.

A twelve-year-old Google Science Fair winner started her TED Talk with "All my life, I've wanted to cure cancer!" She's on her way to producing research that just might unlock a new treatment. And at the other end of the age scale, one of my favorite older and wiser women, the outspoken ninety-four-year-old "Queen of Creole Cuisine," Leah Chase, set the audience buzzing when she shared her opinion:

"Young women just don't know their power. They don't seem to know yet that women are just smarter than men." Leaning forward from her chair to make the point, she added, "You've got to remember about men: you have to build them up, honey. It's not hard; just fill 'em up with cheap gas. That's all it takes."

Mrs. Chase got a big laugh, but the fact is her conversation on TED.com is getting a lot of views as she also shared a bold commitment that she and her husband held firm during the days of civil-rights demonstrations and violence: their restaurant, Dooky Chase, was open to all activists, black and white, making it a popular stop for the Freedom Riders who were risking dangers every day to protest a segregated South.

The privilege of being able to offer the unprecedented reach and impact of a TED Talk to women and, yes, some good men, whose work deserves to be known, better understood, and celebrated; whose ideas can and do ignite important conversations and outcomes; whose commitments to creating opportunities and access are changing lives and communities . . . these are the reasons for me that TEDWomen came to be and continues.

My partnership with TED is work that fully engages my passion and aligns with my purpose as an advocate for other women and my desire "to be in the rooms where it happens"—to paraphrase a popular song from Lin-Manuel Miranda's Broadway hit, *Hamilton.* In these rooms and forums and conferences, history is sometimes made or rewritten, culture is challenged, power paradigms are shifted, communities and connections are created and sustained, and ideas worth spreading are shared.

CONFESSION: I AM something of a conference addict. Last year, I participated in six women's conferences on three continents in four months. I had experiences that enriched my life with new connections, reconnected me with old friends, and stimulated new thinking and plans. I always feel my time at such gatherings is worthwhile, and now new research confirms the value: data collected in a Harvard Business School research study conclude women who go to women's conferences are twice as likely to get a promotion within a year and *three times* as likely to get a 10 percent salary bump! I'm not looking for either at this time in my life, but this is a meaningful outcome for women who could benefit in their careers by their participation in women's conferences, which are sometimes dismissed as a gabfest or as purely personal or social time.

Researcher Shawn Achor, author of *The Happiness Advantage,* adds another layer to the value proposition with the finding that 78 percent of the attendees at women's conferences felt "more optimistic about the future," while 71 percent "felt more connected to others." This feeling of connection, Achor says, brings results: "If people feel like they are trying to get out of depression alone, or fighting inequality alone, or striving for success alone, they burn out and the world feels like a huge burden. But there is a powerful, viable alternative to individually pursuing success and happiness: doing it together."

At one of the Women and Power conferences convened every two years by the Omega Women's Leadership Center in Rhinebeck, New York, I had been asked by the founder and my good friend Elizabeth Lesser and Leadership Center director, Carla Goldstein, to interview one of the women Nobel laureates attending that year—Jody Williams. You may remember she had been awarded the Nobel Peace Prize for her work in negotiating treaties to eliminate the dangers of remaining land mines in areas where they had been used to target civilian populations. I began our conversation with a question about how she was using the power that comes with being a Nobel laureate.

"I'm not powerful," Jody shot back, defensively. "I hate that term and I don't think of myself as having power." I pushed back, reminding her that anyone who can negotiate treaties with difficult governments and achieve the results that her organization had achieved, and the global recognition of a Nobel Peace Prize, had a kind of power or certainly influence. She continued to resist the description, and perhaps, to make her point another way, she kicked off her cowboy boots, a signature wardrobe item for Jody, and did the rest of the interview with bare feet dangling on the main stage. I followed suit, barefoot and toe to toe, in a way I can't quite imagine happening anywhere other than at this women's gathering at Omega, where we are encouraged to connect with nature and nurture body and soul. Jody and I got more personal, unpacking some of the challenging stereotypes and barriers that keep women from owning their personal power and using it collectively.

I acknowledge Omega's Women and Power conferences for putting the subject of power forward, reframing it as a means and not an end in itself; supporting the journey for so many of us to own our power; and modeling through the leaders and programs featured during the conference how we can use it, and share it. Like Jody Williams and other remarkable women I have met at Omega and around the world, I deflected and denied my power for many years after I clearly had some as well as a significant sphere of influence. I've come a long way on this journey, discovering more every day, actually, about how to use my power for the biggest and most significant impact. Today, I have quotes about power on my business cards and call my independent company, POW! Strategies—Power of Women—and if nothing else, interesting and sometimes provocative conversations result when I give someone my card.

In the interest of diving deeper into the subject of women and power, I partnered with former TEDWomen colleague, Ronda Carnegie, and with support from the Rockefeller Foundation, we convened two women leaders forums at the Bellagio conference center in 2017 and again in 2019. With small cohorts of women leaders from the front lines of power in government, civil society, business, media, and philanthropy, we shaped some principles for how power can be used to be a transformative change leader—attributes often associated with women. What Ronda and I have observed in these forums and what I am experiencing in all the rooms and conferences where women come together, share stories, shape solutions, and make things happen is that connected women leaders are the transformative force needed more than ever. As everyone from Speaker of the House Nancy Pelosi to the iconic Beyonce reminds us, "No one gives you power. You have to take it."

Let's take it and use it to make a better world.

DANGEROUS TIMES CALL FOR DANGEROUS WOMEN

In Conversation with Sandi Toksvig

I first met Sandi in one such room where it happens—at the WOW conference in London. I knew who she was long before: she's been a well-known writer, performer, and host of musicals and programs on British radio and television for many years. She hosts the closing-night ceremony called Mirth Matters at WOW every year, and it's a favorite! Currently, she's the host of two of the BBC's most popular shows.

Sandi is also an activist. In March of 2015, Sandi cocreated with journalist Catherine Mayer the Women's Equality Party (Sandi quipped that they gave it that name "because we wanted to be clear") to fight for women's equal pay and equal representation in politics, business, education, health-care research, and more. Today this political party has more than 65,000 members and seventy branches throughout the UK, and according to the Daily Telegraph, *is "the fastest growing political force in the UK." Sandi's TED Talk at TEDWomen 2016 presented equality as an idea worth spreading, and it's become more dangerous and effective in getting more women to run and to win political campaigns.*

When did you begin to think of yourself as a dangerous woman?

Sandi: I'm in my fourth decade in show business and have got used to being seen as a danger to the accepted order. When I came out in 1994, there was not a single out lesbian in the world of British entertainment. I came out partly because I didn't realize anyone thought I was in and because I had three kids and didn't want them to live their lives in the shadow of a secret. I believe secrets are a cancer of the soul, and I wanted my babies to stand up, proud of their family. That week the *Daily Mail*, one of the more reprehensible UK tabloids, published a front-page headline declaring, "If God had meant lesbians to have children he would have made it possible." As I was a lesbian with three kids, it seemed to me the editor was not quite thinking things through, but I didn't really have time to argue.

Immediately the death threats began, mostly from high-minded religious people who wanted to kill me on God's behalf because presumably God was busy and they needed to pick up the slack. It seemed I was threatening thousands of years of belief by merely existing. We had to go into hiding and in the still of the night; it was terrifying. Nearly a quarter of a century later, things have calmed down. I didn't ask to be seen as *dangerous*, but if it is the badge I have to wear in order to get things done then I shall wear it with pride.

Is there an age component to feeling more dangerous?

Sandi: I don't think feeling dangerous has to do with age. I suspect most women can recall a time in their youth when they became enraged for being treated in a particular way based entirely on gender. Maybe age allows us to care less what people think. I hope I grow more dangerous and disgraceful with each passing year.

I suppose my journey toward dangerousness began when I was four and my father came home from a business trip with a rocket for my older brother and a silver necklace for me. I was sure I could build a rocket faster and better than any boy, and I was so angry. It is a rage that sits within me and can still be triggered by the producer who calls me *forceful* in a derogatory way while he smiles at the badly behaved male comics I often work with who are merely being *creative*.

I remember there was a couple who my parents knew well. He worked and she stayed home looking after their two sons. They became like family. He was a big guy and strong. Sometimes he would get mad at something his wife had said or done. He'd put his hand on the back of her neck and squeeze it hard until she apologized. All the other grown-ups just let him do it. No one ever said anything. I haven't seen them for years, but sometimes I think of her. She'll never know that somehow I am still trying to stop her being treated like that.

How does being dangerous play out in your life and work?

Sandi: I think it is very tough for my wife and family; being married to an activist is exhausting and some days I tire myself. It would be nice to just let a few things slide and hope someone else catches the ball.

The hardest challenge is to energize the next generation. Society has become so focused on the self; there is such death of empathy on social media that getting anyone to look up from their phone and out to the world seems a Herculean labor. I'm hopeful that the Women's Equality Party will get women off social media and onto podiums and into political office.

Are you optimistic about women leaders bringing about greater equality in these dangerous times?

Sandi: Amazing women fight every day for a better world. I don't know if I can make a difference, but I believe they can. Maybe together we can inch the world forward.

As we talk, I am about to board a train to Brussels to address the European Women Alliance on the subject of gender equality. Women from twenty-seven countries are gathering together to see how we can help each other. I imagine that the room will be crawling with dangerous women, and that, at least, is a heartening thing and more of these rooms everywhere is where we need to be, together.

Chapter 14

Getting Ready

"LADIES AND GENTLEMEN, we are pleased to present the first-ever recipient of the Women's Media Center Pat Mitchell Lifetime Achievement Award, given to a media professional who has used her work to empower other women through media: Pat Mitchell!"

Healthy applause as the lights dimmed and a carefully curated video chronicling my twenty-five years in media began to play. All my greatest hits were there: my years in Boston, taking the stage at *Yes, We Can,* hosting *Woman to Woman,* peppering DC's famous and infamous with questions on *Panorama,* interviewing Fidel Castro, taking the stage at TEDWomen, and so much more. I should have been filled with pride. After all, here were hard-won triumphs from more than a quarter century of blazing trails, breaking barriers, being the first. Instead, a cruel inner monologue was playing in my head. Why did I wear that sparkly pink pantsuit? Oh my god, I look like a salmon-colored fullback with those huge shoulder pads! Ugh, my hair!

"How could one woman have that many different hairstyles?" I quipped at the podium. "Or bad wardrobe choices?"

I got a big laugh at the time but later wondered, how many times have we, in a moment of great accomplishment—delivering an important speech or accepting an award or hosting a forum or interviewing a world leader—been in our heads judging ourselves rather than being fully present for the full meaning of the moment, thinking instead, "What was I *thinking* with this outfit?"

So much of how we see ourselves and how others view us, like it or not, is to one degree or another determined by appearance. One good friend describes her morning makeup routine as "putting on her war paint." Another refers to dressing for the day as "girding for battle." But in this chapter, I want to set our preparations in a bigger, bolder context: getting ready! Getting ready to go out and fight the good fight. Getting ready to champion the causes that mean the most to us. Getting ready to get really personal, which I am going to do now. This part of my journey began that night when watching my career review. When I was receiving an award that means so much to me, but also worrying about how I looked and judging my choices, I decided to take this thorny issue of appearance head-on in order to truly get ready to be my most effective and dangerous self.

LOOKS HAVE ALWAYS been a loaded topic for me. One of my deepest, most difficult-to-disassemble confusions resulted from my girlhood identity as "Pretty Patsy." Pretty enough to attract comments and smiles from strangers . . . yes. Pretty enough to get attention from boys as I grew older, for sure, so what was the value of *pretty*? Had I been less attractive, would I have gotten the lead in the school play?

Once I got on TV in Boston, my appearance became the property of high-paid consultants who endlessly critiqued my hairstyle, makeup, and clothes—never what stories I should tell or how to communicate them more effectively. "Always wear scarves, darling. They give you a little color and look a little bit like men's neckties."

They wanted me to look like a man—hence the tie stand-ins —but also like a woman—but not *too* much, which meant a lot of blazers. They wanted me to look authoritative but not *too* authoritative, smart but not *too* smart, relatable but not *too* ordinary, attractive but not *too* distracting, colorful but not *too* colorful. If I wore the same thing multiple times in a month, I'd get a letter about it. "Wow, you really like that flowered blouse; you've worn it twice this month." Men never have to deal with that! And let me take a pause to give a shout-out to Australian news anchor Karl Stefanovic, who decided after his female coanchor reported on how viewers criticized her wardrobe, that he would wear the exact same outfit—a cheap navy-blue suit—every day on camera for an *entire year* to protest the sexism. *No one noticed!*

"I'm judged on my interviews, my appalling sense of humor—on how I do my job, basically," he told *People* magazine. "Whereas women are quite often judged on what they're wearing or how their hair is."

The ever-present reminder of my looks in comments or attempts by bosses and boyfriends or consultants to influence what I wore or how I styled my hair sowed deep doubts in me. The most lasting effect of being considered *pretty* was that I couldn't fully believe in my own accomplishments because my outward appearance didn't match my inner life. The conflict deepened with age.

I was forty-six when I returned to NBC to produce the *Woman to Woman* segments for *The Today Show*. I was doing well by all measurements, with good reviews and testing high on those pesky audience surveys that still influenced the fate of on-air personalities. I was even chosen to do some substitute hosting for Jane Pauley herself. Then my boss knocked on my door.

"You're over forty now," he remarked not so gently, "and a lot of women in television start to think about a little nip and tuck at this age. It might increase your chances of being named

Jane's replacement if she doesn't return to work." Jane was then on maternity leave.

I spent a few days depressed and looking too closely in the mirror, finally choosing to take the boss's advice and have a little nip and tuck to give my neck and eyes a more "youthful" look. I liked the results, and I got approving nods from management, but I didn't get the host job, and I was losing my enthusiasm for the "looks trump talent" dilemma that comes at some point to most women on television.

Shortly after the surgery, I decided to leave the network and devote my talents and time to work behind the camera, making documentaries. No more anchor blazers or scarves that looked like ties were needed to report from the front lines of conflict. My hair, of course—never easy to style in any way that survived bad weather or that didn't need strong hair dryers, curling irons, and lots of product—was pretty much a disaster throughout my travels as often none of those necessities were easily attainable. I was on camera from time to time in my first documentary, *Women in War*, but the good news is no one commented about my hair or clothes—at least not to me. Soon I stopped thinking so much about it, too, although I couldn't ever fully banish the judgmental narrative in my head.

MY INTERNAL NARRATIVE about my appearance isn't only about the TV critics or even the male gaze. My harshest judges have often been other women. More than once, I've been greeted with a head-to-toe appraisal by a sister in the feminist movement, too—judged for looking too dressed up or made up, interpreted by some as suspicious signs of subservience to the dictates of the patriarchy—as if there's a dress code for resistance or equality. When *Time* magazine chose Gloria Steinem for the cover story on the women's movement, the responses most often heard were about her hair, her aviator specs, her short shirt, and her good legs. Sadly, our physical appearances, wardrobe, hair, and yes, bodies, are far too often still the focus of comments and conversation about women political candidates and executives.

Let's be clear: there *is* no dress code or hairstyle that defines a feminist . . . although the press continues to try to impose one. Most importantly, I believe it's time to fess up about the time we've spent in the sisterhood talking about each other's appearance and recognize it as a big distraction and source of destructive divisiveness. We're still holding ourselves back, battling feelings of not looking good enough or not having the right clothes or worrying about what other people might say. Yes, if you're in a public-facing career, of course there will be comments, but the challenge for women in public spaces is how much attention is paid to it.

Read the research that the Women's Media Center did on the unequal amount of attention the press gives to women candidates' hair and wardrobe and how unfair and judgmental—and ultimately damaging—this attention can be for a candidate trying to bring attention to her policies and platforms . . . and I don't mean shoes! Numerous studies, such as those from Presidential Gender Watch 2016, indicate strong bias in how women candidates for office are covered. Witness the sexist language used to describe Secretary Hillary Clinton, with criticism of her "cankles," "cackle," and cleavage. Given this bias, I'm not surprised that our numbers at the tops of companies and countries are still shockingly low. Even in 2018, with the largest number of women elected to serve in the US Congress, the reports from their swearing-ins and first weeks on the job included a lot of attention to their clothing choices. And the focus on women leaders' appearance and wardrobe isn't only in the United States.

In the online magazine *BRIGHT*, Rula Ghani, the first lady of Afghanistan, discusses her choice to wear a headscarf to an international development conference called Devex World. She did so to make a point—that a veiled woman "can have ideas and can express herself." As First Lady Ghani told the interviewer, "What I have noticed in my not-very-short life is that people react to who they're meeting based on what they're wearing, and how they're dressed, and what kind of shoes they have. I think it's really the wrong attitude. . . . People attribute all sorts of opinions and ideas to women wearing headscarves that are probably very far from what they're actually thinking." This independent, brilliant woman is choosing to make a powerful statement about her values by wearing her headscarf while engaging world leaders with her ideas for promoting a better future for Afghanistan. The same judgments about whether Muslim women leaders should cover their head have been leveled at the extraordinarily effective Queen Rania of Jordan. She has responded to questions about her lack of head cover with the statement, "I'm more concerned about what is in my head than what is on it." And she proves how much is in her head and in her heart by speaking up for the world's refugee populations, and for supporting girls' education and women's empowerment programs and by staying true to her faith and being focused on positive outcomes for her country.

These women leaders aren't denying the importance of appearance as a leader, but they are prioritizing what matters most. For me, finding a style that reflected what mattered most to me became a priority.

I DECIDED TO view my choices of wardrobe and hairstyle by how closely they reflected what I did or wanted to do. I've given away every structured jacket in my closet. I never felt like somebody who wore those blazers, but it was how executive women were described in every profile I'd ever read: "in her well-tailored suit." I tried so hard as a CEO and president to conform to that made-up standard. Now I've given that up; I've donated all the TV anchor and executive suits and blazers to the nonprofit Dress for Success, which offers important clothing options for women without the means to have a lot of choices and who want to apply for jobs where having a well-tailored suit might make a difference.

For the last ten years or so, as I've made going global a part of my life, my clothes have to be easy to pack and ready to wear when I arrive in Africa or India or Colombia or the Congo. Dresses that roll up and don't wrinkle are a staple. One color scheme per trip, so one pair of heels and flats. I confess I haven't given up heels—being short in stature and enjoying feeling a little taller, and having grown up in the South where you wore heels from an early age, I'm actually as comfortable in them as flats. But I must also confess another aspect of growing up in the deep South is that my feet are accustomed to being barefoot—and these days, I've been known to entertain at home in a total lack of footwear.

One of the most positive aspects of coordinating my travel with my work with women around the world has been diversifying my accessory choices. I buy scarves and jewelry that reflect the style and the culture of places I visit. It's a way of extending the experiences—keeping Jordan with me because I'm wearing a Jordanian designer's earrings or remembering visits to women's collectives in Kenya and South Africa because I met the women who made the bracelets and necklaces. This is how I bring home a part of every journey, every adventure—and a big part of the way I prepare for another one. I call these accessories my *special effects*, a term I borrow from my friend Jacqueline Novogratz, whom you met in Chapter 12. She told me her young niece had referred to her stylish ethnic jewelry as her *special effects* and that felt just right for me, too.

I even joined the board of the Alliance for Artisans so that I could learn even more about the amazing artisans around the world and offer some support other than purchasing their creations, which I still do, of course. Through the alliance's network of artisans, I can support initiatives that create new opportunities for women carrying on important traditions and skills. Buying such products has a double positive special effect—it feels good to wear or carry these works of art, and even better to know that the money spent for the purchase is providing a school or a hospital and, at the very least, employment and independence for the artisan who made it.

For three years, Peggy Clark, who leads the Artisan Alliance, created Global Showcases at TEDWomen conferences so that attendees could meet the artisans, learn about their work, purchase their art, and support their communities. TEDWomen attendees positively responded, and considering the annual revenues reported from these kinds of opportunities, women everywhere buy more when they know their money is going to good causes. According to a recent Case Foundation report, women seek out brands "that—directly or indirectly—promote physical and emotional well-being, protect and preserve the environment, provide education and care for the needy, and encourage love and connection."

Susan Hull Walker, who founded the Ibu Movement (*Ibu* comes from the Malay word for "woman of respect") to help women from thirty-five different countries achieve economic self-sufficiency through sales of their artisanal designs, captured in one of her weekly blogs the special appeal that I feel when I buy something another woman created.

"*To bead . . . or not to bead.* That is the question. For me, I will side with the work of beads; the word, as you may know, means *prayer*, and so to bead is to pray, a legacy coming down to us from the rosary. In the long, slow, painstaking work of ornamentation, a woman is not just making her world more beautiful; she is making it more *hers.* She is connecting the tiny dots of her life into an expansive, liberating story of who she is and what powers she commands and where she sits in this world."

FOR ME, CONNECTING the dots from my earlier fretting about wardrobe choices and hairstyle changes to the *special effects* styles I adopt today likewise exemplifies so many important parts of my life story, including the way I think about getting older.

I started to observe the special power of older women during a series of stories I produced and hosted for NBC's *The Today Show.* No one wanted to do this series, reminding me often that older women weren't an important consumer group for advertisers. Nevertheless, I persisted. The first one I profiled started an important internal shift for me in my thinking about what life could be after sixty, seventy, eighty, or even ninety.

I met the fabulous and famous ceramist, Beatrice Wood, when she had just celebrated her ninety-eighth birthday. This highly regarded painter and actress had first sat down at a potter's wheel in her mid-sixties and had become one of the few ceramists to have her pots displayed in the Smithsonian and around the world. I drove out to see her in her pink adobe home on a mountaintop in Ojai, where she greeted me at the door, clad in a gorgeous sari, with clashing, clanging bangles running up both arms. She introduced the handsome, much younger man standing behind her as her partner—and she wasn't referring to business.

"Women should only wear saris," Beatrice declared when I admired hers. "Saris hide all the flaws." Every day, clad in a different vibrant sari, she'd sit at her potter's wheel and throw pots, unheeding of the spattering clay. Beatrice became one of my earliest models for being a powerful older woman. She didn't care what people thought or said; she was bold and spoke her truth.

"What is your secret to living to one hundred?" I asked at her annual birthday party. "Chocolate and young men," she answered.

Visiting Beatrice in Ojai became a treasured annual pilgrimage. One year I brought my new romantic partner, soon to be husband, Scott. "Pat!" Beatrice exclaimed. "You've always brought chocolate. *Finally* you brought me a young man!" Beatrice lived fully engaged, still taking risks and throwing her extraordinary pots, until she was 105. Because of her influence, I have a closet shelf full of saris, and every time I can find any excuse to wear one, I do, but with consideration of the issues of cultural appropriation: I'm careful to acknowledge with great admiration the women for whom saris are a part of a national and personal identity.

The personal-identity question for older women has profoundly shifted in the past few years, redefined by more older women at the top of organizations. When Susan Zirinsky took over CBS News in March 2019, she became the first woman, and the oldest person, to hold the job.

Her appointment was announced just days after Nancy Pelosi, seventy-eight, was reelected Speaker of the House of Representatives, making her the most powerful elected woman in US history. Meanwhile, Representative Maxine Waters became the first woman and African American to lead the House Committee on Financial Services, at age eighty.

Additionally, in the same week of all this good news about older women in political leadership, seventy-one-year-old Glenn Close received the Golden Globe for best actress, winning over four younger women in the film business, which, until recently, was obsessed with and has a long history of prizing youth.

But the demographic changes in the global population are creating seismic shifts in the way older women are viewed in nearly every country and in the opportunities we now have to create a big shift in every aspect of global life and culture. Statistics indicate that there are more women over fifty in the United States today than at any other point in history, according to data from the United States Census Bureau, and at least in the United States, older women are healthier, are working longer, and have more income than previous generations.

"Age—don't worry about it. It's a state of mind," Ms. Zirinsky was quoted as saying when asked about the effect of her age on her new job leading CBS News. "I have so much energy that my staff did an intervention when I tried a Red Bull."

Because of a greater focus on health and well-being, exercise, and just taking better care of ourselves, age is becoming less defined by looks, too. I notice that older women have a kind of vibrancy and energy that comes from within, maybe as a result of having less of the mothering and nurturing responsibilities that fill so much of our earlier lives and of finding unconditional love and joy in our roles as grandmothers, which is, as one of my friends describes it, "our reward for surviving the adolescent years as mothers."

I have also noticed that men age differently. We used to think this was a good thing—"men get better looking with age; women just look older" was a prevailing mythology, certainly in Hollywood: note the numbers of gray-haired leading men romantically linked to women young enough to be their daughters, an on-screen reality that is still mirrored offscreen in lots of May/December partnerships.

What seems to be shifting in the gender-based aging paradigm is that more and more older women are still eager to stay engaged and active while the men in their lives would rather play a round of golf or take a nap or stay home. I'm glad that's not true of my husband, but it's a phenomenon to ponder in terms of the long-term impact of longer lives on much longer life partnerships than any generations before us experienced.

You most certainly don't need a life partner to be happy, as many women and men are choosing a different path, but if you're going to have one, let me add to the "getting ready" suggestions that you find someone fully supportive of who you are, inside and out! As a woman who never received unconditional love from the first man in her life, her father, I gave away my power far too many times to please a romantic partner, sometimes changing my appearance; once or twice, a career direction; or even whom I spent time with or didn't. I look back on those relationships not with regrets, since gratefully I chose essentially good men who never abused, demeaned, or even judged me as harshly as I judged myself. But I was too much of a pleaser, and that sometimes got in the way of being prepared.

Before I met Scott, at age fifty-four, I had decided that I felt more powerful, more whole, actually, and happier without a life partner—that I would be single and have a full life of work I loved and friends I enjoyed. But then I met the man who changed everything about what I knew or thought I knew about love and true partnership.

With Scott, I am more powerful, more whole, and happier than I have ever been. I never have to hide or diminish my power so as to make him feel bigger and better, and he is always 100 percent supportive of me, my work, my dreams and ambitions. I've certainly never had a greater fan than Scott. He records all my speeches and every moment of celebration or me in the spotlight and sends videos around to all his friends and family, eager to show me off and spread news of the work I'm involved with. I've never met anyone so dedicated, so caring, so up for anything!

But I wasn't sure I was ready for marriage and neither was Scott. By the time he proposed, his four older children were either married or finishing college or working, and he had two granddaughters. But when we first began seeing each other, there was one child still at home—eight-year-old Clark. Clark had not been enthusiastic about our romance, fearing a loss of his dad's time. (He'd also told me he preferred his father's earlier girlfriend, who owned her own private plane; I told him I agreed that was a solid choice.) Scott was wise enough to realize Clark just needed time—and so did we. It was nearly seven years after we started dating that he asked me to marry him.

We had a special wedding at Sundance. Three hundred friends came, and it was an unforgettable weekend, beginning with an American Indian ceremony with family and then a wedding program written by Eve Ensler and performed by various friends and family, including Eve, Jane Fonda, Marilyn and Alan Bergman (who sang their famous song, "What Are You Doing the Rest of Your Life?"), Sir Jeremy Isaacs (my co–executive producer of the Cold War series), his wife and co-producer Gillian, all of Scott's children, the new grandchildren who had arrived during our courtship, and my son, Mark.

Parts of the ceremony featured Eve at her most *provocative*, and my mother, already a bit hard of hearing, asked loudly in the middle of one of the poems Eve had written for me, "What is she talking about?" I'll leave the answer to your imagination.

Among the vows that we wrote and spoke to each other that day was a promise that we would redo the vows and the wedding every seven years. Scott had observed that I changed jobs roughly every seven years—and since science says every cell in our bodies is replaced every seven years, there is something real in that seven-year itch.

So seven years later, we sent out invitations saying "Pat and Scott Are Getting Remarried—to Each Other!" Our second ceremony was at Sundance, just like the first. The third was at Massimo Ferragamo's restored Italian village, Castiglion del Bosco, where Bunker Roy, founder of Barefoot College, did the ceremony and all the guests were attired in saris—thank you, Beatrice!

I'm quite sure I would not have become as bold as I am without the partner I have. Scott is nurturing by nature. His five children give him both Father's Day and Mother's Day cards because he raised them as a single father; and they respect and recognize the role he played and still plays in their lives. If I tell him I'm going to the Congo for ten days, he never questions my decision or whines about how long I'll be away. When I'm having meetings at the house—which is often—he'll say, "Don't spend your time cleaning up the kitchen; I'll take care of that." He believes in splitting household chores 50/50, but if I'm being completely honest—and I am—he does much more, like 80/20 on the household stuff. I confess that I'm not sure how to operate the washing machine, and as he reminds me frequently, "I do my best thinking while folding the laundry or making the bed."

But don't be misled; Scott is also a great businessman and a committed and highly engaged environmental leader, the CEO of a company he started and a force on multiple environmental boards. He's as passionate and purposeful about saving the planet as I am about supporting and advocating for women and girls. As a chemical engineer, he's innovating ways to reuse resources (which sometimes means our pantry is a lab for growing veggies without dirt) and making coatings for grocery bags to make them compostable. He lives his values, and at the center of our fully engaged life is a mutual love and respect that tops my gratitude list every day.

LOVE AS WE age is one thing. Hair is another. Let's talk about it.

For me, it's been a lifetime challenge and barrier to many things, including, perhaps, all the potential accomplishments listed above and more. During my on-camera career, I tried every style—from Jane Fonda's *Klute* shag, which never worked, to Julie Andrews's marmalade pixie (the color orange was terrible on me). Nothing worked well. My hair was always fixed, but only after hours of effort.

Then I hit menopause and started to lose my already thin hair. One day during my annual physical at the Mayo Clinic in Rochester, Minnesota, I stopped in a wig shop. I started trying them on and found one that was the style of my dreams—the one I could get close to on my best hair days. I bought it, and this was a life-changing purchase. For less than three hundred dollars, I avoided spending hundreds more dollars for monthly colors and cuts, and an endless supply of hair-thickening products and hair spray, and more hours than I can calculate on blow-drying, curling, and spraying. The wig is wash-and-wear; I shampoo mine and it returns to its original style in a few hours. With this single purchase, I got back at least an additional *hour* in every day, not to mention that I eliminated so much stress and gave myself more time to focus on what was important. I haven't even begun to calculate the money I've saved already.

Now I want to be clear that I am not suggesting that this is a solution for every woman similarly struggling with her hair, but I am suggesting that for me, the ability to pop on a great-looking wig in five minutes and use the other fifty-five minutes to prepare a speech, create the agenda for a meeting, or write this book or any other more worthwhile activity has been a game changer in my life. That's why, in the spirit of speaking my truth and sharing my story, I'm going public with this "getting ready" secret.

My longtime struggle to better align external appearance—and the time devoted to it—with internal values gets a boost from my "wig" solution, especially when I'm in Eastern Congo, visiting City of Joy, and spending time with the always inspiring survivors of sexual violence. Beautiful women, inside and out. How they manage to keep their colorful pagnes so neatly pressed is their secret, given the power outages and water shortages, but what is even more impressive is how their inner strength, resilience, and courage radiate from every part of their presence. I could be bald and feel beautiful in their presence, but I love popping on the wig, often over unwashed hair, and dancing with them in the rain with abandon.

When I shared the story of my new "friend" and the difference it had made in my life and in getting ready with my other good friend Elizabeth Nyamayaro, the deputy executive director for UN Women, she laughed and said, "Pat, what took you so long? You're just realizing what African women have known for generations. Hair can be your biggest distraction or a great asset and you just have to use it." Elizabeth recently cut off her long hair that she spent lots of time straightening to go for an African version of a buzz cut. When she walked into her office at UN Women with her striking new do, a colleague shot her a horrified look and said, "Elizabeth, you can't go to a UN meeting with that haircut, you know, it's too African!" She went to the meeting, and everywhere she goes, she looks great—and powerful. When I get tired of this wig style, I might try a buzz cut too!

What I'm trying to share is that in this one, small way, I've aligned time and purpose with a practical solution that works for me. I might not have been able to embrace such a solution earlier in my life, but when it comes to clothes and hair,

I'm newly liberated from worry about what others think or the expectations of jobs or bosses or even children or grandchildren—although my grandchildren do approve of my *special effects* and have nominated me for inclusion in the *New York Times* Glamorous Grandmas of Instagram!

GETTING READY TAKES less time, for sure, but managing time remains a challenge.

Having been a CEO for twenty-one years, I'd always had someone helping me manage my overscheduled schedule. When I left the Paley Center for Media, I thought, "Oh, I can get along without an assistant." After all, I was retiring from the daily grind. That lasted less than a month. Could I do it? Sure. Could I be as engaged, effective, determined? No!

When I finally realized I needed administrative help, I had to figure out how to pay for it. How could I afford an assistant anymore, when it was coming out of my own funds set aside for my later life? But I realized this was money I needed to invest in myself.

I advise everyone to make an honest assessment of whether they're giving themselves all the tools and support they need, really investing in themselves, in order to be effective in the world. Creating more time to do what matters should be a line item in your time budget. Figure out what you can pay someone else to do, do without, barter, or do a just-good-enough job on so that you can free yourself up and get ready.

Getting ready means that today I own a pair of boots that resemble the ones the protesters wore during the *Yes, We Can* broadcast as they marched to the stage and joked about my TV-friendly but dreadful pastel pink pantsuit. They judged me on appearance, and I had judged them the same way. No more! Those boots come in handy when walking through the farm that V-Day bought and donated back to City of Joy in Bukavu, a farm that the women and girls have made so productive that it is providing food for the whole community.

In some ways, all my fashion statements today are about place and story, not about what's fashionable or trendy or even age appropriate. What does that mean, anyway? I've had my share of fashion mishaps, and one stands out in my memory and that of my friends who witnessed it.

We were attending a V-Day gala when Eve decided to surprise me with a Vagina Warrior Award. As I practically ran from my chair to the stage to accept the award from Eve and good friend Glenn Close, I noticed they were staring at the scarf on my shoulder. At least I had assumed it was a scarf, but apparently, I'd grabbed in haste from the huge stack of scarves on my shelves without noticing the grommets on the hem where the rings go to hang it. It was a shower curtain! Glenn Close, laughing out loud, asked, "Is that a *shower curtain* you're wearing?" How could I deny it? A standing ovation followed, and I'm sure that in part I was being applauded for going onstage with a shower curtain colorfully draped on one shoulder—a curtain that now hangs in a shower at home and always makes me smile.

Getting ready now means that I'm old enough—no, free enough—to wear what I want, dress as I please, pop on a wig or get a buzz cut, dress up or dress down with equal fun because what matters is whether my outside appearance is aligning with my place, my story, my purpose, and my priorities. I wish I had come to this place of outside-inside alignment much earlier on my journey, and it's my strong hope that in getting personal, I've given you some new ways to think about getting ready.

DANGEROUS TIMES CALL FOR DANGEROUS WOMEN

In Conversation with Ruth Ann Harnisch

Ruth Ann is a fellow media-industry glass-ceiling crasher. The first woman ever to anchor the evening news in Nashville, Tennessee,

Ruth Ann spent two decades as a news anchor, radio talk-show host, reporter, columnist, and coach (she continues to offer pro bono services to support women and girls). In 1998, she became president of the Harnisch Foundation, which focuses on diversity, gender equity, and racial equality. She's also a cofounder of SupporTED, which offers coaching and mentoring to TED fellows. Plus her Awesome Foundation offers one thousand dollars to women-owned start-ups, helping Ruth Ann earn the sobriquet of "the punk-rock fairy godmother of feminism."

When I think of women who know how to reframe definitions, I think of Ruth Ann.

Do you think of yourself as a dangerous woman?

Ruth Ann: I've always been a dangerous person because I will always speak my truth. I will speak against what I think is unfair, unjust, discriminatory, not great for humanity, for peace on Earth, goodwill toward all. And that's always dangerous to people of privilege, whether that privilege comes from their skin color, age, status, or wealth.

Nobody wants to trade their power. Anybody who's white and my age has had to have a tremendous reeducation about race and how much invisible privilege has advantaged anyone with white skin in the United States. The idea of reparations is terrifying to people. What could be more dangerous than justice if you have been on the wrong side of it?

We need to be dangerous to the status quo. Dangerous to privilege. Dangerous to traditional gender roles, which for some people is a matter of religious truth. At this stage of my life, I feel called to use any power I have to give voice to those who have been waiting in line behind me. I used to hope that those who had privilege and power would be generous enough, big enough to give others a chance. Some gave me a chance; now it's my turn to step back and use whatever I've got to be even more inclusive.

What does danger feel like in your life now?

Ruth Ann: What makes me dangerous now is the ability to do things that I couldn't have done when all I had was an opinion. Money equals power. Women have traditionally been herded to spend what little money we get on making ourselves conventionally attractive. We get tricked into wearing expensive shoes that make it hard for us to keep up. We get tricked into wearing clothes that change with the seasons, while men don't invest in their wardrobes in that way. We get tricked into expensive grooming, makeup, hair color, and style.

It's expensive to be a girl, to be an attractive woman, to try to stay relevant. That ties up our money and keeps us from investing in what really counts in ourselves.

Now I own my age. I also own that the real power in this age is recognizing that there's no way that I can be as relevant. It's as impossible as if I were trying to be a teenager. I cannot inhabit the consciousness of that younger self. Part of my power is in self-awareness. Part of my power is in money, knowing where to apply it, knowing that I have to invest in creating power for others. That's where my big investments that are going to change anything have to be. I invest in leaders and leaderful communities, not in myself.

Is there an age component to being dangerous?

Ruth Ann: I used to be young and cute. Being an attractive female was a certain kind of power and currency. I had television, then radio, then newspaper, all available as currency that people wanted to trade. That was powerful, but it's nothing like the obsequious seeking when one has money. There's a joke that says when you become head of the Ford Foundation, you've eaten your last bad meal and told your last unfunny joke, because when you control that kind of money, everybody wants to take you out to dinner and thinks you're the funniest.

What role does financial well-being play in becoming more dangerous?

Ruth Ann: I'm very respectful of that power because I used to be broke, and I know how low it feels, how uneven it feels when the power differential is money. I know how it feels to go hat in hand. I try to use the power of money responsibly and kindly and, for the most part, I try to use it to give people the same kind of opportunities I had, to rewrite their own stories, to find ways to their own power.

Chapter 15

Playing It Forward

"PAT, I WANT to know: Of all the things you've done, what are you proudest of?"

Courtney Martin and I sat close together, our knees almost touching, inside the StoryCorps recording booth. Looking into the eyes of this brilliant, impassioned young woman who inspires so many others through her editing of Feministing.com, her books, and the diverse communities she connects and strengthens, I did feel a sense of pride—not in her accomplishments, which are all her own, or even in mine, but in knowing her and in sharing this conversation about mentoring.

"You once joked that I should make a map of my mentees," I answered, "and I'd love to look at that map, because then I would see a legacy that I'm not sure I'd see in anything else, including the television programs or the documentaries and all the things I'm proud to have been a part of. Those fade; they become the past so quickly. Lives don't, and lives that are changed pass on to the next life touched, and the next. I think I might be proudest of the mentees I've had the opportunity to know and advise and work with. Like you."

I'M QUITE SURE I never heard the word *mentor* while growing up in the fifties in small-town Georgia, but luckily, as I've shared, Mrs. Reid, my eighth-grade English teacher, was the mentor who changed the direction of my life.

I've likewise taken my responsibility to mentor other women (and a few men) quite seriously. In fact, as I tell the organizations with which I consult on the role of women in business, I believe mentoring is one of the strategies that can close the gender gap in leadership in this country and around the world.

Mentoring is one lever we can activate to advance more women in their work, to gain access to capital and economic opportunities they might otherwise miss, and to be better prepared for opportunities when they come. I believe that one of the responsibilities of being a woman who is committed to working toward a more just world is being willing to be a mentor when and where needed. All of us, mentees and mentors, are dangerous women in the making or already boldly declared to be in the sisterhood. We need the support of each other at a fundamental level that goes beyond mentoring and even beyond sponsorship.

Sponsors are what leading Morgan Stanley banker Carla Harris calls colleagues inside organizations who will speak up for others, who are prepared to be more than a mentor. Sponsors are our representatives, our agents, our committed advocates. Harris has been using her sphere of influence and her powerful woman's voice to call for sponsors as well as mentors. "Mentoring," she says, "won't be enough to ensure that you'll get the promotion or the raise you deserve. We need *sponsors*." I recommend Carla's TED Talk, given at TEDWomen 2018, for more instructions on how to be a sponsor and how to get one.

Today I'm committed to being a mentor and a sponsor for other women as a big part of engaging further with my passion and purpose.

How can you be a great mentor? Or a great mentee? With so much at stake, let me share with you some straightforward, how-to advice from my personal experiences as both.

Being a Mentor Takes Time

It's important to specify when and how often you're available to meet with your mentee, and your preferred way of connecting (phone, Skype, Zoom, email, in person, etc.). Are you talking about just a few meetings, or a long-term mentoring relationship that could last months or even years? This is a chance to set clear boundaries; it's all too easy to answer one more email, make one more phone call. If you don't enforce your boundaries, mentoring can quickly become a time suck that leaves you feeling resentful instead of empowered—and certainly not dangerous.

Juliet Asante was one of the first mentees assigned to me when I agreed to be a mentor in a program launched jointly by *Fortune*'s Most Powerful Women conference, the Vital Voices Global Partnership, and the State Department. Juliet was a Ghanaian television and film personality who also owned her own production company and wanted to learn more about how to grow her business, which was producing television series targeted at women in West Africa. This seemed like a good match for my background.

The first time we met, Juliet set down in front of me a single-spaced list of names that covered both sides of a sheet of paper. "During our work together, I would like to meet these people in the United States," she told me. The list started with Obama and ended with Oprah! How could I not love that chutzpah and confidence?

That began what became a two-year official mentoring relationship, with Juliet coming to New York once a month. We'd talk through specific challenges in managing her production company. I also arranged for her to meet with people on her list, walking her through every step so she could make the most of her often-limited time.

I also reached out to each professional connection to give them a heads-up. In some instances, we playacted the meeting; I changed her script if it was either too presumptuous or didn't indicate a deep enough understanding about this particular person's scope of experience or responsibilities. We reviewed the background of every person she met, looking for points on which Juliet could personally or professionally connect so that the meeting had a shared value: in other words, the colleague who'd agreed to give up some of her own precious time might also learn something new or gain a new perspective.

Eventually I did arrange for Juliet to meet and spend time with nearly everyone on her list. Yes, even President Obama, when she was invited to a White House event to recognize this special State Department mentoring program. Juliet used her five minutes with our first African American president well, giving him a quick update on Ghana's presidential election and sharing a quick reflection on how much his first trip there had meant to her and her country. There was no doubt this smart, talented, personally dynamic mentee from Ghana made a positive impression on President Obama.

Oprah was a bigger challenge. We lucked out; Oprah had just established the Oprah Winfrey Leadership Academy for Girls, her school in South Africa, and she was interested in hearing Juliet's perspective on the school and its mission. They had a productive conversation, although Oprah declined to be interviewed on Juliet's Ghanaian television program. She did agree to a photograph that Juliet circulated widely on social media, elevating her following for sure.

Relying on my personal contacts, connections, and friends to supplement in areas where my advice is more limited is always a part of my mentoring process. In Juliet's case, it became an easier decision to connect her with helpful friends and colleagues because I took the time to develop a relationship with Juliet, got a solid sense of her abilities and work ethic, and felt confident that the connection would benefit both parties and that Juliet would treat the introduction with the utmost respect it deserved.

Like me, you've probably spent decades building strong relationships with others. These are your gold; protect them. I had to rein in Juliet's ambitions and expectations once or twice, for example, her request to meet Warren Buffett. Again: you're allowed to enforce a boundary and say no.

Juliet has just been appointed chair of the National Film and Television Institute, started the successful Black Star Film Festival in Ghana, and I am urging her to use her personal power and influence to enter politics and be a force for needed change.

Being a Mentor Means Matching Your Skills and Interests

Check in with yourself before accepting a mentee. Do you have the right skills to help this person, or will you be running yourself ragged trying to find the right answers to her questions? Are you genuinely interested in what your mentee is trying to achieve? If someone looks good on paper but the face-to-face meeting leaves you cold, you're allowed to say, "I don't think I'm the right person to help you." Why waste the mentee's time with a half-hearted, less connected, or less informed mentorship? Find someone who makes the experience mutually rewarding.

Being a Mentor Is About Suggesting, Not Instructing

Resist the urge to provide direct advice. Instead, offer supportive advice so that your mentee has the information to make her own decisions, which she'll then be able to stand by with greater confidence.

Catalina Escobar came through the same State Department/Fortune mentorship program. Catalina had a foundation committed to ending the cycle of violence, unwanted teen pregnancies, and endemic and intergenerational poverty in her home country of Colombia. She'd already served thousands of girls by the time she arrived in my office. She looked like she belonged on the cover of *Inc.*—wholly professional and beautifully and elegantly dressed—and she was all business.

Catalina wanted specific mentoring on how to raise awareness of the challenges in her country so she could expand her programs to other countries and become a global leader for change. We made a plan to get her a speaking coach so that she could put herself forward at global conferences on women and girls. I took her to conferences, introduced her around, and she began to plan a conference of her own. Catalina named it Women Working for the World. It was successful both as a fundraiser for her Juanfe Foundation and as a global gathering of women; it's now in its fifth year and has become the standard-bearer for women coming together to share best practices, to form collaborations across country borders, to support women working for a better world, everywhere.

Catalina didn't need a typical mentor because she'd already created a structure for her foundation, shaped a successful intervention, and proven that her model worked with positive outcomes. What she needed—and this is often the case—was some outside perspectives on how to raise awareness and funding, which I was able to provide.

Being a Mentor Is About Asking Smart Questions, Not Having All the Answers

You will help your mentee more by listening closely and asking questions than by having the answer for everything. I learned this lesson when one mentee turned the tables on me at our meeting. "Could you please ask all the questions instead of me?" she said.

"Why?" I asked, a bit taken aback.

"Because I need to know what questions to ask," she explained. "I can google the answers."

I see my job as a mentor as helping my mentee find her own answers! I'll walk her through the list of questions she'll need to ask, problems she'll need to address, people she'll need to talk to, etc. I want to empower her to have the confidence that she can figure it all out, not spoon-feed her every answer.

Not All Mentorship Ends with a Sense of Satisfaction for the Mentor or the Mentee

Sometimes, mentoring relationships end in frustration. You pour your heart and soul into mentoring someone, and their project doesn't get off the ground. Or the two of you never gel. Or you hear from others that your mentee overstepped. Or you're not able to provide enough of what your mentee wants or needs.

It happens. And when it does, try to resist the urge to fix it by plowing more time and effort into it. Instead, be gracious: "I'm so sorry, but I've come to the end of what I can offer you." The more experience I gain as a mentor, the sooner I realize that a particular mentee-mentor relationship isn't going to be productive or positive and the sooner I can tactfully pull the plug.

You're a Mentor, Not a Mother

It's important to remember that mentees are not your children and mentors are not therapists. This was the hardest lesson for me because I do tend to fall a bit in love with all my mentees, and I value and sustain personal friendships and connections. But I've learned to keep marriages, personal relationships, etc.

off-limits unless intricately related to their business or social enterprise. I try above all to be clear about what I have time to do and what I cannot take on.

As a mother and grandmother, I have to resist mothering, because when I don't, the outcome is a blurring of roles and responsibilities. This hurts my mentee because it degrades her sense of agency and accountability. It hurts me because it takes an emotional toll and eats up a lot of my psychic energy.

Being a Mentor Can Result in Lifelong Relationships that Continue to Nurture and Empower Both Mentee and Mentor

Case in point: I mentioned Courtney Martin at the beginning of this chapter. I recently led a discussion with her on inclusive leadership at the Makers Conference, the annual gathering whose mission is to lead the modern feminist movement to bring women together across all walks of life, in all industries, to advance the agenda of achieving true equality. It's not uncommon for mentors and mentees to become collaborators! I've worked with Courtney to curate and host sessions on several TEDWomen conferences, and our StoryCorps conversation about our relationship remains one of the most emotionally satisfying experiences of my life.

Sitting in that small room with a mic between us, sharing what we had meant to each other, tears and laughter flowed along with the memories of times shared, conversations cherished, and differences made in each other's lives because we came to know each other—first as mentee/mentor, but very quickly and very importantly as friends bound by mutual respect and admiration. This is what good mentoring is all about.

Getting More from the Mentor-Mentee Experience

I'm often asked how to find a good mentor, and the good news is that many organizations now offer mentoring opportunities.

You can find them by contacting trade organizations, career development offices, and the like.

Prepare Before You Approach

The women I most like to mentor are those who have put in the hours to achieve a certain level of proficiency in their field. As a mentee, I expect you to have been working in your field for at least a few years—long enough that you have a fairly firm grasp on benchmarks and ultimate goals; you know what you don't know; and you have a game plan for how you want to get there. You've identified the skills and people you need to help you attain your goals.

Before seeking a specific mentor, I suggest a thorough research of who's the best fit for your needs. You should have enough familiarity with your proposed mentor to know her priorities and existing commitments so that you can shape a reasonable, achievable request.

Appreciate Your Ask

Some of us mentors have a shared weakness: we want to help! We don't like saying no because we've had so many doors slammed in our faces and we remember all too well what it was like when we were young, hungry, and often lacked our own role models to look up to. That means we can be soft touches. Know that you're asking someone for precious time from her (probably overcrowded) schedule and full life. Even when you're asking someone to "take a quick look" at your resume, know that that's no small thing; that's an hour out of a life.

When you're asking for a sustaining mentorship, you're asking for even more of someone's precious time over months or years. Time they could be spending growing their own business, or with loved ones, or contributing to a worthy cause, or making money. That's a big deal. So don't take advantage.

Be Bold but Respectful

I remember when networking parties were big. You came laden with business cards and it was a whirlwind of activity as you danced from group to group, meeting other businesspeople, hoping to make useful connections. By the end of the evening, your purse was stuffed with other people's cards, your face ached from (sometimes forced) smiling, and you left feeling more than a little overwhelmed. Whenever I went to those things, I'd realize after I left that I too often missed what I'd come for: true connection. I wasn't just there to meet the right people so I could get ahead; I wanted to find others who shared my vision and values. If someone approached me just to get to the people I knew, I knew that, and it was a big turnoff.

In today's business gatherings, there are fewer business cards. "Just type in your email here," they say as they hand you their phone. Or "Would you take a selfie and then I'll text it to you and we'll be connected!"

I love technology, but honestly, are these really shortcuts or time-savers? Not for me. I'd rather return home with a bag of interesting business cards and enter them thoughtfully into my contacts. For a true social-media lover, I know this is counter revolutionary, but the fact is that I did design my business cards to say something meaningful about me—each one with a carefully selected quote about power on the back. I actually think about which quote to give which person who might ask for one. So for some of us older women, it might be good to give us options for remembering our encounter.

Be Clear and Specific in Your Requests

I've had several mentees start out by saying, "I want to know everything you know, Pat." Frankly, that prospect is overwhelming. But I appreciate a mentee identifying very specific things you're looking for in the mentoring relationship, the approximate amount of time you think you'll need, and samples of the kinds of questions you need help answering.

It's a good idea to prepare the agenda before every meeting and confirm which times work best for your mentor, and if your mentor has an assistant who can act as a go-between, all the better to establish that as the logistical point for questions and planning.

Give Your Mentor an Out

Always create an easy way for your prospective mentor to say no. (Again, we women sometimes have the disease to please when it comes to setting boundaries.) "Listen, I know how busy you are. Please don't feel you need to say yes to this." "I'm guessing you're already mentoring several other women. If you ever have any time in your schedule for me, I hope you'll be in touch." This level of graciousness and understanding goes a long way, and could turn a no into a yes!

Respect the No

Please appreciate that as much as your mentor wants to help you, she can't always satisfy every request. If your mentor can't do something you've requested, respect the no. You can ask, "Is there anything you think I should do to be better prepared for the request?"

Express Gratitude

Mentoring is a voluntary, unpaid position. It's really important to express gratitude to the person who's taken her valuable time to show you the ropes. No one's expecting a big, expensive present, but a thoughtful gesture can mean so much. Maybe take your mentor out for coffee, or buy her flowers or chocolate. I truly treasure the handwritten notes my mentees have sent me; I have a colleague who keeps hers in a box and takes them out to reread them when she's having a bad day!

I'll say it again: mentoring is perhaps the single biggest lever for positive change we have as women. I encourage all women—particularly those of us with more time available for changing other lives—to consider mentoring. And I encourage women of all ages to identify those mentors who model something important in your development, personally and professionally, and figure out how to make a mentor-mentee relationship successful.

Mentors and mentees, sponsors, advocates, colleagues, friends—dangerous women working for the world, and for each other.

DANGEROUS TIMES CALL FOR DANGEROUS WOMEN

In Conversation with Meagan Fallone

When I think of playing it forward, of someone doing the work of creating opportunities for learning and empowering women in the Global South and around the world—in particular empowering those with little or no access to education, economic agency, or even equal protections, I think of my friend Meagan Fallone, who is currently the head of Barefoot College International, an institution founded by Bunker Roy in 1972 to meet the needs of illiterate and underserved populations. Today, Barefoot operates programs in rural villages across ninety-six countries. It enables women to prosper and reach their aspirations through technical mastery and the development of their enterprise and critical-thinking skills. Training women to be solar engineers and develop sustainable secondary livelihoods has given more than 2 million people access to skills, clean water, and reliable, clean energy. Meagan has multiplied Barefoot's impact through extraordinary partnerships while remaining committed to the shared-value principles of Mahatma Gandhi that have always defined the organization: respect, collaboration, equality, and dignity.

I asked Meagan how she became a dangerous woman on her journey from corporate executive to recently being named the 2018 Hillary Laureate for her leadership on climate, justice, poverty, and peace.

How do you feel about being described as a dangerous woman?

Meagan: I've taken risks in different ways throughout my life. As a young woman in a corporate environment filled with barriers, I was very determined to break as many of those as I could. For instance I fought for equal pay when I was eight and a half months pregnant in one job because I knew I was being promoted and earning half of what other men were earning!

Later, I was determined not to compromise being a really good mother with still pursuing my own professional dreams and projects. That made my three children strong, resilient, self-reliant, and ultimately, they respect women incredibly. People often criticized the time I invested in my own passions and interests, but my children see those very things as what defines me now.

Was there a time or age when you began to feel more dangerous?

Meagan: I became a mountaineer at thirty-six. I started off-piste skiing—I climbed big mountains and skied truly physically dangerous things—but it never felt dangerous to me because I was operating in my zone of calculated risk, physically and mentally. That is something I think women are particularly great at. Women fund managers and others with very high-risk careers tend to evaluate short-, medium-, and long-term risk; calculate where they can manage on that scale; and then go for it, trusting that if they're a little off, they'll adapt and innovate what's needed.

Right now, I'm taking a totally different type of risk, having walked away from a successful for-profit company that I started and loved very much. I wanted to use my skill set to really make a difference, to address inequity and climate change in real time, helping as many women as possible to find their voice. When we take profit-making away from being our first priority, we can have a much larger impact than we imagine. We push ourselves further to be resourceful, efficient, and resilient. I wanted to challenge myself to develop my human skills to the same degree my formal education had developed my business skills.

How do you respond to the idea that dangerous times such as these call for women to be more daring?

Meagan: I feel more dangerous today, at fifty-six, than I did at twenty-five, because I understand my power now, with my network, with my sisters, whether those are the rural women that I work with across the developing world or women who are also doing incredible things in companies, media, government, and other NGOs. We're turning a whole community of the least likely women around the world into dangerous women by making them solar engineers. The power of technology gives them unbridled energy, self-confidence, a different role in their communities, and competence to face all the barriers in their life, because behind a piece of technology, you're gender equal. These women build a solar system and light up every house in their community. Everybody in that community understands they have power, metaphorically and literally. The best way to use power is to give it away to communities.

Becoming more dangerous means letting go of a need to be approved of by everybody around you. You let go of control. There's a great quote that I love: "Growth demands a temporary loss of security." When we are feeling least secure, when we're about to take a huge step, it's so hard. You're tired and you want to say, "It's too much. It's too hard. Maybe I should just go back." Maybe you need to retreat a little bit, gather your forces, get your energy again, and then you leap again, and you realize you're on the other side. You took a huge step.

Becoming dangerous is really, for me, about becoming equally comfortable with moments of great security and confidence, and with moments of great insecurity and self-questioning. Life is this constant flow. It's like walking in the mountains. There's always another up, there's always another down. Those are the sure things in life.

Epilogue

Rewiring, Not Retiring

> I am of the opinion that my life belongs to the community, and as long as I live, it is my privilege to do for it whatever I can. I want to be thoroughly used up when I die, for the harder I work, the more I live. Life is no "brief candle" to me. It is a sort of splendid torch which I have got hold of for a moment, and I want to make it burn as brightly as possible before handing it on to future generations.
>
> —GEORGE BERNARD SHAW

"YOU'RE *WHAT*?"

Frank Bennack, Paley's board chair, was incredulous when I told him I was leaving. And skeptical. "You are pathologically unable to retire. Why are you doing this? You could stay in this job for many more years."

Frank knew about retiring too early. He'd tried retirement, in his words, but had gone back to the Hearst Corporation, and was still CEO at age eighty-four.

"Frank, it's time," I told him. "I'm seventy. My mother died of Alzheimer's with all kinds of regrets. I've had a melanoma, caught early, gratefully, and Scott is commuting more than ever to Atlanta for work. Our grandchildren are growing up, and I'm not seeing enough of them. And I feel I've done what I came to the Paley Center to do. It just feels like the right time to make this decision."

But inside I was asking myself the same questions: Why *was* I doing this now? I told myself it was to have more time, but the reality is that many days, it feels like I have even less of it. I wanted to have more control over my time—and fewer responsibilities for leading a team and reporting to a board. I wanted fewer divided loyalties between what I had to do and what I wanted to do. In reality, I'd felt this conflict less as Paley CEO because this position called on my experience as a journalist, television host, and producer. But a voice I'd learned not to ignore was urging me to give it up.

I also believe that had I been completely honest with myself at the time, I would have seen that I was beginning to feel the urge to take bigger risks than my board at the Paley Center might have approved or that would have been appropriate for my position. I had used my power well as the CEO there—or so I believed—but I wanted to engage more broadly, travel more, do more, move forward again.

Did the decision stem from turning seventy? I'd embraced being fifty and sixty with enthusiasm. I'd started entirely new life acts in those years—from remarriage at fifty-three, to CEO positions at sixty, and a high-profile, well-paying leadership role at seventy. But at seventy, I had to admit that no matter how healthy and active my life was, there were fewer years ahead than behind. That felt different.

No surprise that I celebrated that birthday even more than any before: with seven birthday parties in seven different places with seven different sets of friends. From a surprise party with fifty friends in South Africa to a sixties rock-and-roll party with college friends, all of us dressed like University of Georgia coeds.

No, *retiring* was just not going to work for my next act. I reframed the announcement that I was *rewiring, not retiring.*

Unlike many who step away from full-time employment to pursue their bucket list of places to go or adventures to have, I'd already seen a lot of the world and shared adventures with friends and family as part of my work, so my bucket list was more about things to do, experience, and accomplish—now *that* was a long list!

One of my motivations was a desire to return to Atlanta. Scott wasn't retiring or rewiring—he'd always had a better work-life balance—and being closer to his work was part of the reason for a move out of New York and back to the South. We already owned a comfortable condo in the Four Seasons Hotel, a lifestyle they called *high-class assisted living*—room service available 24/7, maid service, a concierge for everything—an easy transition from our active and independent life of good health should the potential perils of aging catch up to us. But we had no sooner settled back in Atlanta and sold the small New York co-op than we went counter to everything people our age usually do and upsized from the condo to a house. A big house in an old midtown Atlanta neighborhood we had both always loved. To many, especially our children, this made no sense: to go from 1,500 square feet and all that security and support to a 5,000-square-foot, 100-year-old house with a yard and a small pool!

"Nothing grand," Scott assured the children when they protested. "Somewhere where we can have all those nonstop meetings that Pat will soon be organizing and, of course, room for family dinners and overnights with grandchildren."

Finally, we could take our stuff out of storage and enjoy again our eclectic collection of Native American and African artifacts. At last we could hang our beloved paintings and photographs, each one by an artist we also knew and loved. Once again, we were among visual reminders of the life we'd shared during our nearly twenty years together.

On one wall, the wedding gift of Bylle Szaggars Redford's aspen paintings, which so deeply connected us to our Sundance home, a small cottage that is our true retreat. With Bylle's work on our walls, we feel more connected to our shared passions and advocacy for Mother Earth, the driving force behind a multimedia initiative Bylle launched called The Way of the Rain. When we look at her work and the work of so many American Indians, Africans, Cubans, and the two beautiful drawings done by Scott's sister, the artist Susan Cofer, we feel the spirit and the love that were part of each creation. It's a feeling we both cherish in this special place, a part of this new chapter in our lives that defines us more than where we live.

Within weeks, Scott put the new home in perfect order while I packed up my New York office and started the planning for curating and hosting another TEDWomen, flying back and forth to LA and New York for various meetings. "Do you realize that you've only slept in our bed in our lovely new home six nights in the first six months?" Scott asked.

Clearly, I needed to rewire the part of me that has always been in forward motion! I've never had a true off switch; friends call me the Energizer Bunny. "Pat," Scott puffed on one of our morning bike rides through the nearby park, "do you realize you're riding faster uphill than down?" "Yes," I said, puffing, "because I want to get to the top as fast as possible, and the harder it is, the faster I have to go."

And I had lived that way, too. Never braking or pausing or coasting. Always pushing myself to go faster, move further along, do more, see more, be more.

WITH THIS PACE, I was going to fail retirement, and my life wasn't looking all that rewired either. I recalled that my father died one year after he retired, and for me, retirement meant stepping out of life, being too tired to participate, napping or rocking in the rocking chairs I'd insisted we put on our new front porch but have not rocked in once since moving in. I wasn't a good candidate for meditation either, although many friends choose to and thrive because of it. But at least at this point, my rewired life still hasn't hit the pause or snooze button. I hope it doesn't for a long time to come!

But what *was* my life going to be without the regimen and responsibilities of showing up for a job every day? I had aged out of corporate board opportunities, as most corporate boards have age limits of seventy or so—retiring their best, most experienced directors just when we have more time to be more engaged. I understand the reasons for age policies—turnover helps boards stay connected to their customers—and to be honest, I was happy to have all those corporate board meetings off my rewired calendar.

I'm still on many—possibly too many—nonprofit boards, a very important part of my life before and even more so now. I've always been passionate about the organizations I serve, and even though it's hard for me to disconnect from any good cause, I'm trying to further reduce my board responsibilities and further focus my fundraising and my advocacy. I may not have the personal wealth to be as philanthropic as I would like to be, but what I can't give in donations, I give in time.

With my commitments as chair of the Sundance Institute, to Acumen and to the Skoll Foundation, as cochair of the Women's Media Center board, and as a member of Participant Media's advisory board, and of course, my devotion as a founding member and very active supporter and advocate for the V-Day movement, my calendar is full of meetings and my life is full of meaning. With each organization, I am connected to my passions and to truly meaningful purpose: identifying and supporting antiviolence activists all over the world; providing essential funding for social entrepreneurs who are innovating solutions to reduce poverty and restore dignity and compassion to all; and ensuring that independent, marginalized voices are heard and nurtured and that important stories, well told, continue to compel social change. I feel so fortunate to bear witness to this work and to support it in all the ways I can.

But how do I prioritize all the millions of things I want to do, the causes I want to invest in, the friends and colleagues I want by my side? I have a new reality in my rewired life that I have to confess is a bit worrisome: something I call *situational turbulence.* As I've said, part of becoming more dangerous is being more impatient with small things or annoying situations that I might have put up with in the past. I now find certain situations that can create new kinds of turbulence.

I'd flown to the Mayo Clinic in Rochester, Minnesota, for my annual physical. My doctor, Deborah Rhodes, is a woman I admire for many reasons, including how candid she is as well as caring, and how much fun she is as well as a talented, respected physician who has broken through barriers to get her research and new lifesaving, breast-cancer detection technology adapted—watch her TED Talk to get the whole story. She's my personal physician and personal hero!

As she unwrapped the blood pressure cuff from my arm, Deb observed, "Boy, are you lucky to have low blood pressure. That's how you've been able to take on all these stressful activities."

"Yeah, but lately I feel like I'm really pushing it because I'm having all these eruptions of impatience." I told her about what had happened with the flight to Minnesota: I'd been upgraded to business class because of my frequent-flyer status, but when I got to the boarding area, my upgraded seat had disappeared. The gate agent investigated, his frown deepening as he tapped on his computer.

"I probably shouldn't tell you this," he confided, "but I can tell that someone meddled in the system. They downgraded you and upgraded someone else instead, probably a friend. They shouldn't have done that." He couldn't fix the problem, but suggested I call the frequent-mile folks, where I got nothing but a runaround. "I *know* this is a first-world problem," I groused to Deb, "but it's just so unfair, and I'm embarrassed by how upset I am about it."

Deb laughed. "I know exactly what you're talking about!" She told me that she'd flown into an absolute rage because she'd stood in line at a department store for forty-five minutes to return a fifty-dollar blouse, only to have the sales clerk explain that she couldn't return it even with the receipt and credit card because her daughter had made the original purchase. "Pat," she told me, "what you've got is *situational turbulence.*"

The description stuck and now I use it to describe these incidents when my impatience leads to turbulence. "Men don't seem to get upset in the same way by these small things," Deb said. "I think it's because they don't come into these situations with the same history of being treated unfairly. It's like the weathering concept we talk about in medicine. If you experience these microaggressions of racism or sexism over a long period of time, the ability to resist them is weathered away and the body responds differently."

Situational turbulence is the world we're in now, and we're wise to recognize it as a driving force. This isn't about an airline reservation or refund line, of course. I know those are signs of privilege. I'm trying to use my impatience and my privilege to push back against the underlying causes of acts of injustice, however small or seemingly trivial. We're living in a world where so many people are being treated unjustly, a world in which millions of women are dealing with violence and working for less money than male counterparts doing the exact same jobs, being harassed in the workplace, and being turned down for leadership positions. That's why it matters. It's time for women to show up, stand up, and support each other, to be the collective force that we are completely prepared to be. From where I'm standing, we should be impatient about *everything*!

When I tap into situational turbulence, I'm tapping into a vein of righteous anger, which women have so often been asked to disown. I don't want anyone to conflate complaints about injustice with being bitchy or whiny. I was taught as a little girl that expressing anger had dire consequences, so I hid my rage behind tears. Now I want righteous anger to fuel righteous action.

We can't afford to be polite or nice or worry about being acceptable or popular. I'm *done* making decisions based on whether people will like me! No more Ms. Nice Girl! I want to use my "situational turbulences" to raise awareness of the systemic causes of inequality and injustice—and then follow them to the right approach for reparations and repairs.

WHAT'S ALSO RIGHT for me in so many ways, I've discovered, is to continue the global adventures that have been so much a part of my working life as a journalist and activist. I've joined the small board of a travel company, Roar Africa, owned and led by Deborah Calmeyer, a force of nature who grew up in the wild nature of Zimbabwe and now lives in Cape Town and New York. As Scott and I took our first Roar Africa trip to South Africa, we realized that we had an opportunity now to deepen our love of travel and discovery through what Deb calls *learning journeys*, a combination of adventure travel with specially curated experiences with cultures and communities that aren't on tourist itineraries.

Last year, Deb even added a highly curated program of talks and presentations from well-known thought leaders in conservation, culture, community, and women's empowerment—TED Talks on safari is how one participant described the experience at our first Roar and Restore retreat at Segera, one of Kenya's top-ranked safari camps and game preserves. On these journeys that Scott and I now take and invite friends to join, we are noticing an effect that psychologists have called *rewilding*. Especially on our trips to the African continent, we've felt a deep connection with the natural environment; even this Energizer Bunny pauses to flow with the natural rhythms of life in the wild. Psychologists say that the rewilding we've been experiencing on each of our African learning journeys lasts after our return home. On a deeply personal and important level, I now know, at least in part, why I'd been led to rewire my life; I need the time to rewild.

Journalist Richard Louv has documented the importance of these connections in his work on nature-deficit disorder. In his research, he's observed what happens to children who have less time in nature and more time in front of screens, big and small. Watching the complete and total absorption of a three-year-old granddaughter who gets her hands on an iPhone or a TV remote, I don't need research to note the effect, but the studies point to a connection between the loss of time in nature and a loss of curiosity about the world—and, scarier still, a documented loss of empathy among the generation growing up with more virtual reality than human or animal interaction. For this reason and others, we set aside some rewilding funds to take each of our grandchildren to Africa as a kind of rite of passage when they turn thirteen. We compose a journey that provides a deep dive into the communities and cultures of the countries we visit as well as close-up interactions with the animals and their habitats. So far, the outcomes have proven more valuable than any gift we could design; the grandchildren are fully present and perhaps rewilded too.

As an admitted connection addict who actually answers emails under the covers so that I don't wake Scott, I worry for us as a global community, connected virtually as never before, yet with a growing disconnect from other people and places and perhaps even a disconnection from our own better selves. Being aware of this potential disconnection certainly fuels my passion for travel, for being present, and even for pausing, which I am learning to do: to learn patience in a leopard's stalking, feel empathy as we observe elephant families mourning over the bones of a dead relative. These are meaningful encounters and they're changing me. Becoming more present and more patient has been a big part of my becoming more influential as an advocate for the natural beauty, resources, and animals of Africa, all of which are threatened by the very present dangers of human encroachment, poaching, hunters' egos, and ignorance.

I have noticed, too, that I am never tired when I travel. I am energized and more *woke*, as my African American friends say, and I can't think of a better description of how I feel when I step onto soil I haven't walked before, or at least not on the same path or to the same destination. It's about learning about everything: what is wild and beautiful and what is wrong and painful and if there is anything I can do to make a difference.

It's time for women to pack our bags and take a car, train, boat, plane—or all four—and go where we can learn, discover, reconnect with ourselves and others, to be open to adventures that challenge our fears, to experiences that push us beyond our boundaries. Choose a place you haven't been and go there. It may be as close as the community on the other side of town or as far away as Cuba felt to me on my first visit to that magical island, but wherever you go, I hope you find a rooftop and dance.

You know by now in my story that I love to dance. I used to divide friends and dates into the *dance* and *don't dance* categories, knowing I would always prefer the *dance* group for company on and off a rooftop, where I first felt the total freedom that dance can bring, or in the risings of One Billion Rising, where I feel the power of dance to dare, to disrupt, to be dangerous.

THERE'S ANOTHER DISTINCTION, besides *dance* or *don't dance*, that I'm using now in choosing friends, colleagues, even causes. This one comes from my close friend, Carole Black, former president of Lifetime, and one of the most positive people I know. She's also laser-focused on what she wants, unwilling to waste her time, and absolutely clear about what matters and what doesn't. That alone is a characteristic of becoming dangerous that has taken me much longer to understand and embrace than it did for Carole. When I asked her, many years ago, what helped her stay so sure of her needs and purpose, she answered, "I divide the world into two camps: fountains and drains. When somebody walks into a room, do you feel like the energy goes up like the water in a fountain, or do you hear the *gurgle, gurgle, gurgle* of the positive life force going down the drain?"

I took the metaphor to heart and used it to make decisions about whom I hired in my CEO positions. It works—fountains make things happen; drains doubt and dispute and block forward movement. Now I'm applying this same assessment to friends and people with whom I want to work and play, travel and share experiences. If there's a wonderful cause but I feel drained by the people leading it, I'm the wrong person for the right cause and I choose to put my energies elsewhere. It takes rewiring and maybe losing a few friends and dropping a cause or two.

These days, all my friends are fountains. Some friends have remarked, "You have so many friends," as if that indicates a lack of judgment on my part. But I have friends from every part of my journey through this life, and I try to stay connected to them over time and distance as fountains of learning and love.

My college roommate, Glenda, is still my best friend, even though our lives since those days of classes and campus rallies and fraternity parties could not have been more different. She is still married to the same college sweetheart and has lived in Atlanta all her life. Throughout my peripatetic life, I would travel back at least once a year to visit family and always have a sleepover with Glenda and her family. I would share my global escapades, confess my deepest fears, and envy her stable, settled life. We have so little in common and yet we love each other deeply and unconditionally.

I can't think of any single aspect of my very privileged life that gives me greater joy or more meaningful support or better company than my diverse and delicious circle of women friends. Too many to name here, but you know who you are.

To my women friends who are in what Jane describes as *our prime time*, however, I feel a special bond and a big responsibility.

We are potentially the most powerful women on the planet. Think about it. There are approximately *one billion women over the age of fifty* in the world. We're the fastest-growing population on earth! We have the kind of experience that can only result from having seen a lot and done even more. We have the perspective and insights that arise after surviving failures and disappointments, overcoming the challenges that accompany each age of a woman's life. And because most of us are healthier and more active than any generations of older women before us, we're not ready or willing to take to our beds or sit on the beach or be anywhere other than right in the middle of the action.

We're better able to let go of some or most of the daily action of jobs, titles, attending to family. We're ready to leverage all that we know and the lessons we've learned the hard way to make it easier for the generations following us—not only because this makes us feel useful and valued, but because this is the way we can make the biggest difference for women everywhere.

I've thought a lot about how becoming dangerous is playing out in my life now. It certainly means I'm less patient—about very nearly everything, but especially injustice and unfairness. It means expressing anger when I feel it and being ready to fight for what matters. It means caring less what people say and saying more clearly what I think and feel. It has also meant coming to terms with my past, letting go of blame and shame, and bringing forward some of the experiences, buried deep, for better understanding of what my purpose is now. It means facing up to my privilege and harnessing every aspect of privilege and power to open doors, build bridges, heal divides, and fight for possibilities and a more equitable world for all.

Each of us has to find our own way of describing and living from our own definition of danger. For one woman, it's speaking truth to power by dropping a trail of f-bombs. For another, it's volunteering at the local homeless shelter. For others, it's running for a local school board or refusing to shop at a place that discriminates or tithing to a cherished cause or making phone calls for political candidates or simply saying no and setting a clean, strong boundary.

I hope I've made the case with this book that it's time for us to reframe the word *dangerous.* Let me add one more truth about becoming dangerous that I believe more strongly every day: you can't be dangerous from the sidelines! We've got to jump in, be engaged, embrace more risks, optimize all our networks of friends and colleagues, and do more to shape a future where idealogues, tyrants, narcissists, and abusers pose less danger—and have less power.

I am also committed to reframing the word and prevailing stereotypes and definition of *power*. Remember, the word comes from the Latin root meaning "to be able to." I believe that women are able to change the definition of power as Bella Abzug predicted nearly thirty years ago: "Women will change the nature of power, rather than power changing the nature of women." All my faith that the future will be better is grounded by my belief that women are going to come into positions of power and leadership and that we are going to use our power and share our power differently and effectively to improve the lives of other people, especially those without privilege, representation, opportunity, or access to power.

People have argued that historically, women in power governed much as men did, but I believe these leaders were constrained by a patriarchal construct that challenged them to follow the prevailing and dominant model of leadership. In the past, many had to lead without the support of other women. This lack of support is primarily why the United States hasn't had a woman president. What will it take to make that happen? Feminist.com founder Marianne Schnall asked this question in her popular book, *What Will It Take to Make a Woman President of the United States?* Remembering that we almost had a woman president in 2017, when an experienced and well-prepared woman leader, Hillary Clinton, won the popular vote, it's time to ask, what will it take now?

I'm counting on the "supermajority"—that's women in nearly every country—and it's also the name of a new US-based initiative to train, mentor, and support women to put themselves forward to lead, founded by three of the most inspiring women leaders I know: Cecile Richards, Ai-jen Poo, and Alicia Garza. All these efforts to connect women across cultural, social, political, and geographic divides, to unite them around shared values and experiences, can lead to a shift in the power paradigm that still exists in nearly every sector of work and life in nearly every country.

Ted Turner put forward another idea about what it will take when he spoke before the United Nations General Assembly some ten years ago: "It's time for men to step down and let women lead. Maybe for the next hundred years men should be banned from becoming leaders as it will take that long to rid the world of testosterone poisoning."

We don't have one hundred years to change direction, to reclaim the power that has been given up or taken away. We also don't have time to repeat the mistakes of previous movements, which have left many out when fighting for rights or access to power or opportunity. Acknowledging the omissions of the past, we have an opportunity, and indeed an imperative, to lead in a way that truly leaves no one out or behind—not other women, not those without representation, not men or boys. The fears of win-lose can be replaced by win-wins when doors to opportunities open wider than ever, often by activating incentives and strategies for inclusion, and when each of us commits to be an advocate for those not present in all the rooms where decisions are made.

As a global community of women, we are at an intersection where the risks are bigger but so are the opportunities to lead toward a more just world, and I hope I have persuaded you to take up the opportunities (and the risks) to lead for change wherever you live or work, or wherever you may be on your life's journey. At this place and time in my journey, I am prepared to be as dangerous as I need to be to do my part.

As the quotation at the beginning of this epilogue suggests, I am not viewing my life as a "brief candle," but as a splendid torch to be thoroughly used up at the end of this journey.

By sharing my story, speaking my truth, I am not passing the torch but lending it here to light the way forward for others. Braver and bolder, I am dancing in its dangerous light. Join me.

Acknowledgments

To Judith Rodin, who first recommended I write this book and arranged a residency at Bellagio, the Rockefeller Foundation's conference center on the shores of Lake Como, Italy, where I began to compile the memories and consider a memoir, encouraged by Pilar and my fellow Bellagians.

To Betsy Rapoport, whose collaboration supported me through the doubts and delays, whose editor's eye greatly improved the storytelling, and whose curious mind pushed for more meaning in every memory and experience.

To my editor, Laura Mazer, whose personal enthusiasm, professional counsel, and unwavering faith completed my journey to discover the value in this narrative for others.

And to Scott Seydel, who encouraged me, as he does every day in every way, with his unconditional love and support.

To Rutherford, Rosina, Lael, Scotto, Clark, and Mark, our sources of parental joy and pride, and their life partners, Laura, Tess, Nick, and Miranda.

To our grandchildren, Catharine, Michelle, John R., Vasser, Laura Elizabeth, Sullivan, Cole, John, Stella and May, Lizzie, Marisol, and Justin, who love me as Gigi and now know the rest of my story.

I am blessed to know so many dangerous women and brave men, and acknowledging them all would require another book. To end this one, I want to acknowledge with admiration and gratitude: Jennifer and Peter Buffett for the ways they are modeling a values-led life and transforming philanthropy; Jeff Skoll whose innovation, risk-taking, and vision are compelling social change; and to all my colleagues giving time, talent, and treasure to support the work of the Sundance Institute, the Women's Media Center, the Skoll Foundation, Acumen, Participant Media, Alliance for Artisans, Women without Borders, and V-Day, the global movement to end violence against women and girls—thank you for carrying your torches high and bright for others to follow.

WITH SPECIAL GRATITUDE to the Dangerous Women who answered my questions and accepted my invitation to be a part of the book and with admiration for the parts they play in creating a better world.

Here's a list of their organizations, which I invite you to learn more about and support.

Stacey Abrams
FairFightAction.com

Ai-jen Poo
domesticworkers.org

Ava DuVernay
Arraynow.com

Mary Robinson
Mary Robinson Foundation–Climate Justice
MRFCJ.org

Abigail Disney
Peaceisloud.org

Christine Schuler-Deschryver
City of Joy
Vday.org

Dr. Kimberlé Crenshaw
African American Policy Forum
AAPF.org

Zoya
Vday.org

Monique Wilson
OneBillionRising.org
Laura Flanders
http://lauraflanders.org/donate

Jacqueline Novogratz
Acumen.org

Sandi Toksvig
Womensequality.org.uk

Ruth Ann Harnisch
The Harnisch Foundation
thehf.org

Meagan Fallone
Barefootcollege.org

Credit: Lynn Savarese

PAT MITCHELL was the first woman president of PBS, CNN Productions, and the Paley Center for Media, as well as an award-winning producer of documentaries and TV series. She is the cofounder and curator of TEDWomen and the Connected Women Leaders Initiative, chair of Sundance Institute and the Women's Media Center, trustee of the Skoll Foundation, and advisor to Participant Media. She lives in Atlanta and Sundance, Utah—but mostly on airplanes.